NO PLACE TO HIDE

*Facing Shame So
We Can Find Self-Respect*

Michael P. Nichols, Ph.D.

A Fireside Book
Published by Simon & Schuster
New York   London   Toronto   Sydney   Tokyo   Singapore

FIRESIDE
Simon & Schuster Building
Rockefeller Center
1230 Avenue of the Americas
New York, New York 10020

Designed by C. Linda Dingler
Manufactured in the United States of America

1   3   5   7   9   10   8   6   4   2
1   3   5   7   9   10   8   6   4   2   (pbk)

Library of Congress Cataloging in Publication Data
Nichols, Michael P.
No Place to Hide : Facing Shame So We Can Find Self-Respect /
Michael P. Nichols.
p.   cm.
Includes bibliographical references and index.
1. Shame.   2. Self-Respect.   I. Title.
BF575-S45N52   1991
152.4—DC20   90-47416
CIP

ISBN: 0-671-68784-0
ISBN: 0-671-68181-8 (pbk)

To my aunt Camille Solomon,
for the gift of her unqualified love,
and the example of her lifelong commitment to social justice.

∎ ∎ ∎ ∎ ∎ ∎ ∎

Thanks to Laura Yorke for editing this book.

CONTENTS

■ ■ ■ ■ ■ ■ ■

PREFACE

∎∎∎∎∎∎∎

When we think about self-respect, in whatever terms, and wish we had more, the natural tendency is to look for ways to make ourselves stronger, more secure, more confident. Perhaps if we were better-looking or smarter or more successful, we'd feel good about ourselves. The last thing we want to think about, certainly not to dwell upon, is *why* we don't respect ourselves. Occasionally, in moments of difficulty, we've all had to face the fact that we suffer from insecurity. We tend to think of this insecurity as an irreducible fact of character. If, deep down, we're insecure, that must be the truth about us, and we're stuck with it. Some people worry about insecurity, others try to forget about it; most of us blame our parents. But few of us ever look long enough and hard enough at ourselves to realize that the root of insecurity is shame.

This is a difficult book, because it asks you to look at one of the most deeply repressed and ugly emotions in human experience. Even reading about shame makes us wince. But the truth is, every one of us is controlled by a sense of shame and humiliation. It's a universal problem.

Why delve into such a painful subject? Because only by digging down and confronting our painful fears can we ever be free of them. The alternative—ignoring the problem, pretending it doesn't exist—feels better, in the short run. But it doesn't work. How can we build secure self-respect on a foundation of denial?

I first began to recognize the central role that shame plays by witnessing it in the lives of my patients. It takes a long time to get to shame, because it is layered over with so many defenses. But once I realized the extent to which shame was responsible for so much insecurity, vulnerability, and avoidance, I became a more understanding and better therapist. That was the easy part. Facing my own shame was harder.

When I was a young psychotherapist, I used to get annoyed when anyone suggested that a therapist had to have an experience before he could understand it. For example, that you had to be married and have children before you really knew what it was like. I didn't want to think that way because it was too limiting, too threatening. Gradually, however, I've come to realize that no one can ever fully understand what he hasn't experienced. Let me tell you a story about how I learned to face painful truths.

When I was a kid, monsters lived in my backyard. When I took the garbage out at night, they were there, lurking in the dark. The scariest moment was when I turned to come back to the house. That's when they could get me. So I had to run like crazy—up the steps, onto the porch, and slam the door as fast as I could. Most kids are afraid of the dark, but my fears were my fears. They were truly terrifying, and they lasted a long time.

Snakes lived in my room. You couldn't see them—they might be hiding in the closet or under the bed. The only way to be safe was not to look. The only escape was sleep. But sometimes the snakes slithered into my dream. I was scared a lot.

Finally, I resolved to conquer my fear, and set out to do it by forcing myself to look into dark places. When I took out the garbage, I made myself walk back real slow. I shuddered with fear that the monsters might get me. But I did not run. If I was going past a dark alley and felt scared, I made myself walk down it. I knew I was winning over fear when one night, after a late movie, I made myself walk through the parking lot behind the Safeway. It was supposed to be a bad place where drunks hung out and hoods got into razor fights. I walked from one end of that parking lot to the other and then back again, real slow. There was nothing to be afraid of. What a brave kid I was. Maybe. But maybe there was something I was more afraid of than the dark: my shame about weakness.

This fear of mine—fear of being weak—has helped me overcome a lot of difficulties; I try not to let cowardice be a reason to avoid doing what needs to be done. It's also made me do some things that were about as smart as walking through the Safeway parking lot alone at midnight: take stupid dares, drive my motorcycle 130 miles an hour, attack authority figures just because I was afraid not to. This is one of the ironies responsible for the controlling power of shame: We'll do anything to avoid facing it.

I once had a patient I had a hard time figuring out, a young husband and father who couldn't stop screwing around. I didn't have any trouble understanding how he could succumb to sexual temptation, once. But even after his wife found out and his infidelity almost destroyed his family, how could he do it again and again? Why, I wondered, wasn't this man more ashamed of his selfishness, his betrayal of his wife, and his exploitation of other women? The answer was that he was more ashamed of something else: a sense of himself as deficient, fundamentally inadequate. He needed the reassurance he got from seducing young women, like an anemic needs massive doses of supplementary iron.

When we hear about someone behaving as badly as this faithless husband, we're tempted to fall back on labels and blame. He's "immoral," "incorrigible," "addicted to sex"; "something is wrong with his superego." We do something similar to ourselves. When we run into our own weaknesses and inhibitions, we condemn ourselves—or blame someone else—and then try to forget about it. The alternative—asking ourselves why we're insecure, what we're afraid of and why—is difficult and painful. Bear with me, it's worth it. The very things that make shame hard to talk about and hard to face, make it urgent to do so. By looking at shame, discovering how it works and how it holds us back, we can begin to overcome its grip on our lives. Once we stop hiding from our dark fears, we can accept ourselves more fully. This enlightened self-acceptance releases us from pretense and frees us to live with more confidence and more dignity.

I

....

THE
ROOTS
OF
INSECURITY

1

•••••••

The Search for Self-respect

It's really quite remarkable how our sense of well-being depends on the vagaries of circumstance and the actions of other people. Minor events, often unexpected, can spell the difference between a good day and a bad one. One of the kids comes down with a cold and your whole schedule is thrown out of whack. Your spouse snaps at you for no apparent reason and the evening is ruined. A pointless, boring meeting is canceled and suddenly a free afternoon opens up. The sun breaks out and your whole mood lifts. Who's in charge of our happiness, anyway: the unforgiving clock, a cranky boss, an unsympathetic mate, the weather—or ourselves?

When satisfaction eludes us, we usually have a reason. Too much work and not enough play: "There just doesn't seem to be enough time." "By the time I finish the things I have to do, I don't have enough energy left over for the things I want to do." Health problems and job frustrations rank high on the list of things that stand in the way of our getting more of what we want out of life: "If it weren't for my headaches (allergies, trick knee, bad back), there are a lot of things I'd like to do." "This damn job is killing me." And, of course, most of us would be a lot better off if it weren't for certain recalcitrant others: nagging wives and withdrawing husbands, greedy children and stingy parents, unappreciative bosses and coworkers who don't do their share.

We worry about the future and regret the past: "Why didn't I get a better education?" "If only I'd married someone else." Our many regrets and various dissatisfactions seem to have one common denominator: What keeps us stuck is something we cannot control. The point is not that most of us are miserable or even seriously unhappy. Rather, our own efforts seem to take us only so far in the direction of satisfaction and meaning, until we reach a plateau beyond which we cannot go. Meanwhile, our everyday happiness appears to fluctuate at the whim of events.

Triumphs, all too brief, and disappointments, all too frequent, produce striking swings in self-esteem. Sometimes this seems reasonable, as when a major success at work or a new relationship (or an outbreak of affection in an old one) makes us feel great. Likewise, it's no surprise when losing out on a promotion or getting into a major argument with someone we love makes us feel dejected. What's harder to understand—and harder still to accept—is how vulnerable most of us are to even minor slights and rejections, especially from certain people. Why should criticism deflate us so, and why are we so easily hurt? Why are we so insecure?

At times, it seems that life is one long defense against insecurity. We worry about what we're going to wear, what we're going to say, what we're going to do. Will people be impressed? Will they like us? What's missing is a sense of constancy and self-worth. What's missing is *self-respect*.

Self-respect is the conviction of being whole, worthwhile, and valued from within. With self-respect we have the security to pursue satisfaction, the capacity for intimacy, and the ability to be alone. Whatever we choose to do, self-respect enables us to feel that our lives are useful and that we ourselves are worthwhile, that what we do and who we are matters. Self-respect stills self-doubt.

In *The Ambassadors*, Henry James wrote, "Live all you can; it's a mistake not to." Good advice; unfortunately, most of us are constrained by nagging self-doubt. Easily wounded, afraid of failing, fearful of rejection, we narrow down our lives to avoid risk and concentrate our concerns in limited avenues of expression. What is it that holds us back? Insecurity—the antithesis of self-respect.

The undercurrent of insecurity in our lives helps explain the infectiousness of strong-willed, confident personalities. Self-respect confers dignity. Humphrey Bogart had it, and his manifest faith in himself is one reason for his enormous appeal. Another person who knows who she is and can stand up to anyone is Katharine Hepburn. You probably have your own favorites. We admire film stars for many reasons—Cary Grant for his charm, Fred Astaire for his style, Grace Kelly for her quiet dignity, Meryl Streep and Jack Nicholson for their talent and their willingness to play "unattractive" roles—but in all the actors who have become great stars one thing stands out: They radiate self-confidence.

Despite the enviable self-assurance movie stars present to the world, we wonder: Do they really feel good about themselves, or do they just act that way? Maybe the confident manner is a facade; after all, they *are* actors. Most of us can and do seem sure of ourselves in certain contexts, although inside we may feel more like Woody Allen or Diane Keaton than Humphrey Bogart or Katharine Hepburn. This same duality—confidence in one setting, anxious uncertainty in another—is striking to observe in other people. I remember, for example, the day I gave my first lecture as a college professor. I was so nervous that I could hardly get through it. My throat was dry, my heart was thumping, and I couldn't stop shaking. It was awful! Later that day, I went to talk to one of the senior professors, a graceful, charming man who always seemed at ease. I told him how nervous I'd been and that I didn't want to have to go through that again. "What do you do to get ready?" I asked. I still remember exactly what he said: "I stay up all night, and in the morning I vomit." This man I admired so much was twice as nervous as I was! He just learned to live with it.

Maybe you've known people who are competent and confident at work but completely out of their element at a party. Or women who run a household with authority and assurance but feel ill at ease and uncertain in a committee meeting—or vice versa. That's why it's important to distinguish between self-confidence and self-respect. Self-respect is basic and global; self-confidence is specific and limited to particular situations. For example, a woman might be self-confident about her professional ability, but at this point in

her life she may not value her work as much as she does relationships, and since she hasn't had a man in her life for over a year, her
global self-respect may be low.

People with self-respect aren't just confident about their ability
in certain endeavors, and they aren't likely to be brash or arrogant.
They accept themselves and are at ease with who they are. Their
sense of self-worth is constant, even when they attempt something
they don't do well, and they have no need to prop themselves up
by putting other people down.

The first time it struck me that another person was genuinely
self-respecting was in the seventh grade. His name was David
MacLean, and he scored B+ or better on all the requisite pread-
olescent virtues: He had regular features and dark, wavy hair—
B+. (When it comes to looks, B+ looks may be the best of all
possibilities.) He was as smart as anyone in school—A; and he was
among the better athletes—A, again. It was something completely
unexpected, however, that really impressed me about David. He
didn't feel the need to constantly be raising his hand in class to
answer teachers' questions. As you may or may not remember,
school children are so ardently eager to be recognized as knowing
the answers that they compete to be called on, frantically waving
their hands in the air—"Me! Me!" Some kids raise their hands even
when they don't know the answers, hoping to seem knowledge-
able, hoping not to be found out. Not David MacLean. The only
time he raised his hand was when nobody else knew the answer.
He was cool.

So impressed was I with David MacLean that I, too, stopped
raising my hand, except when no other hands went up. Of course,
what I was doing was totally different. I was copying the first in a
long line of people I admired.

A good place to observe people's self-respect is when they're
willing to try something new and unfamiliar, or even something
they already know they aren't good at. They don't mind being
incompetent at some things, because their self-respect isn't at
stake.

Most of us are sufficiently confident most of the time that we
don't spend a lot of time worrying about insecurity. It may be,

however, that we keep self-doubt at bay only by confining ourselves to familiar territory. Our composure starts to slip when we
find ourselves in unfamiliar situations, or when we're deprived of
some of our props. The army knows this; that's why they start
basic training by stripping the recruits of their Levi's and leather
jackets, and cutting off their proud hairdos. If you want to see
some lost looks on people's faces, visit boot camp on The Day of
the Haircut.

What constitutes the opposite of self-doubt? Pride, self-esteem,
confidence, assurance, poise, self-respect. These are some of the
words. Read them again, slowly: Pride. Self-esteem. Confidence.
Assurance. Poise. Self-respect. These words have an evocative res-
onance. They are what we wish we could be. Still, they are only
words, and no single word sums up what it means to be free of
self-doubt. When asked to define the opposite of self-doubt, the
people I spoke to agreed that it had to do with a sense of dignity
and self-assurance. But, interestingly, there was a split between
the images of men and women. Men tend to associate self-respect
with a secure knowledge of one's powers. Women, on the other
hand, emphasize being comfortable with oneself, which means
accepting weakness. You don't have to be beautiful or brilliant or
masterful to be secure; you have to accept who you are and what
you can—and cannot—do.

MAGIC MEMORIES

Somewhere, locked in the heart, most of us have cherished memories of moments when we felt the proud glow of self-worth. For
men, these memories often involve personal triumph. Here's an
example from a forty-year-old lawyer who, despite a very successful career, never seems to be very sure of himself.

*The proudest day of my life was when I won the high school
declamation contest. I used to entertain my friends by imitat-
ing people—teachers, parents, especially anybody with an unusual accent. Thinking about it now, I suppose my imitations*

*had a hostile edge, but back then it was just something I did to
show off. Entering the declamation contest was a natural for
me, but I had no real thought of winning. It was a big school. I
was lucky to get into the finals. I'll never forget that feeling
after we all spoke and they announced the winners. I was
afraid to get my hopes up, but secretly I thought I had a shot
at finishing third. As they read off the names, starting with fifth
place, I got dizzy with excitement. I couldn't think clearly. But
when the principal read the third place name and it wasn't
mine, I was crushed. The next few moments were a blur. And
then I heard him say that I had won. I couldn't believe it! It
was wonderful. I can still hear his voice: "And the winner
is . . ." and then my name, and then that applause—that wonderful, wonderful applause.*

*For days afterward, I walked around feeling proud. No mat-
ter what else was going on, I was a winner. The winner.*

*I've competed in many things since that day, but never have
I had so clearly the sense of being the best. Did winning that
contest give me more self-respect? Probably not. It gave me a
tremendous temporary rush—a moment of living out the
grand dreams of achievement my head was always filled with.
But it was success of a very limited and specific sort. So, big
deal, I can read a poem with feeling. There are a lot of more
important things I can't do.*

Clearly, achievement does not create self-esteem; it only reinforces it. In fact, self-esteem may create achievement.

The following story, from a college professor, may be more
typical of a woman's relationship-oriented sense of personal worth.

*My father died when I was thirty-six. It was totally unexpected.
He was such a powerful man, the dominant force in a large
extended family. When the news came that he had cancer, no
one could believe it. I guess we never thought anything could
happen to him. The doctors did all they could for him in the
hospital, and then he came home. I took a leave of absence
and moved in to take care of him. I wasn't ready to let him*

*go. There was still stuff I needed from him. Like I wanted him
to tell me that he loved me.*

*After the radiation and chemo he was pretty weak, so I had
to do everything for him: I fed him, bathed him; I even had to
help him go to the bathroom. At first he was embarrassed. But
what could he do? He had to accept it. All that closeness—it
was very intimate.*

*The weaker he got, the less he talked. We listened to his fa-
vorite operas and watched a lot of TV. Then one day he mo-
tioned for me to turn off the television and come over to him.
All he could do was whisper. "You're the only one who was
never afraid of me," he said. "Yeah," I said, "like the time you
didn't want me to go to graduate school. You said I wasn't going; I should come to work in the business with you. And I said
it wasn't fair. You always told me I should be a success, but I
had to do it my own way." "You were right," he said. "And
now you are a success. You always made a success out of everything." I told him that I loved him, and he said, "I love you,
too. I always have."*

*In that moment of love spoken, her heart soared and she
felt complete. Now she knew she was loved. But nothing can
completely heal the hurt of thirty-six years of doubting it.*

Perhaps you can recall a time when you felt really good about
yourself. If you are a man, it may have been a major success or
accomplishment that made you feel powerful. If you're a woman, it
may also have been an achievement, or it may have been a time
when you felt loved completely. In either case, you felt content, no
matter what might happen next or what someone might say. You
may only have had a fleeting glimpse of that feeling, but you know
how special it is. My guess is that remembering a proud time in
your life will make you feel sad, exposing as it does the contrast
between that wonderful, elusive feeling and your usual doubts and
uncertainties.

We don't usually spend a lot of time thinking about our level of
self-esteem. We're too busy trying to get ahead—or trying to get
by. Most of the time we're looking out, not looking in. Still, even

though we may not think about it, most of us are plagued by insecurity.

Look at people walking down the street. Notice people who walk with their heads held high, make unself-conscious eye contact, and seem sure of themselves. These people appear to have a self-contained dignity; because they are in the minority, they stand out. Most people don't have this presence, this visibly apparent sense of self-worth. They glance down or away when someone looks directly at them. You can almost see insecurity written on their faces the minute they become conscious of being looked at.

Notice that as long as people are engaged in doing something, whether it's talking or window shopping, you can't tell how they feel about themselves. As long as we are fully engaged in *doing,* we are not self-conscious about *being.* As Sartre said, "I *am my acts* and hence they carry in themselves their whole justification. I am pure consciousness of things."[1] It's only when we become aware of being watched that we show our insecurity. With the consciousness of being looked at comes the awareness of being vulnerable.

Sartre illustrates the sudden switch from being "lost in the world" to becoming an object of "the gaze" with the example of looking through a keyhole. Once you yield to the temptation to peek, you become caught up in curiosity. Then all of a sudden you hear footsteps in the hall. Immediately you become self-conscious. As Sartre said, "I see myself because *somebody* sees me."[2] With this awareness comes the consciousness of feeling worthy or unworthy. Instant insecurity.

THE ROOTS OF INSECURITY

There are many ways to ward off insecurity by giving a temporary boost to self-esteem. I put on my best suit, an elegant shirt, and a no-nonsense necktie. My clothes say, "Here's a man with self-respect." And it works—for a little while. Some people find that meditation helps; and, of course, a lot of people think insecurity is soluble in alcohol.

Overcoming insecurity is the theme of countless self-help books, and the popularity of these books attests to the universality of the wish for greater self-esteem. Their continuing flow proves that self-doubt doesn't go away easily. Most of the usual advice boils down to trying to talk yourself out of being insecure. Some authors advise identifying your "critical inner voices" and then talking back to them. Here are one book's recommended rejoinders to the voice of insecurity: "This is poison. Stop it!" "These are lies." "No more put-downs." Behavioral psychologists call this technology *thought-stopping*. Dale Carnegie called it "the power of positive thinking."

There's nothing wrong with trying to ignore or talk yourself out of self-doubt. Positive thinking can help you over an anxious moment and give you the courage to do what needs to be done. This is the same kind of encouragement we often turn to friends for. Tell a friend that you feel bad about yourself, and most likely he or she will try to cheer you up by telling you that you're just fine the way you are. It feels good, and after a while, you get to know how different friends will respond to your worries.

The trouble with reassurance is that it doesn't last. You can turn from one book to another and go from friend to friend for pep talks and inspiration, but none of this encouragement will have a lasting effect on stilling self-doubt or instilling self-respect. You can't create self-respect by sealing over self-doubt or by talking yourself out of it.

Self-respect confers a natural grace and ease. Instead of thinking of others as providing what you need, you become the primary source of your own approval and well-being. With self-respect, you can be independent, spontaneous, and self-accepting; your actions can match your feelings; you have an appetite for life because you approach the world with confidence in yourself. Without self-respect, you cannot be your own support system, and so you continue to be dependent on others. We make our own lives, but as long as we're plagued by self-doubt we're not open to the possibilities life presents to us. Insecurity holds us back.

As long as the foundation of the self is shaky, our efforts to shore it up with accomplishment and reassurance only create the illusion of self-respect. We don't get beyond insecurity by masking it.

Instead of taking insecurity as a regrettable but irreducible fact, perhaps we should ask, "Why are we insecure?" Exploring this question takes us to the heart of the self. Unfortunately, between self-discovery and self-expansion stands much that is painful, much that we've learned to deny.

What lies at the root of insecurity? Dig down and you'll find shame, a feeling we've run from all our lives.

We've all known shame, and each of us has memories of humiliation we'd rather forget. Perhaps you can recall striking out with everyone's eyes on you, or getting caught cheating, or the cruel laughter of mocking children when you made a fool of yourself, or the hot flush of shame when somebody rejected you and everyone else knew it. Most of us associate painfully public memories of humiliation with childhood and adolescence. All we wanted was to be loved and included; all we got was laughed at and left behind. Parents and playmates mortified us with criticism and mockery. Some of this was a deliberate attempt to mold our behavior, some of it was inadvertent, and some of it was just plain cruel. (Unfortunately, we do unto others as was done unto us.)

A woman I know, who has struggled all her life with being overweight, remembers a very painful incident when she was ten. Her parents went out for the evening, leaving her alone and feeling lonely. So for supper she had two TV dinners. Apparently, her older sister (also overweight) discovered the missing packages and wrote to their brother (also overweight) at camp. When he came home, he tattled at the dinner table and hissed at his sister, "Greedy pig!"

Acquired interpersonally, shame gradually becomes internalized. Images of the self as flawed—greedy, lazy, stupid, dirty—are rooted in unconscious memories. The memories fade, but the shame endures. Now insecurity is no longer about how someone made us feel, it's about who we are.

The shamed child disowns parts of the self. Depending upon the child's experience, this may be certain emotions, or it may be needs, or it may be playing games, or competing with others. Each one of us, in our own characteristic ways, narrows our life in order to escape and avoid shame. Ashamed of shame, we learn to live with it but keep it out of awareness. In the process, however, we choke off natural human emotions and desires. Unwilling to face shame, we settle instead for alienation: Conditioned by a deep fear of shame, we become alienated from ourselves, from other people, and from full participation in life. This alienation takes many forms and goes by many names: shyness, modesty, uptightness, rigidity, timidity, embarrassment, and (turning the attack on others) arrogance and contempt. These many ways of paralyzing the heart's feelings have one thing in common: avoidance. And it's shame that lurks beneath avoidance, at the heart of human experience. We don't ever get away from shame, we just bury it.

Let me pause here to review the thread of my argument so far. Self-respect is undermined by self-doubt. Self-doubt is the conscious tip of insecurity. Insecurity isn't merely a passive absence of confidence; it's an active product of deep-seated shame. We're insecure, at least in part, because deep down we're ashamed of important aspects of ourselves.

Chief among the effects of shame are lack of self-confidence and experience avoided. "If only I had more self-confidence!" How many times have we heard that—and thought it ourselves? The underlying problem is lack of self-respect (roughly synonymous with self-esteem and self-worth), but we more often experience a lack of self-confidence because we don't think of ourselves as persons-in-general but as persons-facing-situations. The nagging doubt that one is not good enough as a person holds us back, and the painful awareness of our dependency on the opinions of others—not just anyone, but those we elect as arbiters of our self-esteem—haunts us all. The shame-sensitive individual meets other persons not as an equal but as a frightened and vulnerable child, burdened anachronistically by troubled memories of past humiliations. If only we were stronger, strong enough not to need anybody, surely then we would be free.

Herein lies a sad paradox: Self-worth is not something you can develop on your own, like building muscles at the local health club. Shame-sensitive individuals with shaky self-esteem need to do precisely what makes them feel vulnerable—that is, build bridges to other people and develop trusting relationships in which the self can be supported and confirmed.

How can we start to reach out to others, overcome our insecurities, and bolster our self-worth? To begin with, we can recognize that shame underlies low self-esteem. Although shame comes to be felt as shame of the whole self, we first learn shame in connection with specific actions and personal traits. To say that one lacks self-confidence is to say that one is afraid to risk feeling shame by exposing a particular aspect of the self. Knowing this fact points the way toward change. It's easier to begin taking risks if you know what *the* risk is: It's not something awful in a vague and ineffable way; it's shame.

In the following chapters I will show how, by taking risks and building a network of support, we can begin to unfreeze the possibilities of life and find renewed satisfaction—at work, in relationships, and within ourselves. I will explore and explain common patterns of avoidance that are conditioned by shame at the psychic center of the self: work and success inhibitions in women, allergy to intimacy among men, avoidance of anger, not taking time for friends or play, holding back one's natural inclinations, and turning our backs on our goals, retreating from life, and seeking gratification in passive escapism. It isn't just stress or overwork that gets us down and wears us out. It is a system of negative thoughts, driven by shame, that plays such a major role in human suffering and significantly limits our healthy strivings.

This book is designed to bring shame out of the closet. Shame plays a poorly understood but central role in our lives. It's poorly understood and insufficiently appreciated because of the wordless nature of this affect and the primal anxiety of exposure. By illuminating the dynamics of shame—what it is and how it works—I hope to provide the intellectual basis from which conscious control can evolve. By including numerous examples, I hope to involve you, the reader, emotionally as well as intellectually. Examples drawn from my psychotherapy practice, supplemented with interviews and schoolroom observations, will illustrate the development of shame and stir personal associations so that you can begin to recognize cycles of shame and avoidance in your own life.

As you read further, you will begin to recognize how shame holds us back in our own lives, and by remembering past humiliations, you may begin to understand how shame becomes a part of us and then alienates us from full life. Humiliation is too painful to be "recollected in tranquillity," but I hope you will discover how to put it into perspective, and how, by facing shame, you can unfreeze habits of avoidance and begin to live life more honestly, and more fully.

2

Shame

The Alienating Emotion

The first stab of shame comes from sudden and unexpected exposure to the critical eyes of another person. We stand revealed, painfully diminished. The genesis of this emotion is a process that moves from the outside in. Shame has to be taught. We learn to be ashamed of, and even disown, those parts of ourselves that are rejected, ridiculed, or humiliated by our parents. Conflicts that originate interpersonally, with anxiety or shame generated between parent and child, then become internalized and eventually unconscious. The result of this process of internalization is a selective disowning, which alienates us from shamed parts of the self, and a gradual lowering of self-esteem, which alienates us from other people.

One of the problems with discussing shame is that, because it is so painful, it's buried—not dead, just buried. Most people have very little idea of the role shame plays in their lives; it's buried too deep. The way to achieve self-respect is not to deny shameful feelings of inadequacy, but to face them. Let's begin by examining the experience of shame.

THE PHENOMENOLOGY OF SHAME

Thus far I have been speaking of shame as though it were a singular phenomenon. In fact, it is not. Shame is an *affect*, an *attitude*, and an *anxiety*. The immediate experience of shame is an *affect*, the conscious component of an emotional response, and it has two parts: feeling upset, plus thinking one is bad or worthless. This affect state may be short-lived or may endure to become an attitude. Some people live with shame, such as Hawthorne's Hester Prynne, who was branded with a scarlet *"A"* for all the world to see, and people who sink into degradation from which they cannot seem to emancipate themselves—such as alcoholics, drug addicts, and sexual deviants. More typically, however, shame is an *attitude* that manifests itself in insecurity and avoidance of any situation that might lead to humiliation. As we shall see, this attitude shows itself in embarrassment, shyness, and low self-esteem. An unmodified sense of shame, and the resultant need to keep hidden a defective sense of self, prevents self-assertion and healthy strivings, sexual or aggressive. *Shame-anxiety* is the fear of imminent danger of exposure, humiliation, and rejection.

Shame as an Affect

The immediate shock of shame is sudden exposure. It has the quality of an unexpected, caught-in-the-act feeling, like dropping through a trap door. Shameful exposure can come about when someone penetrates our privacy or when we lose control. The prototype of shameful loss of control is when a child wets the bed and is then scolded and punished for it. One of the most important lessons of childhood is that our bodies, "temples of the soul," are filled with disgusting discharges that must be hidden, put in special places, and gotten rid of as quickly and noiselessly as possible. "Full of shit" did not start out as a metaphor.

As children we learned the imperative to gain and maintain control over strong desires and weak emotions: "Don't touch yourself *there!"* Don't you speak to me that way, young lady!" "Big boys don't cry." *"That* isn't very ladylike!" So much to learn, so much to hide.

By the time we reach adulthood, we've been inculcated against "losing control." We've learned that, for adults, it's shameful to give way to lust or violence, cry more than a little, get mad and start yelling, look where we're not supposed to, be seen when we're not supposed to be—give up, give in, let go, fall down, or reveal what should be concealed. Much depends on the setting. Imagine an exquisitely gowned, superbly coiffed, subtly scented, beautiful woman who suddenly belches.

We have rituals for relaxing control—"Loosen up, have a drink"; "It's a party, enjoy yourself"—and taboos against overdoing it— "Get a hold of yourself"; "Don't be a baby"; "What do you think you're doing?" and, of course, "You should be ashamed!"

The experience of shame is bipolar. At the subject pole is the actor; at the object pole, a witness. The critical aspect of the subjective experience is *what* one is ashamed of, originally something specific, eventually the whole person. Shame is an affect with an inverse relationship to self-respect and integrity. The more shame we feel, the less we respect ourselves. It is a self-related, narcissistically oriented feeling. Beneath pretense and self-doubt, we are objects of our own affection. Shame is a piercing awareness of ourselves as somehow fundamentally deficient—instant self-hatred.

Shame as an Attitude

We think of humiliating experiences as causing shame. Consider: At the moment of passionate embrace a man's erection wilts and the woman he's with gives him a scornful, disgusted look. After a woman delivers a very important presentation, she discovers that her dress is spotted with menstrual fluid. You can imagine how these two burned with shame, and you'd be inclined to say that these terrible incidents "made them ashamed." But that's not quite right. The humiliations of adulthood don't *cause* shame, they expose it. Pay attention, this is important: *The shame is already there.* We don't normally notice, because it's repressed, but deep in our hearts, most of us have a vast reservoir of self-loathing. That self-loathing is unbearable, so we stuff it down and lock it away.

Repression seals it in. We feel shame, not when something happens to *make* us ashamed, but when something happens to *expose* the shame that's already inside us.

Shame is a painful discrepancy between our image of who we'd like to be and our perception of an ugly reality. The experience implies being caught, being observed by an outside witness who condemns. The original witness to our shame is, of course, a scolding parent; later, the superego will do. Yet shame is doubled when it's exposed to the eyes of others.

Public humiliation is worse than private for two reasons: It exposes us directly to the judgment and condemnation of people we care about, and it makes it harder for us to forget painful truths about ourselves. We know the truth about ourselves, but we also know how to forget it. Exposure evokes shame and makes it conscious; witnesses make it harder to put out of mind.

Even the most apparently shameless public figures are brought low by public disgrace. We've seen a lot of this lately. Spiro Agnew, Jim and Tammy Bakker, Jimmy Swaggart, Gary Hart, Bess Meyerson, Zsa Zsa Gabor, and maybe even ex-marine lieutenant colonel Oliver North—a whole parade of people who warped the laws and mocked the rules. One minute they're among the elect, immune from the laws of simple decency, next minute they're down in the ditch. According to journalist Hunter Thompson, a man not fond of pretense, there's a special kind of hell reserved for shamed politicians and disgraced guardians of the public morality: "A place where the beasts are blind and the doomed scream all night in the darkness."[1] A place where those rare and rotten ones sink down after their perfidious behavior has been thoroughly exposed.

It's hard to know how much shame disgraced public figures feel. For that matter, it's hard to know what anyone feels. We don't even know how bad someone else's headache hurts, much less how much shame they feel. When a disgraced politician slithers off and crawls back under a rock, is it from shame or merely to escape the glare of public criticism? How much disgrace evokes how much shame? It depends upon the available supply.

Repeated reexposure to shame in adulthood recapitulates the process by which a shameful image of the self was laid down in the first place. Isolated experiences of shame are like cold drops of water. When there are enough of them, the drops run together into one big icy puddle. The result is an abiding sense of not being good enough as a person—defective. In this way, shame becomes part of one's identity. "I *feel* ashamed" becomes "I *am* shameful." The conscious experience of internalized shame may be feelings of inadequacy, rejection, or self-doubt; feeling guilt-ridden or unlovable; and permanent loneliness—but the underlying problem is shame.

Shame as an Anxiety

Shame is also a form of signal anxiety, evoked by the imminent danger of exposure to humiliation. Anxiety is a primitive physiological reflex pattern; shame is this biological response plus the idea that the upset is due to one being despicable and worthless. What is feared is contemptuous rejection. This anxiety can be acute when, for example, we're called on to perform or speak in public. The wish is to parade one's self with pride, to feel the opposite of shame—honor, dignity, respect; the fear is that you'll fall flat on your face.

This shame-anxiety can lead to a general attitude of bashfulness and the avoidance of situations and actions that might bring about humiliation. The many forms that insecurity takes are, in fact, shame-anxiety expanded and generalized. Embarrassment, shyness, social phobia, inferiority feelings, and low self-esteem—all of these radiate from shame-anxiety. Anything that can radiate that far must be highly charged indeed. Shame is hot. It burns. On some people it even shows. One thing you can't hide is blushing. Here, for example, is Tennessee Williams's account of how shame anxiety becomes a self-fulfilling prophecy.

I remember the occasion on which this constant blushing had its beginning. I believe it was in a class in plane geometry. I happened to look across the aisle and a dark and attractive girl was looking directly into my eyes and at once I felt my face burning. It burned more and more intensely after I had to face front again. My God, I thought, I'm blushing because she looked into my eyes or I into hers and suppose this happens whenever my eyes look into the eyes of another?

As soon as I had entertained that nightmarish speculation, it was immediately turned into reality.

Literally, from that incident on, and almost without remission for the next four or five years, I would blush whenever a pair of human eyes, male or female, would meet mine.[2]

We blush, we burn, our hearts pound from fear of shame. What is it we're so ashamed of?

"WHAT'S WRONG WITH ME?"

We may speak, incorrectly, of being ashamed of certain actions, but shame is about who we are, not what we do. We feel guilty about breaking the rules, ashamed of ourselves for doing so. Shame is closer to identity than action; no single act is seen as wrong and, therefore, reparable.

If you lie to a friend and feel guilty, you can confess and apologize. If you lie to a friend and get caught before you can confess, you may feel so ashamed that you can't even face that friend. In shame, it is the self that feels worthless. If you are bad, you can make amends. If you are worthless, *there's nothing you can do about it.*

What is it about the self that is so unacceptable? What is the basic content of shame? According to Leon Wurmser, one of the most astute psychoanalytic students of shame, human beings are ashamed of three things above all else: weakness, dirtiness, and defectiveness.[3]

Weakness

Children, in their naive cruelty, mock each other with these shameful traits. What do they call weaklings? "Sissy," "wimp," "namby-pamby," "fraidy-cat," "big baby," "chicken," "momma's boy," "teacher's pet." Most of these names are so overworked that they lose their sting—unless *you* are the kid they call "chicken" *and* you're afraid it's true.

We may outgrow the name-calling, but we don't outgrow the fear of weakness. As we grow older, physical weakness becomes more acceptable but not incompetence, stupidity, or moral cowardice. The worst weakness is where we're supposed to be strong: impotence, literally or figuratively, for men; selfishness for women. A person who prides himself or herself on brains may even feel ashamed of not being able to remember answers to Trivial Pursuit questions. In our culture, even old is bad, shameful. When we get old, we become "feeble," "invalid," "incompetent," "incontinent," "senile," "old fogies." Better stay young—and strong.

Dirtiness

The shame of dirtiness applies literally to uncleanliness and figuratively to moral corruption. "Dirty" is the word we use for unchecked human appetites. Giving way to any of the seven deadly sins—pride, covetousness, lust, anger, gluttony, envy, or sloth— makes us vile, foul, and filthy—but, after all, human.

There is, of course, a difference between, for example, instinctive sexual desire and desire twisted into perversion. Ironically, secret deviance is likely to be a product of frustration due in part to shame of natural sexuality. Anger, too, can be a natural wish to fight back against injury, or it can be a poisonous hatred against everything and everyone. But because the ideational content of shame remains unconscious, we cannot subject our deepest fears to rational scrutiny. And so we live with shame about our natural humanity.

This same lack of acceptance applies to physical bodily discharges. We bury human excrement for a reason. Shit stinks and it's riddled with disease-causing bacteria. But some people seem to think they must always be on guard lest they be exposed as dirty, messy, and disgusting. The result of this anxious vigilance may be fastidious cleanliness, reticence, or both.

If you have any doubt about how anxious people are to avoid the shame of being exposed as dirty, take note of the number of advertisements for personal hygiene products—not to make us beautiful, just to hide our dirty smells. It's not enough to take a shower and brush our teeth. We have to scrub, scour, disinfect, deodorize, scent, spray, powder, and perfume ourselves. We disinfect our homes and then cloud the rooms with scents of pine and flowers. We deodorize our kitchens and bathrooms and rugs and cars and the cat's litter box. We can even buy deodorizing bone-shaped biscuits for Bowser, in case he has doggie bad breath. Much worse, of course, is the dread prospect of human bad breath. So gargle twice a day with Scope (Listerine if you're tough), freshen your breath with Clorets, and spray it with Binaca if someone attractive approaches. To protect ourselves from an outbreak of BO, we can choose "long-lasting protection," "longer-lasting protection," or "super-long-lasting protection"—depending, I suppose, more on how anxious we are than on how bad we smell. Some deodorants are "manly," others are "strong enough for a man but made for a woman." Ladies are also advised to . . . well, you know . . . use Summer's Eve. And don't forget Odor Eaters for your shoes. God forbid you should smell like a human being.

In the same way, extreme politeness, which most of us admire, may be a negative achievement, driven more by shame about what is natural and spontaneously human than by consideration for other people's feelings.

When I wrote to friends to ask them for some embarrassing memories, one very dear friend wrote back several examples that had to do with bodily functions. Her letter surprised me. I know her as a successful, considerate person. What I didn't know—had no idea, really—is how anxious she is about cleanliness.

My grade school was very, very old, and the girls' rest room was in a dark and dingy basement, with no partitions between the toilets. Heaven forbid someone else should be there using the bathroom at the same time. I don't think I ever used the bathroom in eight years of school (fortunately, we lived only six blocks away and I went home for lunch). I developed very good bladder and bowel control, so I suppose it wasn't a complete loss. On the other hand, one of my recurring nightmares (the one besides the test in the course I've forgotten to attend) is that lots of other people are around when I'm trying to go to the bathroom. Oh, yes, when I went to Girl Scout camp, we had four-seater outhouses, so I always tried to find an excuse to use the staff outhouse (a one-seater).

Embarrassing moments? When I was a teenager and discovered after a party that there was parsley stuck in my teeth after I had been smiling and talking to people.

Of course, girls live in constant fear that they'll get their periods when they're not prepared, or that they'll "leak" even when they think they're prepared.

You realize that you forgot to put on deodorant and now you worry because you're sweating and you think everyone can smell you.

You did use deodorant but you're standing next to someone who didn't, and they smell, and you're worried that everyone thinks it's you, instead. This was actually a problem I faced during graduate school, when a girlfriend had very bad body odor, and I didn't quite know how to tell her, but I was concerned that people would think it was me. The smell got so bad that I really found it difficult to be with her, so I found myself avoiding her more and more. Would it have been more embarrassing to tell her and risk her displeasure? I don't know.

God, I was a prude back then, and still am, to some extent, today— for example, the word "fart" was not one I ever heard used at home, and I think most members of my family would have died rather than pass gas (actually, I don't know that we even had a word for it) in public. Even when I was in the hospital after having Amanda and after my operation, I was not thrilled about being gassy and not being able to control it. I still sort of cringe when I hear the word "fart."

Your own threshold for embarrassment may be different, but every one of us is vulnerable to shame about being dirty. Search your experience, you'll find that it's true.

Defectiveness

The third of the three shameful qualities is defectiveness. We are ashamed of physical or mental shortcomings. The content of this shame, what anyone considers defects in the self, varies greatly. Some people are ashamed of anything that makes them conspicuous—their height, weight, hair color, facial features— especially if it runs counter to sex-role stereotypes. A young man may be proud of being tall, a young woman may be ashamed of it. Culture shapes shame, and every now and then we have public campaigns to rescue certain groups from shameful regard. It's now officially okay to be black, female, crippled, homosexual, or old. But how real is our acceptance when we sugarcoat reality by relabeling these variations on the human condition? So far, women are still women, but homosexuals are "gays," crippled people are "handicapped," elderly people are "senior citizens" or —yeuch!—"golden agers," and, as of this writing, there is a campaign to substitute "African-American" for those we used to call blacks, and before that Negroes.

Prejudice is ugly and stupid. It should be crushed. But the hardest place to crush prejudgment is the cruel judgment we bury in our own hearts about ourselves.

One example of how cruelly people can judge themselves as defective is Franz Kafka, who was deeply ashamed of his body, which he considered disgracefully skinny and weak. Not until he was twenty-eight years old did he feel able to appear at public swimming pools. Kafka's profound alienation from his body led to profound difficulty in relationships.[4] Most of us manage to show up at the pool before twenty-eight, but who among us cannot remember being ashamed of defects—real or imagined—and remember as well how that shame made us hang back?

Who knows how much adolescent anguish lies behind S. J. Perelman's delicious self-mockery?

Blue as an auctioneer's jowl, the pool of the Hotel Belshazzar in Bel Air, Southern California's most opulent suburb, lay shimmering in the noonday heat. Around it, barbecuing themselves an expensive cordovan, a dozen guests drowsed and gossiped languidly, narcotized by the remorseless sun. Suddenly, without warning, the loungers by the pool were galvanized into attention. A man of imposing mien, who wore his white terry robe with the dignity of a toga and whose profile might have graced some early Roman post office, had approached the diving board. As he slipped from his robe, there stood revealed a body as flawless as a banana: the shoulders small and exquisitely formed, a chest that would have shamed Tom Thumb's, a magnificent melon-shaped paunch that quivered like junket at its owner's slightest command. With the ease of a born gymnast, he dropped on all fours, crept out warily to the very end of the diving board, crept back, and, sides heaving painfully, collapsed on a beach mattress.[5]

This is black humor, a cathartic attempt to master shame by scoffing in defiance. Perelman says, Ha-ha, look at me! I'm skinny. Shame says, Hide.

HIDING FROM OTHERS BECOMES ALIENATION FROM THE SELF

Just as exposure is the immediate cause of shame, the immediate response is to hide. In fact, the linguistic root of the word "shame" is to hide or cover up. According to the *Oxford English Dictionary,* the word "shame" is derived from a Teutonic root *skam/skem,* meaning "sense of shame." Earlier still, it can be traced back to the Indo-European root *kam/kem,* meaning "to cover, to veil, to hide." The prefixed *s* (*skam*) adds the reflexive meaning: "to cover one-self." The wish to hide is inherent in and inseparable from shame.

Imagine, for a moment, the soul-chilling humiliation Hester Prynne had to endure when not only was her adultery exposed, but she was forced to submit to the scornful eyes of the community, shackled to the stock and branded with the scarlet letter *A.*

There can be no outrage, methinks, against our common nature . . . no outrage more flagrant than to forbid the culprit to hide his face for shame . . . under the heavy weight of a thousand unrelenting eyes. . . . Hester Prynne, meanwhile, kept her place upon the pedestal of shame, with glazed eyes, and an air of weary indifference . . . her spirit could only shelter itself beneath a stony crust of insensibility.[6]

Small children hide their faces or run to their rooms when they are shamed. The adult version of this wish to disappear is withdrawal. When we're shamed, we want to be alone, to regain equanimity and avoid further humiliation. In time, shame leads to a pattern of withdrawal and avoidance. Shame casts a large shadow over relationships, eclipsing the pleasure of companionship with fear of further exposure and with it rejection.

You don't have to move your feet to hide. Psychological retreat is every bit as isolating as physical seclusion. Perhaps more so.

Even when the habit of avoidance becomes stamped in character, it is still a defense aimed at external danger: the danger of exposure, shame, and rejection. What happens when the enemy is within, when shame is internalized? Defenses must now be aimed at one's self. Avoidance is transferred to the inner life, where it is installed as selective disowning of potentially shameful parts of the self.

How can we live with ourselves if the self is shamefully flawed? We do to ourselves as was done unto us. We disown those parts of the self that were rejected when we felt helpless in a hostile world.

One of my patients was the youngest of four children in a highly competitive Boston Brahmin family. The children anxiously paraded their achievements for their parents' approval and just as anxiously belittled each other's accomplishments. Mockery flowed downhill. The fact that the mockery her three older brothers dished out was a projection of their own anxiety did not lessen its mortifying impact. When they allowed her to play with them at all, they relegated her to subhuman roles. If the boys were cowboys, she was a dog. Not wanting to be left out, she complied. Later, when prizes were won in school, the boys scoffed at any accomplishments their little sister might dare to share with them. So she first learned not to share and then, to make her defense complete, she learned not to succeed, not even to compete. Today, the brothers are successful attorneys like their father. Their sister, with her 140 IQ, works as a secretary for some man with half her talent.

We know so little about ourselves, least of all the nature of painful feelings against which we protect ourselves by forcing them out of consciousness. This is perhaps more true of shame than of any other unhappy emotion. We underestimate the importance of shame in our lives because it's too painful to bear. So we keep it locked away where we don't have to face it.

Another painful emotion with which we are more familiar is guilt, which is often confused with shame.

SHAME VS. GUILT

The primary distinction between guilt and shame is the difference between the evil of being too powerful and the disgrace of being too weak. We feel guilt for being bad, for transgressing against others; we feel shame for being weak and worthless. Guilt is bad, shame is worse. Guilt is about something you've done; shame is about who you are.

Guilt is the inner experience of breaking the moral code. We feel bad about what we've done—worse than that, terrible—and we imagine being punished. But it's punishment for what we did, not for who we are.

Shame, on the other hand, is the inner experience of being looked down on by others; it is a painful feeling of unworthiness. Shame involves the entire self and the self-worth of a human being. We feel shame as humiliation and embarrassment, a sense of being diminished or insufficient. A pervasive sense of shame is the deep conviction that one is fundamentally bad, unworthy, inadequate, defective, and, ultimately, unlovable.

Guilt restrains strength; shame hides weakness. Guilt-anxiety warns us not to cross the boundary around the rights of others, and the affect of guilt is the punishment for having done so. Shame-anxiety marks the boundary around the private self, beyond which one cannot permit others to intrude. The affect of shame is the feeling we get when the boundary around the self has been violated. Guilt limits action; shame limits exposure.

Both shame and guilt lie close to the heart of human experience, and yet we hear so much about guilt, so little about shame. Why is that?

We're more conscious of guilt than shame because we remember the lessons of morality better than those of self-worth. Much of childhood is taken up with learning what to do and what not to do. Once we learn what's expected of us, we take it upon ourselves to restrain our actions, using guilt in the service of self-control. When loving parents teach their children right from wrong, they do so deliberately; in fact, passing on the cultural code of conduct is one of the primary functions of the family. The messages we get about our self-worth come earlier and are less intentional. Before they begin teaching us to control our motor activity, parents have already conveyed a great deal to us about our value.

Shame is more archaic, more encompassing than guilt. Guilt relates to a code of actions; shame relates to the core of the self. Guilt is the more familiar concept because it is simpler—easier to explain and easier to understand—and more immediately tied to deliberate action. (Guilt has long played a larger role than shame in psychoanalytic writings because it is so directly tied to conflict between unbridled libidinal and aggressive wishes and the mechanisms of social restraint, Freud's primary concern. As the psychology of the self begins to correct the unbalanced emphasis on the psychology of conflict, however, we will see shame becoming a topic of much greater concern.)

Although shame is at least as powerful a motivating force as guilt, guilt-induction is more deliberate and more familiar than shame-induction. Methods for dealing with guilt have been institutionalized in custom, religion, and law. For example, parole boards consider it essential that prisoners not only admit their guilt but also express remorse for what they've done. It's not enough to feel bad. Before he is considered rehabilitated, the jailed criminal is expected to feel guilty for doing wrong, not just ashamed of getting caught.

Rituals of atonement, confession, penance, punishment, repentance, reparation, and forgiveness are universal and well known. Not so with shame. Shame cannot be forgiven, only concealed. We confess our guilt; we hide our shame—from others and from ourselves.

Once the distinction between guilt and shame is spelled out, it's easier to understand the difference: Guilt is the feeling of *doing* something bad; shame is the feeling of *being* unworthy. Guilt is for wrongful actions; shame is for an inadequate self. But when we move from words on the page to experience in the world, things aren't always so clear. For one thing, the same action can evoke a mixture of guilt and shame.

Suppose a woman gets fed up with nagging her son to pick up his toys and starts screaming at him. She's had it, and she really lets him have it. He's not used to seeing his mother this way and so he becomes frightened and runs to his room, crying unconsolably. She's determined not to go in there and try to make up, but, listening to him sobbing, she feels awful. What in fact does she feel? Most people would say guilt. Women aren't supposed to shriek at their children—"nice girls" aren't even supposed to get angry. So she's broken the code of motherhood, twice. She feels guilty for what she's done, but she's also likely to feel shame. She's let herself down; she's not the calm, rational person she thought she was. In fact, she's turning out to be just like her mother. She's ashamed of herself.

Whenever you've done something that might cause either shame or guilt, you can try to figure out which is the predominant emotion by asking yourself which you feel worse about: violating someone else's rights, or letting yourself down? And which consequence do you fear most: punishment for transgressing, or rejection for being unworthy? As I said, you can *try* to figure out which is which. But human emotions are never simple. Shame, like guilt and depression and so many other emotions we cover with a single word, is really a complex phenomenon made up of a number of different feelings. By the time you finish reading Chapter 7, you will have a fairly comprehensive understanding of the dynamics of shame. This understanding will enable you to better know the workings of your own emotional life, but it won't make emotions simple. If you want simple emotions, get a dog—better yet, a goldfish.

Shame, "the alienating emotion," is ugly and painful. It turns us against ourselves and drives us away from other people. Like other ugly emotions, including hatred and anxiety, shame is a blight and a curse. And yet, like all things human, shame serves a purpose.

3
The Adaptive Function of Shame

Every emotion propels us toward some human action, and every emotion has its uses. Grief is the sorrow of loss; it makes us weep and remember, mourn and, finally, let go. Guilt is the inner anguish of transgressing against others. Before the act, guilt holds us back; after the act, guilt makes us seek punishment and restitution for having done wrong. Anxiety is the fear of danger, known or unknown; it urges us to run. Contempt has the aim of eliminating a person by rejection. Love's aim is union. Shame makes us want to hide.

Hiding has its uses. Shame is linked to the human need to protect that which is vulnerable. The self cannot function effectively without protection. Shame acts as a barrier to shield the self from physical intrusion and psychological attack. Shame also ensures the self's integrity by enforcing fidelity to ideals and honor. Shame safeguards our identity and protects our privacy.

PRIVACY

The contemporary estimate of privacy is at best ambivalent. Disillusioned by politics and worn down by indefatigable pressures at work, many people seek satisfaction and security mainly in the private realm. But for this very reason, others regard the private realm with suspicion as a retreat from the more demanding but ultimately more important public realm. Privacy, in this view, is an evasion of social opportunity and responsibility—a haven for selfish indulgence.

Personal privacy conflicts with public curiosity, a fact that is shamelessly exploited by the press. Newspaper reporters and television crews, unhampered by any scruples of modesty or tact, swoop down on the rich and famous like sharks in a feeding frenzy. If heavyweight boxing champion Mike Tyson wants to visit ex-wife Robin Givens, even after their bitter and very public divorce, he may be ashamed to be spied on by the American paparazzi. He may need privacy to work out his feelings and his relationship. He has a right to feel embarrassment at being exposed and angry at being intruded upon.

Some things *ought* to be private. Parents need privacy to discuss disagreements about disciplining their children, and they need privacy to make love. The closed door acts as a barrier to ensure the integrity of the marital unit; it permits the couple to deal with each other and it bars outside interference. Every unit, every system, every relationship, and every person needs protective boundaries. Lovers discussing the possibility of getting married need to be alone. Teenagers facing themselves in the mirror, practicing their smiles or inspecting for pimples, need to be alone. Shame makes them close the door.

Intrusion arouses shame; shame protects the privacies of life. Friendship and love, sex, birth and death, prayer, nakedness, elimination, even eating—these things belong to the private realm of experience. These private acts make us vulnerable. Our own modesty and other people's discretion protect us against violation.

Exposing the intimacies of life to public view is obscene. The more personal the intimacy, the more obscene the invasion. It's embarrassing for someone to walk in on you when you're picking your nose, worse if you're taking a crap, and worse still if you're making love. It's not that you're doing something wrong; you feel shame because what you're doing—grooming, going to the bathroom, or making love—is a private experience, not necessarily one that is negatively valued.

"Privacy" is a loaded word; it's hard to argue with "the right to privacy." To labor the need for privacy is to risk moralizing as well as unbalancing the truth. But nothing is inherently private, and most things are better shared, if they can be. Take a strong man's private weakness, for example. Most men, if they cry at all, prefer to do so alone. Perhaps it would be healthier for them to own up to their feelings, to be more open. And yet some things feel too private, too embarrassing, to show openly. Perhaps the point is that privacy is necessary to protect us when we're vulnerable. Maybe you can relate to the following example from my own experience.

I never really learned to dance as a kid. At thirteen, I grew nine inches in one year. Suddenly tall, I was gawky, awkward, and extremely self-conscious—much too self-conscious to risk tripping over my own feet, especially in front of a *girl*! From fifteen to eighteen, I was busy playing football and basketball and running the high hurdles when other kids were going to sock hops. Now I love to dance—but only in private. The energy might come from good news or the bottled up tension of a long week; the safety comes from the privacy of my own house. I'll put on Merle Haggard or Chuck Berry or Aretha Franklin, turn the stereo way up loud, and let the driving beat move me, giving in to my feelings and letting go with my body. It's wonderful. But I'd be mortified if anyone other than the cat saw me.

Intrusion arouses shame, but not all intrusion. Shame does not restrain all exposure; it protects against defiling exposure. Shame guards the separate, private self and prevents intrusion during activities that make us feel vulnerable. Some of these activities rightly remain private, others need protection because they're tender, in the process of development. Earlier I talked about behavior as public performance. Some things we can't perform in public until we're ready. We need time offstage, time for rehearsal, before we try out certain difficult performances in front of an audience. The sense of shame protects this private time.

In his book *Shame, Exposure, and Privacy,* theologian Carl Schneider has written eloquently about our need for shame as protective covering:

> Processes of growth need protective covering until a certain aging or mellowing gives form to emerging values and unarticulated commitments. The sense of shame protects this process. This protection is against ourselves as much as against others, for what is sheltered is not something already finished, but something in the process of becoming—a tender shoot. Like a darkroom, shame protects against the premature exposure to light that would destroy the process. It functions like the protective cover during the period of gestation, until the embryo—whether seed or soul—has come to full term and is ready to emerge.[1]

Shame tells us our limits and acts as a boundary, but it would be a mistake to think of this boundary as merely enforcing separateness. Psychological boundaries help us maintain a balance between autonomy and social participation. In the wild, predatory animals can share the same region because they respect each other's territories. In the city, human beings use shame to afford them a bubble of privacy. We can walk in a crowd and still maintain our personal integrity and the privacy of our relationships. The lowered voice and the averted gaze cushion life in public. As we move about, our privacy is protected by the sense of shame. "Good fences make good neighbors."

Shame not only protects us from intrusion, it also enforces fidelity to social values. What is valued changes from generation to generation, and from culture to culture.

THE CULTURAL USES OF SHAME

When anthropologists speak of "cultural relativism," we often think of quaint customs in faraway places. What They do is odd, charming but peculiar; what We do is . . . well, the way things are done.

When it comes to culture, we're like goldfish in a bowl who don't see the water they swim in. Whether it is "magical and primitive" or "scientific and civilized," culture scripts our lives in countless unseen ways. The question is not whether we are products of culture, but merely how conscious we are of that fact. Usually, we aren't conscious of the controlling forces in our lives—dictates of the superego, traffic laws, or cultural mores—until we break the rules.

Conflict with culture is punished by shame and guilt, culture's police force. Parents transmit the demands of society in the form of guilt in order to socialize their children. Guilt protects the physical integrity of others, helping us live harmoniously in social groups. Social conformity achieved through guilt takes the form of *submission*. Shame plays a complementary role to guilt, protecting the psychological and moral integrity of the self and ensuring fidelity to the ideals of the culture. Guilt helps societies ensure conformity and cooperation; avoiding shame enables individuals to be secure and accepted. Whereas guilt is a product of obedience, shame comes from comparing and competing with peers (siblings, playmates, work associates, social class, etc.). Social conformity achieved through shame takes the form of *identification*.

Anthropologists distinguish between the "shame culture" of primitive groups and the "guilt culture" of advanced societies.[2] I'm not so sure this distinction holds up. Perhaps, as philosopher Eric Hoffer suggests, the prevalence of shame is less a matter of social primitiveness than of social compactness. Primitive societies were tightly compacted. But a technologically advanced society, like Japan, in which the individual is totally integrated with the group, has as strong a sense of shame as any primitive tribe. Americans get claustrophobic thinking about such regimented social pressure. Long past the time when we were a nation of wide-open spaces, we still like to think of ourselves as rugged individualists. We distrust social pressure.

Culture has always been a favorite target of radical protest because it seems to be antithetical to freedom, something imposed upon us by repressive authority. Thus social critics attack the authoritarian family, repressive social morality, literary censorship, and the work ethic. Psychologists are among the most self-righteous critics of anything that smacks of opposition to individual autonomy. In the 1960s, for example, R. D. Laing—the Morton Downey, Jr., of British psychiatry—described children as helpless prisoners of family and culture. So oppressed is the natural child, according to Laing, that his only recourse is to develop a divided self, offering a compliant "false self" to appease his jailers while hiding away the real self that their tyranny threatens to annihilate.[3] Although Laing's assault on the family was dramatized to extremes—the "concentration camp" of modern society—it was enormously popular, demonstrating our fondness for imagining ourselves innocent victims of malevolent culture.

Writing in this same culture-bashing tradition, Gershen Kaufman and Lev Raphael described America as a shame-based culture, but one in which shame is hidden. In their article "Shame as Taboo in American Culture," they argued that there are three cultural scripts in contemporary America that foster shame.[4] The first of these is the *success ethic,* which enjoins us to compete for success and to be ashamed of failure or mediocrity. "The injunction to compete for success inevitably strangles our capacity for caring and vulnerability."[5] The second cultural injunction is to be *independent and self-sufficient.* Our cultural hero is the cowboy, who stands proudly alone, never needing anything or anyone. Needing people makes us vulnerable—that is, makes us weak—which we're ashamed of. The final injunction is to *be popular and conform.* Being different is shameful.

Kaufman and Raphael acknowledge that these cultural injunctions create conflicting scripts, but that's their point: cultural injunctions foster shame by generating conflict. The point is well taken (as I shall explore when I examine the impact of cultural norms on American children) but one-sided. While it's true that cultural expectations can produce shame, it is not true that culture is primarily repressive. Cultural expectations may at times seem oppressive, but culture isn't imposed on us; we create it.

Culture is a collective expression of the human need to regulate personal drivenness for the security of group loyalties. We are born with an inner compass that directs us to find our own personal identity—"Follow your bliss." But we also have a second heritage, the heritage of culture.

Every group of persons living in a single area—from Aleuts to Zulus—builds up a set of ways of coping with the environment and of living together cooperatively, which form their culture and its instrumentalities. Culture is the cumulative wisdom of the group. Shame, culture's instrument, ensures group cohesiveness by enforcing standards of conduct, from the personal to the collective and from the sacred to the profane.

Every culture has its objects symbolizing achievement and respect. Whether the trappings of self-respect depend upon the accumulation of cowrie shells as on the Rossel Islands in the Pacific, arm bands and necklaces as in the Trobriands, or German automobiles and Italian clothes as in the canyons of Wall Street, the culture's role in defining symbols of pride is similar.

Likewise, every culture has rules, backed by shame, about eating and elimination, sex and nudity. Although we like to think of those *National Geographic* pictures of naked South Sea islanders as proof that some cultures aren't ashamed of the human body, most cultures have strict taboos against displaying the genitals. The primeval association of sex with shame is, like the taboos against incest and endogamy, part of an apparatus devised to control the destructive capability of this potentially antisocial impulse. Sex, of course, is not the only threat to the group. Cowardice, weakness, uncleanliness, and bad manners are also dangerous, and they, too, are associated with shame.

Conformity with accepted standards of behavior reflects a dual allegiance to the proprieties of the group and the dignity of the self. Eating and elimination are physical activities that belong to the private realm and, therefore, need protection. Engaging in such elemental bodily functions makes every creature vulnerable. Animals are vulnerable to attack when eating or defecating; human beings are vulnerable to embarrassing intrusion. At both ends of the digestive cycle, we are reminded of our animal nature. We, too, are bound by the involuntary.

In all societies, eating is a ritualized activity, invested with social meaning and regulated by custom. It's hard to see the ritual significance of a family sitting around in front of the television set eating fried chicken from a cardboard bucket. Erosion of ceremony in our culture has obscured our awareness of ritual and ceremonial meaning, but even eating a meal takes on more ceremonial significance when we are in public. A meal shared with friends in a restaurant is an occasion for communion. When we dine out alone we are exposed. That's why most people hide behind a book or distract themselves by focusing their attention elsewhere.

We humanize and dignify elemental activities with custom and etiquette. Shame and concealment cover revelation of anything that reminds us of our animal nature. That's why it can be embarrassing to be intruded upon while eating unceremoniously. Sex, of course, is even more private. But the one room in American homes sure to have a functioning lock is the bathroom.

Excretion is very private. Our anxiety over exposure and humiliation is expressed vividly in our fear of "getting caught with our pants down." The cultural taboo surrounding elimination is rooted in the sense of the body as dirty and its products as disgusting. Repression weighs heavily on anality.

Cultural anthropologist Ernest Becker describes the problem of anality, in vivid language, in his Pulitzer Prize–winning book, *The Denial of Death*.

Anality and its problems arise in childhood because it is then that the child already makes the alarming discovery that his body is strange and fallible and has a definite ascendancy over him by its demands and needs. Try as he may to take the greatest flights of fancy, he must always come back to it. Strangest and most degrading of all is the discovery that the body has, located in the lower rear and out of sight, a hole from which stinking smells emerge and even more, a stinking substance—most disagreeable to everyone else and eventually even to the child himself.[6]

According to Becker, the anus (and its repulsive product) fills us with disgust because it reminds us of our physicality and our boundedness. As Montaigne put it, "On the highest throne in the world man sits on his arse." Usually this epigram makes people laugh because it deflates artificial pride and snobbery, and lowers us back down to earth. On closer examination, the joke, like most jokes, is about something truly fearful. Anality is disgusting because it reminds us of our fate. We refuse to concede that we are rooted in nature, because to be rooted in nature is to share a common fate with things physical: decay and death.

Shame does double duty, reflecting the dualism of human nature: individual privacy and social connectedness. Shame preserves the integrity of the individual—shielding the self against exposure—and enforces allegiance to the norms of the group.

In exchange for security, society extracts loyalty. A society is not only essential to its members, but it has an existence of its own, and its culture is its heart, which its members will defend with their lives because without it they are rootless and lost. No wonder we honor the loyal and brave, and shun the disloyal and cowardly.

When I was a kid, I often wondered what motivated soldiers to risk death in battle—and would I do it? Shooting my friends with my trusty six-shooter always seemed like fun. ("Don't mess with me, sucker—bang! bang!") But what about running across a field where real people were shooting real bullets? What would make somebody risk that? When I was drafted in 1968, I found out: humiliation, disgrace, dishonor—ideals drilled into us from day one, and backed up by the threat of court-martial. For those who disgraced themselves by disobeying orders, punishment was sure and swift.

War once galvanized national loyalty as nations fought for their very survival. In our time, however, we have seen ugly little wars, fought not for survival but merely for political influence. These neocolonial conflicts tear powerful nations apart. The war in Vietnam split our own country into two angry camps, one side decrying the war as a shameful abuse of power, the other side demanding that we fight on to avoid the shame of abandoning an ally. (Cynics said we were fighting to save face—and the face was Lyndon Johnson's.) Weakness and disloyalty are shameful, but violence against a small and weak adversary is also shameful. Sober assessment was muddled, on both sides, by anger and shame.

War is certainly not an everyday occurrence. Most of us are normally more concerned with the office wars and the private struggles of our personal lives, and yet real war brings the dilemma of social allegiance into sharp focus (just as serious psychopathology shows us what quirks of character look like magnified). The everyday dilemma that war dramatizes is the potential conflict between one's personal ideals and those of the state. Shame serves the need to identify and belong by enforcing the rules of culture, but shame also serves the need to be true to one's own ideals by enforcing the rules of conscience. Trouble comes when loyalties collide.

Sometimes one's own internalized social ideals are clear, and conflicting laws of the state are clearly wrong. For an inspiring few, personal ideals may even be held higher than life itself.

Socrates loved life, but allowed himself to be put to death by the state because he refused to deny his beliefs.[7] After being condemned, but before being sentenced to die, he did not swerve: "The unexamined life is not worth living." And when sentenced: "I would rather die having spoken after my manner, than speak in your manner and live." After his disciples urged him to escape from jail, he engaged, in the *Crito,* in a "dialogue" with the laws of the state.

They would say, "Now you are doing what only a miserable slave would do, running away and turning your back upon the compacts and agreements which you made as a citizen. . . . Do not make yourself ridiculous. . . . All patriotic citizens will cast an evil eye upon you as a subverter of the laws. . . . Will you go to them without shame and talk to them, Socrates? . . . Will there be no one to remind you that in your old age you were not ashamed to violate the most sacred laws from a miserable desire of a little more life?" "This is the voice," said Socrates, "that I hear murmuring in my ear. I cannot hear any other."[8]

Some people prefer death to the shame of betraying the integrity of their ideals.

Socrates's martyrdom is inspiring; real-life conflict rarely assumes such mythic proportions. Nevertheless, as we shall see, the struggle of ordinary men and women to reconcile their own best judgment with the dictates of culture has its own kind of drama, and its own kind of nobility.

Yes, shame has a socially useful controlling influence on behavior. But if shame has a domesticating effect on the wild human spirit, most of us are overly domesticated. Unfortunately, when we are taught shame, the lessons are not always rational or deliberate.

A social behavior theory of shame, which focuses on criticism to inculcate values, is superficial because it fails to account for all that is unconscious and contrary to reason. Parents deliberately transmit a more or less rational set of values and norms, showing approval for culturally valued behavior, like honesty and loyalty, and disapproval for violations of cultural mores. But parents also foster shame unthinkingly. They betray disgust and contempt both for taboo behavior, like playing with feces, and for perfectly healthy forms of behavior that they simply aren't comfortable with, like crying, perhaps, or spontaneous exuberance. Moreover, parents also allow shame to take root merely by failing to foster healthy pride.

So, while shame is one of the instruments through which culture shapes personality, it is a blunt instrument. The process miscarries for at least three reasons. First, cultural traditions change slowly. Culture's stubborn attachment to the past means that we are heirs not only to the wisdom of our ancestors but also to the ghost of their fears. Consider the lingering stigma of divorce, which still adds to the burdens of those who find it necessary to change the shape of their families. Second, subcultures may enforce conformity to unhealthy norms. In the 1950s, for example, it was shameful for teenage boys *not* to guzzle beer at parties. Third, as

I just mentioned, parents inculcate excessive shame by their inadvertent failure to actively validate children's good feelings about themselves.

Once you understand shame and what it does, you begin to see signs of it everywhere—no, not shame itself, that we keep hidden, but the defenses against it.

4

•••••••

The Mechanisms of Defense

Shame is so painful that we hide it, file it away and try to forget it. Forgetting about shame does not, of course, heal the hurt. It festers. Hidden beneath our insecurities, shame acts on us, and we react to it in automatic and uncritical ways. Before we can face shame and get past it, we must uncover it, and to do that we must understand where and how it is hidden—our defensive coping strategies.

A WORRIED MIND

In the course of every child's life, painful emotions—anxiety and depression, guilt and shame—come to be associated with certain thoughts and actions. When this happens, psychological defenses are instituted to minimize or, if possible, eliminate the unpleasant affects in question.

Deliberate actions can be deliberately curbed, but unbidden impulses cannot so easily be regulated. The heart-racing, shaky fear of anxiety warns us how dangerous our impulses can be; gut-knotting guilt damns us to suffer for wrong acts; and burning shame makes us feel deep-down dirty and worthless. Feelings and thoughts such as these are more than most people can bear. They must be warded off, defended against as effectively as possible.

One reason for the continuing appeal of western movies and detective shows is that when cowboys and private eyes face danger, they take action. Unfortunately, the atavistic options—fight or flight—are rarely appropriate for the stresses of modern life. Instead, we have defense mechanisms.

Defense mechanisms edit our awareness, filter our emotions, and divert unruly impulses into safe channels. They are attentional tricks we play on ourselves to avoid pain; they protect us, but at a cost. We prevail against anxiety by sacrificing some of the full range of life. We don't *have* the experience from which we might profit. After a while we get stuck, caught up in defensive rituals that cost us the simple, unattainable art of taking things as they come.

In Psychology 101 we learned the standard defense mechanisms: *suppression, repression, denial, projection, reaction formation, isolation, sublimation, displacement,* and *rationalization.* Or perhaps you learned a different list, one that included *intellectualization* but not *denial.* Actually, any alteration of attention or awareness can be defensive, whether it takes the form of psychic filtering, distracting action, or diverting fantasy. Active strivings that we don't normally consider defensive, like aggressiveness or sex, can also be used for defensive purposes. Active or passive, defenses are useful shelters, hard shells into which the self can retreat.

The mind defends itself against anxiety by any and all means available. Despite their diverse nature, however, there is something that all modes of defense have in common. This is opposition to facing shame, and even stronger opposition to exposing it. Every defense has an element of denial or negation.

Among the most common defenses against shame are: withdrawal, arrogance, contempt, ridicule, defiance, disavowal, numbness and boredom, envy, rage, and obsessions and compulsions.

WITHDRAWAL

When we're ashamed, it's natural to want to hide. Little children run to their rooms to escape a parent's tirade or a sibling's teasing. Retreat gives the child a chance to pull himself together. Just think of all the ruses to which children resort to avoid being buffeted about at school. They "get sick," sleep late, cut classes, work on special projects, and sit in the corner looking sad. Grown-ups have their own ways of curling up under the covers.

A colleague of mine once submitted a journal article that was accepted for publication but with several criticisms that required rewriting. Chagrined, he put the manuscript away and never again submitted an article to the critical eyes of an editor. Temporary respite can become self-defeating habit. Another friend stopped giving talks at professional meetings a couple of years ago. When I asked her about it, she said that although the response to her talks had been generally favorable, one of the feedback forms had called her "boring and pedantic." She was so hurt that she refused to submit herself to that ever again. "I'm sorry," she said, "but it just hurts too much."

Sure it hurts. Everyone is stung by criticism—if the criticism strikes a nerve. My friend who was so hurt by being called "boring and pedantic" probably worries that it might be true. Another friend flew home from giving his first professional workshop burning with shame after reading the comment that he was "shallow and superficial." This friend, however, responded by polishing up his act. Now he's one of the most popular speakers in his field. When a five-year-old sits in the corner looking sad, someone will probably come over and ask what's wrong. At five, but not thirty.

A familiar example of the unhappy consequences of withdrawal is the person with few long-standing close friendships. ("Close" because casual friends have limited capacity to hurt us.) The lonely are vulnerable, old hurts keep them from making new friends. Most friendships go through predictable stages, from initial attraction, to the first tentative steps toward each other, to intimacy. It's a courtship without the intoxication. Inevitably, somewhere between getting to know each other and developing trust, something will go wrong. The other person hurts your feelings. You ask her to save you a seat, but when you get there she's sitting with someone else. Or you begin to realize that you're always the one who calls. Or your friend always seems to be busy when you invite her to your house. In the course of friendship, we all wonder how much the other person *really* likes us, and we all feel rejected sometimes. When this happens we have essentially three choices: withdraw, pursue the friendship despite feeling bad, or say something about our feelings. Some people who feel like withdrawing let their feelings dictate their actions, others don't.

ARROGANCE, CONTEMPT, AND RIDICULE

Arrogance, contempt, ridicule—nasty words that suggest defensiveness is willful and mean. But have you ever considered the narcissistic value of a bull session in which a group of friends sit around and take others apart? "She thinks she's so smart!" "Oh, I liked him at first, but then I realized the only person he really cares about is himself." Everybody has a marvelous time (it's a form of consciousness-lowering). Why? Because self-esteem is heightened by a mutual lowering of others. Is this good or bad? It depends. Nobody likes nasty, mean-spirited gossip. Gossip is like any other form of aggression: If it's too flagrant, we're turned off; otherwise it's a source of pleasure. It's only our conflict about—shame over— natural human tendencies like criticism, sex, or violence that disgusts us if they're too blatant, if they exceed our tolerance.

Our favored defenses become habitual mental maneuvers. When faced with anxiety, we naturally turn to whatever has been successful in warding it off in the past. Introverted children and those from disengaged families move away from threats to the self: A boy who insulates himself from rejection by not joining in may grow up to be aloof and arrogant. Extroverted, expressive children, from emotionally crowded families, are quick to blame and attack: A girl with a nasty mouth may grow up to be critical and contemptuous. They become the men and women who never apologize.

Acting superior is likely to cover a deep, lurking sense of inferiority. Arrogance in particular is a cover-up for shame, a means of
turning passive rejection into active rejecting. Its shape reflects
experience and culture. For example, shamed boys in many cultures grow up to be men who strut their aggressive machismo as
a defense against castration anxiety and shame over flawed masculinity. They act tough, talk dirty, and mock tenderness. They're
not sissies!

Some people make snide or sneering comments directly and
with venom, others pass off contempt with a joke. Fortunately, the
headlines deliver up a steady stream of characters who invite
ridicule by their own actions; they *are* ridiculous: Spiro Agnew, for
his puffed-up polysyllabic statements; Jim and Tammy Bakker, for
his peccadilloes and her crocodile tears; Imelda Marcos, for her
forty thousand pairs of shoes; and Gary Hart, for his flagrant infi-
delities. These easy targets are public property. We don't pull our
punches because we forget that these people are human beings.

Haughty arrogance and contempt cover a person's own fears of
ridicule. But in some instances arrogance isn't so obvious.

Last year my son's teacher was arrested for child abuse. We
were shocked, numb, confused. Nobody knew what the facts were,
and fears abounded. Many parents turned this teacher into the
monster of their own imaginations, assuming that he must have
molested generations of children. These people were frightened
and angry. Some demanded a cordon of police protection around
the school in the event that this poor unfortunate showed up with
an automatic rifle to shoot up the place. Some of us were more
reasonable, and we were horrified by this thirst for revenge. I
remember how disgusted I was when parents stood up to demand
that the authorities revoke this teacher's parole, throw him into
jail, and throw the key away. How can people be so cruel, so
vindictive?

Two weeks later, walking with my son in the Bronx near Yankee
Stadium after dark, I heard footsteps behind us and felt a shiver of
fear. For an instant my mind flashed to the possibility that some
stranger might try to hurt my boy. It came to me that I would kill
him, or at least want to. Then it hit me: The vindictive parents, the

people I was so contemptuous of, were feeling just as I was. The only difference was then I didn't feel my child was threatened, now I did. We're all arrogant; we just don't all know it.

DEFIANCE

Defiance is combative, bellicose and brave; its defensiveness is hard to miss (at least in others). If arrogance is cold, defiance is hot. Instead of being paralyzed by anxiety, defiant individuals confront any situation that threatens humiliation. As blatant as a teenager's argumentativeness, defiance is blind, irrational, and potentially self-damaging. But at least it's proud.

Some people make a career out of defiance. They become known for their aggressive, flamboyant contrariness, and divide opinion according to whether we're taken in by their manic defense or see through it to their deeper shame: weakness. Does anyone still think of Norman Mailer's public pugnacity as heroic, or Ernest Hemingway as "a real man"? Sometimes knowing what's in the background of a person's public posture alters our attitude. I remember James Baldwin's courageous and uncompromising opposition to racism, and I remember being electrified by his writing. But I also remember that life wore him down, and that he died from drink in expatriate decline.

Baldwin grew up poor, the illegitimate stepson of a bitter, mean man who told him that he was not only poor and black but also the ugliest child the stepfather had ever seen, with a weak little body and pop eyes.[1] As a child, this sensitive boy, convinced that he was ugly and unloved, was desperate to fit in. Unfortunately, the neighborhood children weren't kind. They taunted him: "Hey, Frog Eyes!" For years he cried himself to sleep at being so unlucky. Baldwin's life was a long struggle to rise above humiliation, to conquer his shame and harness his rage. His successes include a legacy of breathtakingly beautiful novels, of which *Another Country* is the masterwork, a devastating account of all that stands in the way of relationships between black and white, and men and women. Sadly, though, his unmetabolized rebellion against his stepfather led to a string of celebrated feuds. Defiance consumed him. In time, he became embittered and disillusioned with the civil rights movement, but perhaps even more by the erosion of his own powers. Bitterness turned him from a witness against injustice to a hateful critic of White America, and brought him to a sad end of loneliness and despair.

James Baldwin was a tragic hero, a man of courage who defied false convention and social injustice, but also a man ashamed, driven to rebellion and defiance in order to prove that he was not a weak, pop-eyed little boy. Our own defiance is likewise often double-edged: half bravery, half bravado.

DISAVOWAL

Defense, as Freud said in "The Unconscious," is always against emotion. Whatever the form of defense—repressing a wish into the unconscious and keeping it there, or projecting an unwelcome reaction onto someone else—the purpose is always to banish painful emotions. Although disavowal may not be a familiar defense mechanism, its operation is elegantly simple. Instead of forgetting or denying that something happened, disavowal merely subtracts the affect, "Yes, it happened, but it didn't bother me, so why get upset?"

The reason disavowal is less familiar than other mechanisms of defense is that students of psychoanalysis have followed Freud's belief that affect always signals instinctual impulses. Therefore, all defensiveness is assumed to mask an instinctual conflict, sexual or aggressive. As we have seen, however, painful emotion is not necessarily linked to instinctual conflict. Self-regard stirs strong feeling every bit as much as instinctual impulses. Shame, the prototype of painful feeling, is not about what we're doing, or even thinking about doing; it's about who we are. When it comes to instinctual impulses, effective defenses must curb action, but when it comes to painful feelings about the self, forgetting will do. Disavowal is a special case of forgetting.

In disavowal, shameful memories are conscious, but the painful emotion is split off: "Oh, yes, I was a klutz in junior high, but it didn't really bother me." We remember the details, the clumsiness and the teasing; what's repressed is the pain of it; we take in the facts but not the feelings that go with them. With disavowal we mold the past into something palatable, something we can live with.

NUMBNESS AND BOREDOM

In a snowball fight without gloves, the stinging cold soon numbs your hands. It takes longer, but a heart full of hurt also gets numb.

Perhaps you can remember discovering that you'd become so used to enduring unhappy emotions without complaint that you were beginning to get numb. Your grandmother died and you couldn't really feel it, or you saw the bloody aftermath of a crash on the highway and you were curiously distant. Like boxers who don't fight back, we absorb so much emotional punishment over the years that we become a little insensitive. Unfortunately, a heart inured to pain isn't as easy to warm up as are cold hands.

Numbness, by definition, is something we aren't usually aware of. What we are aware of is boredom, which is a derivative emotion that masks conflict and throws blame on something (or someone) else. The reason we're bored is that "We can't afford to have any fun," or "He (or she) never wants to do anything." The fault is not in ourselves but in the stars. Boredom is defensive. What we don't want to face makes us anxious; what we don't want to risk holds us back. Life becomes monotonous when shame and insecurity hold us back from venturing beyond habit and routine. Boredom isn't pleasant, but it is protective. When they're bored, some people daydream of tropical beaches or big-city nightlife or mountain meadows; others imagine that absent friends would make them happy, or that romance would provide the excitement missing from their lives. Not too many think about real life avoided, and why.

ENVY

I remember my first James Bond movie, *Dr. No.* I was seventeen, working as a dishwasher on Nantucket, and I went to whatever happened to be showing on that rainy afternoon between lunch and dinner. What a surprise! Having no idea what to expect doubled my pleasure. How I wished I could be like Sean Connery—so suave, so self-assured! I ached with envy, just as I had years earlier when Lash Larue dispatched bad guys with his whip. Grown-ups usually don't allow themselves such unguarded identification and envy, but most of us have fleeting moments when we wish we lived in the house on the hill or drove a Jaguar or had the easy elegance of men and women in Ralph Lauren clothing ads.

As unpleasant as envy is, it's less painful than its counterpart, shame. Wishing I were James Bond, I was aching for the impossible. But at least it was better than facing my feelings of being skinny, shy, and lonely. My daydreams were full of bittersweet adolescent longing, but they were easier for me than facing my anxiety about getting out and making friends.

NARCISSISTIC RAGE

As we've seen, when faced with shame, some people retreat, others attack. Narcissistic rage embodies both defensive strategies, because attacking others allows us to withdraw self-righteously. Rage is a reaction very close to shame. When we show ourselves to others and get ignored or rejected instead of the hoped-for appreciation, we feel ashamed. We all react to narcissistic injury— and subsequent shame—with hurt and anger. But the most shame-sensitive individuals flare up at the slightest criticism. Shame is the wound criticism hurts on the inside: When someone bumps against a wounded self, it's only natural to lash out in anger—much as an injured animal lashes out with instinctive self-protection against anything that hurts a tender spot. Unfortunately, since shame is hidden and hard to see, sometimes we only see the rage, and it often seems to come out of nowhere. Narcissistic rage, then, is the reaction of a self attacked.

Nobody is surprised if you kick a dog and it snaps at you. Similarly, we know that a direct assault on another person is likely to provoke a counterattack. Sometimes, however, we're surprised when an innocent comment—"All I said was, Is that what you're planning to wear to school?"—is met with an outburst of rage. (Innocent comments like this hide our controlling sentiments only from ourselves.) The response seems to be all out of proportion to the stimulus: "Goddamn it, you're always picking on me! Why can't you just leave me alone!" The person who is oversensitive or who overreacts is like a wounded animal, even a nudge can hurt.

A mild form of narcissistic rage occurs when a stubborn ("easy-to-assemble") appliance defeats our attempts to make it work and we flare up in frustrated rage. It's not just the frustration, it's the feeling of being made stupid that gets to us.

Whenever someone responds with an aggressive reaction—a hot retort or sharp retaliation—it's a safe bet that they felt attacked in a way that made them feel diminished, ashamed. Sometimes it's obvious what they're responding to; in other instances, some people just seem mean and spiteful. The dynamic is the same.

Narcissistic rage is the emotion that drives the two strutting *Tin Men*, BB (Richard Dreyfuss) and Tillie (Danny DeVito), to a war of revenge after their gleaming Cadillacs collide. The more you invest in a car (and I don't mean money), the more painful the dents and scratches. And, of course, it was narcissistic rage that drove the Glenn Close character in *Fatal Attraction* to a mad hysteria of revenge after the Michael Douglas character loved her and left her.

The desire for revenge is a way of hanging on to the rage. As long as we can hang on to our anger, we can focus outward—"I'll get them!"—instead of accepting the hurt and the shame. It's the kind of emotion that turns men into vigilantes. Wounded and bested, they become bent on avenging an attack against the self. Humiliated fury can be as little as slamming a door after an argument, or as much as murder.

Captain Ahab's relentless, hateful hunt for Moby Dick illustrates the enormity of rage that can come from a profoundly shameful injury to the self. Ahab sought revenge against the white whale that defeated him and took his leg. As long as he was in the grip of interminable narcissistic rage, he could concentrate on the whale and not dwell on his unbearable narcissistic injury.

Narcissistic rage serves a vital, self-protective function by insulating the self and keeping others away. This may seem inherently counterproductive, a good example of what is ordinarily meant by "defensiveness"—showing an inappropriate reaction—but it isn't necessarily. Withdrawal can be healing. What begins as an angry "I don't need them!" becomes a way to increase one's own self-reliance and autonomy—if the withdrawal is temporary.

OBSESSIONS AND COMPULSIONS

As we've seen, the patterning of defense is double-edged. While some aspects of experience are closed off, others are highlighted. We dwell in those zones of experience that are free of anxiety, or mostly free. We feel at home there. So we organize our thoughts and actions around very striking and compelling—and very narrow—themes. We become fixated. We artificially inflate small areas of the world, and these become our obsessions and our compulsions.

Some compulsions are addictive, in the true sense of the word. Alcohol and other drugs act as tranquilizers, which numb anxiety, and releasers, which lull inhibitions to sleep. Other involvements are addictive only metaphorically, in the sense of becoming controlling, though not chemical, habit. Obsessions, like addictions, offer illusory release, simultaneously a form of expression and a form of escape.

Most obsessions have the double advantage of furthering some of the self's aims while avoiding some of the risks of insecurity and shame. The helpful caretaker derives, from other people's neediness, a sense of being needed. Lovers, desperate seekers like the women Robin Norwood described in *Women Who Love Too Much*, try to acquire through fusion with a partner all that they lack inside. Hoping that new love will undo old scorn, they give themselves in masochistic surrender. The result is a cycle of romance with starry-eyed beginnings and tearful endings. The perfectionist does things just right so as not to feel just awful. Workaholics, most of whom have intimations of what their compulsive industry costs them, lose themselves in their profession, blinded by the kudos that success offers (or promises), and blind to the gentler satisfactions of family, friendship, and fun.

Obsessional people must always be in control. Of what? Their own feelings of inadequacy, of which they are ashamed. The hypochondriac, preoccupied with and perplexed by the workings of the physical plant, doesn't have time to worry about other things. (Maybe we're all hypochondriacs, only some of us don't brag about it.)

Just as healthy defenses are flexible, cushioning and protecting without trapping us, healthy preoccupations are also flexible. We do what we do because we love it, not because we're anxious if we don't. Compulsions are traps we walk into and are afraid to break out of. The way out—moving toward experience and toward other people—is guarded by insecurity and our fear of shame.

SHAMELESSNESS

Perhaps by now it's occurred to you that some people don't seem to be ashamed of even the most outrageous behavior. When Oliver North or Bernhard Goetze justify their crimes in the name of higher principles, even those of us who don't support their actions can at least understand their motives. But what about Al Sharpton, the minister who exploited Tawana Brawley for the publicity value of her audaciously fabricated story of gang rape? Or Leona Helmsley, the vainglorious hotel queen, who, when indicted for tax evasion, brazenly declared that "paying taxes is for little people"?

Why are some people so shameless? How can they openly do

such things as lie, cheat, and steal—actions that would mortify most of us with guilt and shame? The easy answer, that they are corrupt, won't do, because it's only a label. The explanation it implies is that some people grow up shameless because they aren't given a proper moral education; they don't have worthy consciences. This is only a slight improvement, for it confuses shame with moral standards.

Over the years I've seen a few patients that many people would consider shameless. One was a rich kid from Westchester who regularly stole from his parents and lied about it with innocent outrage. Another was a government official who calmly asked me to help him extract double payments from his insurance company. Frankly, I didn't like either of these two, but I could understand why they did what they did. The boy from the suburbs felt so deprived emotionally that he thought he was entitled to his parents' money; the crooked government official was a drug addict who did whatever was necessary to feed his cocaine habit. Neither of these two people were shameless: What they did, they did slyly.

"Shameless" means acting without restraint *and* doing so brazenly. I remember treating a handsome couple in which the husband regularly slept with other women on business trips. His promiscuity was hard to understand: His wife was gorgeous and gentle, a successful executive, and both of them said their sex life was good. I remember thinking what a jerk he was to hurt his wife and jeopardize his marriage by acting like an adolescent in heat. But I also remember thinking, if it was the thrill of sex with a stranger that he craved, why wasn't he at least more discreet? Another fellow with whom I had trouble empathizing was a doctor who owned his own clinic, a large estate, and two summer homes, as well as property in four states. When he divorced his wife of twenty years, he admitted to only $50,000 in assets, and settled by paying her less than half of that. (Unfortunately for his wife, the divorce took place in a state where the "deep pocket" spouse can hire the best and most ruthless attorney and divulge as little information as possible.)

What really stood out about these two charming characters wasn't only that they had no scruples, but that they were so blatant about their abusive treatment of their wives. They were proud of themselves. That's shamelessness.

A closer look into shamelessness reveals that some people provoke (external) humiliation to avoid more painful (inner) shame.

Early in *The Brothers Karamazov*, Dostoyevski describes a scene in which Fyodor Karamazov and his sons are invited to the monastery for a solemn meeting with the revered elder, Zossima. As usual, Karamazov acts the fool, deliberately patronizing the saintly Zossima, making up sacrilegious stories, and provoking the volatile Miusov to a tirade. Watching his performance, Karamazov's sons are mortified, but when he asks the elder, "Do I insult you with my high spirits or not?," the response comes back:

"I beg you earnestly not to disturb yourself and not to be put out," the elder said impressively. "Do not be disconcerted, make yourself quite at home. And, above all, do not be so ashamed of yourself, for that is the root of it all."

To which Karamazov responds:

"Quite at home? You mean be my natural self? Oh, that is much, sir, too much, but I accept it—touched to the core! Though, you know, blessed father, you must not let me be my natural self—it's too great a risk! As a matter of fact, I won't go as far as that myself."

He continues shortly thereafter:

"By your remark—'Don't be so ashamed of yourself, for that is at the root of it all'—by this remark, sir, you seem to have seen right through me and read my innermost secrets. For it does seem to me every time I go to see people that I'm more contemptible than anyone else and that everyone takes me for a clown. That's why I say to myself, 'All right, let me play the clown! I'm not afraid of your opinion, because you're all without exception more contemptible than I!' That's why I'm a clown, great elder. I am a clown from shame. Yes, sir, from shame! It's my sensitiveness alone that makes me kick up a row. If only I could be sure when entering a room that everyone would accept me at once as the kindest and wisest of men—Lord! what a good man I'd be then!"[2]

Karamazov's game, acting foolish—shamelessly foolish—to avoid the greater shame of being rejected for being himself, is one most of us are familiar with. The class clown, the cutup, the practical joker, the wisecracking cynic—these characters are familiar to us. We know them, or we are them. We're amused or not amused, but at least we understand the comic pose. The joker flaunts wit, risking no more than occasionally appearing foolish. But what about those people who flaunt those qualities that most of us are ashamed of: promiscuity, ruthlessness, treachery? They're deliberately bad. What's more painful than being bad? Being weak.

Shamelessness is a reaction formation against shame, a defiant, counterphobic attempt to deny and overcome a profound inner fear of weakness.

Another of my patients who behaved shamelessly was Clarence, who sought therapy to control his violent temper. When I learned that he regularly slapped his wife around, I insisted on seeing the two of them together so they could face each other directly, and put into words what they had been putting into action. I was sure I could help, because one person's "bad temper" often turns out to be a problem in communication. She's more verbal, and he, cowed and inarticulate, builds up rage until he can no longer contain it. Then, often drunk, he smacks her, striking out in the only way he knows how. She's furious, but she loves him and perhaps feels a little responsible, so she puts up with what no woman should.

My first session with Clarence and Maria confirmed my suspicions. When Maria complained, she got shrill. The louder she got, the quieter and angrier Clarence became. After a few minutes he got good and mad and started screaming at her. The result? Maria got attacked instead of understood. At home, this sequence is precisely what led to physical abuse.

I told Maria that when she asks for something by complaining, Clarence only feels attacked and doesn't hear her. I told Clarence that his wife needs him, "It's a shame you can't hear her." And I also said that it was odd that Maria was the only one with complaints—and enough guts to put them into words.

The next week they came back all smiles. Maria said, "I never realized how I was coming across to him. On Wednesday, I told him I was tired and asked him to take the baby for a while, and he said, 'Sure.' " Clarence added with obvious pride, "She's my kid, too, you know." Unfortunately, my quick cure was illusory. They learned to communicate in my office but forgot at home. The beatings continued. I was puzzled, why couldn't (wouldn't) Clarence stop hitting his wife?

Then I started noticing a pattern: How Clarence repeated with an almost stagy concern, "I guess I'm just naturally violent." How dramatically he described his intimidating and uncontrollable outbursts and Maria's cowering. And I noticed how when Maria talked about his brutality, a hint of a smile played around the corners of his mouth. These suggestions of a willful, motivated quality to Clarence's "uncontrollable temper" were a clue to his shameless behavior.

Clarence didn't want to control his temper. He was proud of it. He fooled himself—"I can't help it"—he fooled his wife, and he fooled me. Acting ashamed of himself, Clarence was actually pleased with his power to intimidate his wife and the manliness it implied. His attacks may have been triggered by a "problem of communication," but they were propelled by his own unrecognized fear of weakness. I figured this out about a week after they dropped out of treatment.

Shame shapes character in harmony with standards of society. Thirty years ago most parents were ashamed if one of their children moved in with a lover before marriage. Today, parents often recommend it. Standards change and we all have to adjust, but sometimes it seems as though our whole culture is becoming shameless. You can walk into your local video store and rent X-rated movies featuring nonstop anal and oral intercourse, and the kid behind the counter will smile and say, "Have a nice day." Shock television journalists, like Geraldo Rivera and Morton Downey, Jr., invite volatile and controversial guests and then goad them into shouting matches with attacks on their integrity. When they succeed in provoking someone like Roy Innis, director of the Congress of Racial Equality, into punching out someone like Al Sharpton, or getting hit by a flying chair, these shameless sensationalists are happiest. (The closer talk shows come to the bughouse antics of the Three Stooges, the higher their ratings.) Even people who choose not to watch these trashy programs are shamelessly insulted by the network news, where substance and integrity have given way to the slick, the smooth, and the superficial. As ratings become the arbiter of taste, television news programs become as thoughtful as the front page of the *New York Post*.

It can be argued that the legalization of pornography and the unfettering of television productions are not all bad. These developments can be seen as signs of openness and honesty, signals of hypocrisy breaking down in favor of freedom and acceptance of the human condition. Maybe. Or maybe ours is becoming a culture of shamelessness.

Unrestrained exposure of bodies and emotions and lurid details of personal lives is not uncomplicated openness. The unmasking of sex and violence, the scorn and derision of modesty and privacy and the rights of others, is a sickness of our time. Wolfish appetites for power, ambition, opportunism, and revenge seem to displace conscience, ideals, fairness, and even everyday self-protection. We expose badness, but weakness and failure are more deeply hidden. The shameless cynic usually turns out to be someone who was tragically humiliated and learned to defend woundedness with a defiant show of strength. Similarly, the shameless cynicism of our time may be a reaction to a succession of blows to our national pride and prominence. Personal or communal, shamelessness is defensive, a mask for haunting fears of failure and lovelessness and emptiness.

Defending against painful emotional truths is not like putting something away in the attic and forgetting that you put it there; defensiveness requires constant psychic energy to maintain. The fact that this effort is unconscious does not make it any the less draining. Most people are tired all the time not because they work so hard but because so much of their energy is tied up in psychic conflict.

Successful defenses become habit; habit molds personality. These protective reactions become automatic, so that whenever shame confronts us we retreat to these familiar tactics. We close off certain avenues of experience and limit ourselves to what's safe. We may not even be aware of what we're missing. When we ransom vitality to pay for our safety, we're driven away from ourselves, from self-knowledge and self-reflection. Slowly, gradually, our insides, our very selves, become foreign to us.

Other people's defenses are, of course, easier to see than our own. Study them; with practice, you may see yourself. Defenses are signposts to shame.

We need defenses. Impulses must be stopped and searched, because some of our knee-jerk reactions are self-destructive. But defenses can outlive their usefulness. Next we'll see what remains conscious from our struggle with shame: a residue of insecurity and a vulnerability to embarrassment.

5

·······

Living in the Shadow of Insecurity

Deep down, we're ashamed of certain aspects of ourselves. And that shame, or the fear of it, haunts us like nothing else. That's why, as we've seen, each one of us has an elaborate system of defenses to avoid facing shame, to avoid even knowing it's there. What remains, the residue of shame, is insecurity.

Peggy Rosario was a forty-two-year-old administrator in the State Health Department who requested psychotherapy to work on a problem with men. A stormy, on-again-off-again relationship with a disarmingly attractive man was off again, and she wanted to understand what kept driving the two of them together and then apart.

The problem as she saw it was she was too outspoken: "I'm blunt. I'm blunt with men. I'm blunt at work. I'm blunt in my family, but everybody in my family is blunt; that's the way we were brought up."

Frankly, I didn't see the problem. There's nothing wrong with being outspoken and direct, and I had the sense that Peggy didn't think so either. Rather than impose my own point of view ("What's wrong with being direct?"), I tried harder to understand hers. "You seem ambivalent about your directness. On the one hand, you're telling me that it's a problem, but on

*the other hand, you seem to think of it as legitimate and hon-
est self-assertiveness."*

*"You're right," she said. "I'm not sure whether it's me or the
relationship."*

"Can you tell me about one of these conflicts?"

*The example she chose was of her last fight with Bob, the
man she was in love with. When she offered to help him rewrite a report he was having trouble with, he told her in a
clipped tone of voice that he could do it himself. Later, when
they went out to dinner, he seemed bent on antagonizing her.
The restaurant she picked was "a typical Yuppie fern bar"; he
took exception to everything she said; and, most aggravating
of all, he made a point of looking at other women. "He was
deliberately playing on my insecurity about my looks." The
final insult came when a showy blonde in a tight dress walked
by, and Bob said, "Mmmm . . . look at that." That was it! She
told him she was sorry if she'd made him feel bad about his
writing, she hadn't meant to, but she would not put up with
being treated this way. He was being stupid and cruel, and if
he was that insecure about being inarticulate, that was his
problem; she wouldn't tolerate his taking it out on her.*

*I didn't know what to make of this example. Her boyfriend
insulted her, and she told him to stop. What's wrong with that?*

*The fact that Peggy's confrontations occurred mainly with
men made me think that maybe the problem was not her, but
sexual politics. Perhaps the men Peggy met simply weren't
comfortable with a strong, honest woman. It happens.*

*"Does this, ah . . . problem [I didn't know what to call it]
come up with your women friends?"*

"Not often. Sometimes."

*She went on to tell me of a recent argument with an old
friend. Peggy had called Sheila to go out and celebrate Peggy's
new look. At forty-one she'd decided to do something radical
about her looks, so she dyed her hair auburn and had a bilat-
eral breast augmentation. She bought a green silk dress for the
occasion and met Sheila halfway between Albany and Spring-
field at the Red Lion Inn.*

"Right away I could tell she didn't like my new look. When I asked her what she thought, she said, 'You certainly look different.' That was bullshit and I called her on it. I told her I had a right to change my looks and if she were a true friend she wouldn't be so disapproving. She said maybe I was right. Maybe it was just going to take some getting used to. The rest of the evening was pretty tense. But I've spoken to her since and everything's okay now."

I still wasn't sure I understood Peggy's problem. What struck me, though, was not so much something she said as something she didn't say. In all of her explanations and examples of conflict, she made no mention of being hurt or feeling bad. Her "bluntness" was the only half of the story she talked about.

As I used to tell my students: In psychotherapy, the customer is always wrong—at least in one respect. Unhappy people usually have an incomplete range of experience. A critical emotion is missing. The most common example is people who are afraid of their anger. These people talk about anxiety (or headaches) and about other people hurting their feelings, but they hardly mention anger. Anger is repressed, and it is usually repressed emotion that causes problems.

In Peggy's case, I guessed that behind her "bluntness," she was easily wounded by criticism. The examples she gave of outspokenness seemed like legitimate expressions of an assertive self. She did not, like some people, fly into a rage when her feelings were wounded, and yet by her own account she seemed to have a lot of trouble getting along with people. Maybe the trouble was hurt, not anger.

So I tested my conjecture with an interpretation. "You've talked about your bluntness and how it seems to get you into trouble with people, but, as I've said, it usually seems reasonable. On the other hand, I've noticed something interesting. You haven't said a word about your feelings getting hurt. I don't really know yet, but maybe the problem has less to do with how aggressive you are than with how easily your feelings get hurt and how vulnerable you are to criticism."

She started to cry; and then after a few moments she said,

"I've been insecure all my life, and I've worked hard at achieving self-respect."

The customer may always be wrong, but here was one perceptive enough to have faced her own insecurity—and gutsy enough to have worked at overcoming it. She spoke with feeling about how hard she'd struggled to overcome her defensiveness and insecurity. I thought she'd done a good job, becoming more direct and honest but without the usual aggressive edge of defensive people. Still, although Peggy had done a good job of compensating for her insecurity, she'd really only covered it up. Maybe it was time to dig down to the roots of that insecurity.

"Let me mention something else. You seem to have done a good job of working toward self-confidence, but maybe you've just covered up your insecurity rather than resolved it. From some of the things you've said, I get the idea that your insecurity goes very deep and that perhaps it has something to do with how you feel about your body."

That struck a nerve. Peggy told me she'd never been comfortable with the way she looked. *"I've spent my whole life feeling inadequate about my body."* She remembered her mother teasing her since before she was a teenager. "She was always making jokes about my small breasts. I remember the first time I bought a bra; I didn't want her to tease me about it, so I washed it in the bathroom and hung it out my window to dry. When she found it, she showed it around to everybody in the family. 'What's this for?' she asked, laughing. When I told her it was to cover my breasts, she just laughed some more. 'Those two peas?' That's exactly what she said, 'Two peas.'"

So. We'd gone from the problem of being "too direct" to being "insecure" to Peggy's "feeling inadequate" about her body. Peggy was quick to argue because she was easily wounded. She'd worked hard not to act insecure, but deep down she was ashamed of herself. We'd get to the connection between the body and the self later, but this was a start.

Peggy is like a lot of us. We know insecurity but not the shame beneath it.

"Insecurity" is one of those fuzzy little words we evoke to explain what, in fact, we do not understand. Why do we hang back? Why do we have such trouble speaking in public? Why do we find it so difficult to meet other people's direct gaze? We call it insecurity—as though giving it a name explains it. Insecurity is nothing more than a lack of confidence that helps us avoid tests we are afraid we won't pass. The problem isn't lack of ability, it's lack of self-worth. Insecurity conditions avoidance, an avoidance that is not random but highly efficient. We avoid that which might expose us to shame. A person's life space is a topographical map of painful—that is, shame-sensitive—areas. We travel where we feel secure and don't venture where we feel vulnerable. Those areas that threaten self-esteem are posted "off-limits."

Shame and our attempts to avoid it pervade everyday life. We don't often think about shame and we rarely encounter it. It's too painful. Instead, we encounter insecurity and low self-esteem—several layers closer to the surface than humiliation, mortification, and shame. The closest we come on a regular basis to shame is embarrassment, the social edge of shame.

EMBARRASSMENT

Embarrassment is one of the most prominent and painful ways that insecurity manifests itself. As novelist Anita Brookner's protagonist Edith Hope discovered in *Hotel du Lac*, "Quarrels can be made up; embarrassment can never quite be forgotten."[1]

When we think of embarrassment, the first thing that comes to mind is some experience that exposes ineptness or impropriety. "Don't be embarrassed," a mother says to her little girl. "Tell Daddy what you did." "Don't be embarrassed," a man says to his wife. "Nobody cares how well you can dance." Don't be embarrassed. Don't let that silly little feeling stand in the way of your doing what needs to be done. It's only a mild case of self-consciousness, don't let it bother you. After all, it's only your self.

At a party, you meet someone you haven't seen in a while. After a few minutes chatting, another friend comes over, but you can't remember the first person's name. In that moment of awkward silence, you feel like an idiot. You're embarrassed. It's only a mild case of shame, but it still isn't any fun.

The fact that we suffer embarrassment in awkward, unpredictable moments makes embarrassment seem like a chance occurrence, a more or less random collision of circumstance and sensitive feelings. That's because we systematically avoid risking embarrassment. We only suffer it by miscalculation.

Only occasionally does severe embarrassment pierce those layers of decency and defensiveness that make up our adult characters. You may never have been in a situation like the woman in the following example, but I'm sure you can identify with her feelings. The experience of shame is like the smell of a skunk: It may not be common, but it's unmistakable.

Through the soot-fogged train window she stared at the passing Hudson landscape. What would it be like to live in one of those grand mansions on the hillside? she wondered. To live in all that splendor and look out on the sky and the river? Something about riding on the train shook loose buried longings. Her dreams were endless.

She was wearing her good wool suit and carrying the matching heels in her bag; she was on her way to the city and an important interview. Feeling good. She knew the interview would go well; she was at the peak of her powers. Just then she became aware of the rush of wind and felt the hot, humid air coming through the door behind her. Why doesn't someone get up and shut that door? Nobody seems to take any responsibility anymore. Never mind, she thought, I'll do it myself.

Swaying for balance, she tugged on the rubber flap to pull the sliding door closed, but she couldn't budge it. Then she looked up and saw a knob protruding from what must be the door-closing mechanism. When she reached up and pulled the knob, she heard a loud whooshing sound and the train sud-

denly came to a stop. Oh, no! Was that the emergency brake?
It hardly seemed possible. Wouldn't the emergency brake be
clearly marked?

Feeling like a fool, she went back to her seat. Heads turned.
Anxious faces fixed her with inquiring eyes. If only she could
disappear. She still couldn't believe that little knob could be
the emergency brake. And yet the train had stopped dead in
the middle of nowhere. She realized that she'd have to tell the
conductor what she'd done. Waiting for him to come took five
minutes and seemed like an hour. She could feel the other
passengers' eyes on her, and she burned with shame.

Embarrassment—actually, the fear of embarrassment—is a powerful motivating force, a charged barrier that surrounds our self-esteem like an alarm system. When we enter the presence of others, they commonly seek to acquire information about us. We, on the other hand, take preventive measures to avoid possible embarrassment, revealing some but not all of our real selves. We *express* ourselves, and others are in turn *impressed* in some way. We're cautious to avoid the possibility of suffering chagrin. The more cautious we are, the more we become self-conscious and socially ill at ease. If the feeling is strong enough, it leads to isolation.

We're embarrassed when we momentarily lose muscular control and trip, stumble, fall, drop something, bump into someone, make a slip of the tongue, scratch, twitch, belch, yawn, or fart. We're embarrassed when we show ourselves too much or too little concerned; when we stutter, forget what we wanted to say, appear nervous ("Never let them see you sweat"), guilty, or self-conscious; or when we give way to inappropriate laughter or outbursts of anger. And we're embarrassed by inadequate attention to costume or setting, either of which may not be in order or may become deranged during a performance.

I was very anxious to make a good impression the first time I
was invited to give an all-day workshop to a large audience of
family therapists, so I dressed with extra care. I wore my

*special-occasion blue suit, a new shirt, and a flowered tie that
said, "This guy is jaunty, in a subdued sort of way, flashy but
restrained, a sort of laid-back bohemian." It was a talkative
tie; I was counting on that.*

*Three cups of coffee and a serious case of performance anx-
iety gave me an adrenaline rush that carried me right through
the morning. Things went so well that I even forgot to worry
about my appearance. Half an hour before lunch I stopped
lecturing to answer questions. When I sat down I felt the chair
directly against my skin. Uh-oh.*

*As soon as the break came, I went into the bathroom and
discovered that my pants had split down the back. The old
seam had just given up the ghost. Fortunately, I had enough
time to get to a clothing store and buy a new pair of pants in
time for the rest of my presentation.*

*I began the afternoon with a weak joke about my split trou-
sers. It wasn't funny, but it served its purpose. For me, it was a
minor catharsis for a minor case of social embarrassment; for
the audience, it was a signal that I was aware of my exposure
and didn't feel too bad about it—they didn't have to protect
me by pretending to be blind.*

Most of us have suffered the embarrassment of split trousers or
raveled stockings or unraveled plans, but these things are relatively minor, little annoyances hardly worth worrying about. Slip-
ups by which we reveal something that everybody understands are
nothing compared to dark secrets exposed when others intrude
where we don't expect them.

*A man goes into a variety store on the far side of town. Just
this once he decides to violate his usual sense of propriety and
picks up a pornographic magazine. His first reaction is surprise. The pictures are far more graphic than he imagined. He
starts to get turned on. Someone says "Excuse me," and he
quickly returns the magazine to the shelf. Too late. The someone is someone he knows, and he knows she saw what he was
looking at.*

A woman is lying uncomfortably on a rotating table in a bright theater of light. She's taken a barium enema so that her lower gastrointestinal tract can be X-rayed, and now they're taking the pictures.

"How much longer?" she asks anxiously.

"Be patient," a disembodied voice answers.

Did they give me too much? she wonders. She can't keep it in. She feels the barium begin to dribble out, down her leg and onto the table. She feels terribly exposed. The chalky white flow turns slightly brown.

"Can't you wait?" the disembodied voice says, accusingly.

A boy, twelve, climbs the ladder to the high dive, but when he gets to the top, panic catches up with him. Six other kids waiting on the ladder for their turn all have to climb off so that he can back down.

As Erving Goffman so brilliantly demonstrated in *The Presentation of Self in Everyday Life,* social life is like a stage on which we, the performers, strive in countless ways to manage the impression we give. A performer tends to conceal or underplay those activities, facts, and motives that are incompatible with an idealized version of himself or herself. According to Goffman, "A status, a position, a social place is not a material thing, to be possessed and then displayed; it is a pattern of appropriate conduct, coherent, embellished, and well articulated. Performed with ease or clumsiness, awareness or not, guile or good faith, it is nonetheless something that must be enacted and portrayed, something that must be realized."[2] Character is performance.

Embarrassment is a protective barrier around the public performance of self. We feel embarrassment when facts are revealed that discredit our performance or weaken the claims about the self we try to project. We aren't quite what we pretend to be. We're embarrassed to be seen at the movies when we're supposed to be sick; we're embarrassed if we're out with friends and discover we don't have enough money to pay our share; and we're embarrassed if unexpected company shows up and the house is a mess. Embarrassing revelations can be well-kept dark secrets or flaws that everyone can see but no one refers to. The private, guarded self behind the public performance can be exposed by unmeant gestures or inopportune intrusions.

But why are we *so* embarrassed? Or to put it differently, What makes embarrassment so painful? This question takes us from the experience of insecurity—one form of insecurity—to the deep fears that underlie and create insecurity. The really mortifying instances of embarrassment involve more than just dropping our act. The most painful embarrassment comes about when we expose the most unacceptable thing about the self: shame. It isn't possible to dissect embarrassment without opening up shame.

Again I refer to Leon Wurmser's triad of unacceptable traits: weakness, dirtiness, and defectiveness.[3] We are most deeply embarrassed by anything that touches upon these unacceptable characteristics.

The controlling fear of embarrassment exposes our preoccupation with other people's opinion of us and our own insecurity. Why are dirtiness, defectiveness, and weakness such dark secrets? Because they make us unlovable—the ultimate insecurity.

What is the most embarrassing thing that ever happened to you? Got it? If you allow yourself to remember something truly and profoundly embarrassing, it was a time when you were exposed in front of others as being worse than you could tolerate. That terribly embarrassing experience probably made you feel one of three ways: dirty, weak, or defective. This constellation of traits goes to the core of our concerns about ourselves. What it takes to make you embarrassed about being dirty, weak or defective varies according to what you expect of yourself—and who's watching. It might be okay for a teenage boy to pee in the bushes on a camping trip, but if he tries the same thing in the alley behind a tavern, he risks indecent exposure.

The triggers for embarrassment also vary between men and women. Take a highly successful professional man, send him up to bat in a softball game, and he'll be embarrassed if he doesn't hit the ball out of the infield. He could be forty-five years old, vice president of his company, a man people look up to, but if he strikes out he's a wimp. What a woman considers to be a weakness is more likely to be a selfish indulgence. I'm reminded of this every time one of my women patients begins a psychotherapy session by asking how I am. Men rarely bother. It's not a matter of politeness; many women just seem to feel that there's something self-indulgent about taking a whole hour for themselves.

Men and women alike can be embarrassed by compliments, especially when the praise is unfamiliar. Men are often embarrassed by compliments about their appearance. They aren't used to being noticed so openly. Women may be more accustomed to compliments about their appearance—after all, isn't that a woman's most important quality?—and more embarrassed by compliments on their achievements. Compliments are embarrassing when we're insecure.

When it comes to being the object of attention, we can easily feel embarrassment or pleasure. We enjoy being noticed and admired; we dread looking foolish or being laughed at. By the same token, we can laugh or cringe when we witness ineptitude in someone else. When I asked several of my friends for examples of embarrassment, some told me they were embarrassed watching Dan Quayle's pitiful performance in the vice presidential debate against Lloyd Bentsen. Others thought it was funny. There's a fine line between feeling uncomfortable for someone out of sympathy and distancing ourselves with the catharsis of laughter.

Embarrassment is so painful that it's hard to tolerate even minor episodes. On the scale of personal discomfort, embarrassment is far above physical illness. Most people would rather have the flu for a week than suffer ten minutes of painful public embarrassment.

To avoid such incidents, defensive measures are practiced by performers and audience alike. We lead stage-managed social lives. We specialize in fixed settings, keeping strangers out, and giving performers some privacy to prepare themselves for the show. Audiences are tactful in order to protect performers, both because they're considerate and because they identify with the performers. Most of us deliberately refrain from overhearing other people's conversations. Worse than listening is looking. Sustained eye contact may be the most intense form of human interaction. If someone does something that might possibly be embarrassing, we lower our eyes and look away.

"Performers," "audience," "impression-management"—something seems false and phony about this analogy. It makes us sound calculating and deceitful. The device is deliberate. Reducing complex interpersonal interaction to simple performance emphasizes our enormous concern with what other people think of us. No matter how much or how little we reflect upon it, we're always concerned with what we reveal about ourselves. The word "person" itself comes from the Latin *persona*, an actor's mask. Impression-management may sound dishonest, but it's something we do. When our concern with impressions is excessive, it isn't so much about being dishonest as it is about being insecure. The more insecure we are, the more elaborate our social front.

The amount of openness of the performance of self depends on the audience as well as the performer. The safest audience for most of us is our friends. We know they like us. With good friends it's even safe to expose ourselves to criticism. A friend might rebuke us for behaving badly or pan something we're proud of, but we can tolerate the criticism because we're not worried about being rejected. We may be closer, more intimate with our spouses, but, as I shall discuss later, we ration openness in marriage to protect ourselves from hurts too close to the heart. There are things you've said to complete strangers that you'd never tell your spouse. A stranger might disagree or disapprove, but who cares?

Perhaps the most important thing about embarrassment is that it conditions avoidance. Embarrassment keeps us from talking openly about certain subjects, wearing fun clothes, or playing games at which we might be awkward. We're embarrassed to be silly. If we tell a joke in which the hostile element is too blatant for the audience, we suffer acute embarrassment. So we guard what we say, restrain the playful child inside, and withhold ourselves in a thousand ways, all because we can't bear to appear foolish or childish. Embarrassment hems us in.

Fear of embarrassment kills spontaneity. Gradually we lose the ability to be careless, to disregard appearances, to relax and laugh at the world. This inability to unbend is a favorite figure of fun in the movies. What makes those ossified old fuddy-duddies so funny? They're us. We laugh at what we're afraid of.

Being uptight may not seem like such a terrible thing. So what if we're a little reserved? So what if we don't want to make fools of ourselves? Make no mistake: Putting on a show before others is a form of alienation from oneself. The system of defenses we erect to shield the self from social embarrassment also closes off the world and fences us in.

Fear of embarrassment plays a large role in our lives, but most of the time we're too busy avoiding embarrassment to think much about it. If we do, we think of it as something in the situation—doing such and such is embarrassing. Actually, it's us. We're embarrassed because we're insecure.

We live always on the edge of insecurity. However, because we organize our lives to avoid that awful, uncertain feeling, we do not have a clear idea of either the nature or extent of our insecurity. We avoid, as much as possible, situations that make us insecure and concentrate instead on those things that make us feel competent and confident. In the process, two things happen: We construct more or less secure and useful lives, and we close off avenues of experience and parts of the self.

We've seen how psychological defense mechanisms seal away shame, leaving few memories but a residue of insecurity and a protective barrier of embarrassment. In the following chapter, we'll see some of the ways we deliberately distract ourselves from feeling insecure.

6

■ ■ ■ ■ ■ ■ ■

You Can Run But
You Can't Hide

Distracting Ourselves from Insecurity

In 1941, just before his first heavyweight title bout, a reporter asked Joe Louis how he would cope with the skillful evasive tactics of Billy Conn. Louis replied, "He can run but he can't hide." It's the same with insecurity. We have many strategies for avoiding insecurity; beating it is another thing.

The psychological defense mechanisms we use to protect ourselves against shame operate automatically, outside of awareness. What we are aware of is insecurity, and since even this is hard to bear, we distract ourselves in a variety of ways. Distractions differ from defense mechanisms in being deliberate and conscious. The most general strategy for avoiding insecurity is a self-limiting and self-protective avoidance of risk.

LIFE AVOIDED

We protect ourselves against insecurity the way any creature would: by narrowing the world in order to make our way in it, damping down experience, and avoiding anything that stirs too much anxiety. Otherwise we would be crippled for action. Self-restriction is self-protection.

We anesthetize those parts of ourselves that might expose us to conflict or shame, in the process crippling some of our many selves. *Many selves?* Yes. Within the self there are many partial selves, subpersonalities, real and potential. The psyche is like an ensemble troupe of actors. When we are all that we can be, any of a large cast of characters can be activated under different circumstances. When the time is right we can call forth a playful child, an artist, a contemplative, a tough kid, a consoling angel, and more. But those members of the company who are hooted down often enough will go backstage and stay there. We, the observing egos, know they're back there; they just won't come out.

That's the most painful part of life avoided: We know what we could be, we just *can't.* . . . The old bright focus is gone.

Most people could tell you one or two major changes they could make in their lives that they know in their hearts would be good for them. But fear—ultimately, the fear of shame—holds them back. And so our lives are haunted by the ghosts of unborn dreams, unrealized hopes, and undiscovered talents.

I know a woman stuck in a clerical job she hates despite a hot ache and an enormous talent for writing. She'd rather endure stagnation than risk the possibility that her work might be rejected. By the way, she has very little trouble tolerating criticism of her everyday work. Her writing, on the other hand, is too close to her to dare exposure. You probably know men and women chained to numbing routines who would love to find more time to have fun and be with friends. They'd like to, but somehow they just can't.

We lead lives of systematic self-restraint, and the result is that the less we do, the less we can do. Parts of the self wither like unused muscle. When we fall out of the habit of hard exercise, creative play, and easy sociability, other habits take their place, and simple avoidance grows to almost phobic proportions.

People who lead fearful and prudent lives look at the world with longing, wishing they could embrace life more fully—or at least one or another attractive corner of it. They do, fleetingly, and these are cherished moments. Perhaps at a party, a few drinks put defenses to sleep and allow the playful self to venture out of hiding. They manage to loosen up and have a good time. Because hard physical exertion is as good as or better than alcohol at relaxing anxiety, a swim or perhaps a game of volleyball may enable them to relax and feel fully alive.

But too often life is a drama seen through a curtain of protective self-restraint. Our own experience has an "as if" quality—remote, blurred, hazy, not quite real—and we look on with longing as other people enjoy themselves.

Experience means sticking your neck out, but shame-sensitive people can't bear to. They don't want to risk disappointment, and they don't want to risk their self-image. They don't want to fail, they don't want to be rejected, and so they hesitate to open themselves to other people. What they aim for is freedom from humiliation; what they get is estrangement.

Among the more specific strategies for avoiding insecurity is shyness—painful self-consciousness that makes us try to avoid the anxiety inherent in human relationships.

SHYNESS

Shyness is shame in the presence of a stranger. It is rooted in the fear of appearing foolish, clumsy, or stupid. After a while, we may turn this fear around and cover our shyness with arrogance, distrust, or contempt. When it's extreme, self-doubt—known or disowned—seals us inside a cocoon of loneliness.

Human beings are social beings with a natural inclination to enjoy the company of others. We long for friends to relax with, a group to identify with, and a special someone to be intimate with. No matter where we go, there is no need to be alone. The great human capacity for companionship makes it possible to find friendly people happy to share in easy, informal conversation. Few human strivings are as compelling as the need to belong. So powerful is that striving that we'd do almost anything to avoid loneliness. *Almost* anything, because stronger even than the yearning to belong is the need to protect one's dignity as a human being.

That's what shyness is all about: protecting our precious dignity.

When unwillingness to expose ourselves becomes habit, we call it shyness.

No matter how well we hide it, we all suffer some measure of shyness. "Shy" means avoidant. Because we can be bold in one context though timid in another, we can fool other people. "*Her*? She's not shy!" And we can fool ourselves. Some shy people don't think of themselves as shy. They avoid others because they find small talk tiresome. They don't want to talk about the weather, they don't want to hear about other people's jobs, and they don't want to listen to a steady stream of stories about the kids. They're not shy; they just want to be left alone.

Some people are so painfully shy that they arrange their lives so they can avoid situations where they might be put on the spot. If those situations are hard to avoid—like informal group conversations—the shyness will be apparent. If the uncomfortable situations are easier to avoid—like speaking up in a committee meeting—the shyness may not be so obvious.

Interestingly, among the 20 percent of people who don't consider themselves shy, most acknowledge reacting with such symptoms of shyness as blushing, pounding heart, and butterflies in the stomach in certain social settings.[1] These "situationally shy" people don't consider themselves shy; it's not them, it's external events, such as walking into a room full of strangers, that cause temporary discomfort.

Lack of ease in the society of others is only the most obvious form of shyness. Some people don't seem shy because they learn to avoid exposing their insecurity by cultivating independence. They don't need anybody, they go their own way. In fact, conspicuously independent people may only appear autonomous. Independence is an illusion if the sense of the self as independent of others cannot be maintained except in isolation.

Behind the tight-lipped masks, the smiling masks, the earnest masks, and the satisfied masks that people use to bluff the world and themselves about their vulnerability, you will find deep-seated insecurity. If you look closely, you'll discover a fear of dependence, a fear of vulnerability, a fear of shame.

One reason we underestimate other people's shyness is that

those of us who know we're shy—timid with self-consciousness—
and who hold back from informal sociability find it hard to imagine
that other people who don't hold back may also be shy. The truth
is that we're all cautiously averse to exposing ourselves in some
way.

The essence of shyness is avoidance out of fear, but some people shrink from self-assertion so gracefully that we find it charming. If bluster, arrogance, pride, and aggressiveness are vices, then
shyness must be a virtue. Gary Cooper's charm was his naturally
quiet and retiring nature. His shyness was disarming, a refreshing
change from men who are assertive, aggressive, and obvious in
social encounters. The shy man, the strong silent type, seems
sensitive. Maybe, but his greatest sensitivity is to the possibility of
his own embarrassment.

Shame shapes character. When we live in fearful anticipation of
embarrassment, ridicule, inadequacy, and failure—even though
these fears are buried deep in the heart—we cut ourselves off from
easy social spontaneity. When you're inhibited from acting out of
a deep fear of exposing yourself to shame, you'll only be safe if
you're not seen and not heard. The bashful little girl, struck
speechless before strangers, hiding behind her mother's skirts,
seems cute. But if she fails to outgrow that shyness, its inhibiting
impact is not so cute. It's fun to hide, not so much fun to live inside
a shell.

INTROVERSION

Another way to play it safe with freedom is to become an introvert.
Rather than merely avoiding certain social situations, the introvert
avoids people altogether. The shy person is uncomfortable in the
presence of others; the introvert avoids others and turns inward.
When it comes to avoidance, the shy person is an amateur compared to the introvert.

At this point you may be thinking, Wait a minute, introverts
aren't necessarily defensive. Isn't introversion just a different—

and perfectly legitimate—way of experiencing the world: thought-ful, quiet, self-contained? It seems reasonable to suppose that being a private and reflective person is a legitimate alternative to being active and expressive. And it's certainly not my intention to criticize anyone's adaptation to life. However, I do believe that introversion is rooted in avoidance. Consider this: How flexible is the introvert? It's one thing to choose to be alone and contempla-tive; it's another to be unable to open oneself socially and enjoy the company of others.

Introverts protect their shame-sensitive selves by creating dis-tance between themselves and others. They are more concerned with what it means to be a person with individuality, all unex-pressed, than with the satisfactions to be found in company. They enjoy solitude and withdraw periodically to reflect, perhaps to muse on ideas about their secret selves, their hopes and dreams. Introverts are more comfortable with books, ideas, objects, and the great outdoors than with other people. They would gladly have traded places with Thoreau. (What they may not realize is that he visited his mother every single afternoon while he stayed on Wal-den Pond.)

The benefit of solitude, recently elaborated on by the British psychiatrist Anthony Storr,[2] is that it provides space for rest and reflection, time for looking within the self, and time for creative endeavor. Solitude provides rest and respite from the noisy claims of everyday social living. A restful break is good, but some people—especially men—are beguiled by solitude until they're lost in its charms. When these private men attempt to impersonate husbands, the result is often a pursuer/distancer marriage. Wives, starved for affection, hurl themselves against their introverted hus-bands' reticence with little success.

Introverts resist being sucked up into standardized social activ-ities. If they cannot be true to themselves—their private inner being, their specialness—in company, at least they can blame oth-ers for being "shallow" or "intrusive." Introverts are, after all, basically insecure. They feel their uniqueness but do not risk exposing it, especially if it might lead to a confrontation. Here's a rather extreme example.

Years ago, when I was working in a university counseling center, a young man came to see me for "help with relationships." He was a nineteen-year-old music student, so talented that he was already performing as a soloist with a well-known orchestra. His was a world I knew little about—the consuming dedication to art that kept him practicing six hours a day alone in a windowless room—but helping people with relationships was right up my alley.

He had met a young woman at the conservatory where he was studying and was immediately taken with her. She was serious and kind. It was a pleasure just to be with her. A tender friendship grew into an infatuation. Then something awful happened.

One night after dinner he played for her. When he finished, she told him that it was truly beautiful, she was much moved. Her praise was as sweet to him as warm sun on a winter day, and so he opened his heart and tried to put into words some of his deepest and most private thoughts about music. She listened with interest to his rather unique ideas and then, because she had ideas of her own, she disagreed with him spiritedly. To a heart laid bare, her dissent was devastating. What was to her a discussion of music was to him an attack on his very self. He ran out of the room and avoided her for the rest of the week.

His story was sad, but it was like many stories from young and wounded hearts. Then he clarified for me what he meant by "help with relationships." He wanted me to help him become strong enough never again to need anyone. "Never, never again."

When an individual with an introverted nature is forced to contend with excessive shame—excessive beyond his or her ability to cope or find comfort in supportive relationships—that individual is likely to fall back on the natural tendency to withdraw deeper into the self. These individuals develop an intensely private posture. Their relationships are highly ambivalent. Sometimes they're intensely involved; at other times you knock but no one's home. If feelings are disowned, we might see a person who lacks either awareness or expression of feeling. Such a person is hard to know.

Even more than shyness, introversion seems to be a fact of character, not a deliberate choice. True, the way we live in the world becomes habit, and habit is hard to change, but we choose the way we live and, with sufficient motivation and courage, we can rechoose if we so decide. Similarly, we can blame our problems on other people, or face up to our contribution and our own power to change the problems that plague us.

INSULATING OURSELVES FROM DIFFICULT PEOPLE

Most of us can relate with reasonable confidence to the majority of people in our lives, but each of us has special trouble with Certain People. Not just individuals, but types of individuals. When we run into someone who's very frustrating to deal with, it's natural to assume that the problem is that person's personality. The person who's always finding fault; the one who never lets you know what he's thinking; the abrasive, abrupt, and intimidating person who *always* lets you know—these people are maddening.

Robert Bramson, an organizational psychologist, wrote a book with the compelling title *Coping with Difficult People.*[3] Among the difficult types he describes are Sherman Tanks, Snipers, Exploders, The Compleat Complainer, The Unresponsive Person, Know-It-All Experts, and Indecisive Stallers. Sound familiar? I've come across my share of these charmers, and I found Bramson's suggestions quite helpful. But after reading the book, I decided that the most difficult people in our lives are not the most outrageous curmudgeons we run across. Those people are difficult, all right, but we can often avoid these extremely unpleasant characters. It's not the truly outrageous people who do us in, it's the ones who provoke in us feelings that we don't know how to deal with. The most difficult people in our lives are the ones who have the capacity to make us feel ashamed.

Difficult people provoke our insecurity because they evoke needs and feelings we're ashamed of: narcissistic strivings, dependency needs, sexual feelings, and anger. Sometimes the source of the insecurity isn't obvious.

Liz works for the state government in a job she really loves, except for one thing: Her office mate drives her crazy. As Liz describes her, this other woman is easy to dislike. She's moody, irritable, takes forever to get her own work done, and turns nasty if anyone infringes on her prerogatives. Not your ideal office mate. In fact, however, what drives Liz crazy is not this woman, but what she evokes: anger. Liz is ashamed of feeling angry, *and* she is ashamed of being too weak to confront her colleague for being obnoxious.

The solution? Bear with me and resist the urge to look for a simple answer to a complicated question. For now, please consider some of the most difficult people in your life and see if you can figure out how your difficulty with them is a clue to the nature of your insecurity. Consider their personalities and the roles they occupy, but examine your reactions. *They* are difficult because *your* needs are exposed in relationship to them, and they respond in ways that are frustrating. It's not that they're powerful; it's that they mobilize longings and ambitions that make you acutely vulnerable to their response. Bosses evoke the need to be accepted and approved of, especially in regard to valued talents. Lovers have the capacity to make us feel lovable and so, after we've trotted out our best selves, we risk exposing our most vulnerable selves. When someone awakens impulses we're insecure about, we need the other person to be especially attuned to us. When they stubbornly insist on responding like separate human beings with their own agendas, rather than conforming themselves to our needs, naturally we get annoyed. So it's not them and it's not us; it's the combination. There are exceptions, of course. For example, I've discovered in recent years that I have a very hard time with editors. It must be them. All seven of them.

It's hard to give up the belief that what happens to us depends upon the favors of benevolent others. "If only he (or she) would stop doing this, and start doing that, then I'd be happy." If only!

"Loosen up." "Relax." "Just be yourself." Hell no, you might accidentally alienate one of the five or six most important people in your professional or social life and have to spend years atoning for the blunder.

Not only does passive self-protection pull us away from life, it doesn't always work. No matter how well we guard our insecurity with avoidance, we still feel it directly sometimes. It always hurts.

If they rob us of full life and don't always work, why are habits of avoidance so hard to break? *Negative reinforcement.* Anything that helps us avoid anxiety is powerfully reinforced.

Some people don't like to hear about reinforcement as an explanation for human behavior. (These days "addiction" is a much more popular concept. It does sound dramatic.) "Reinforcement" seems so mechanical; it robs us of dignity. I feel the same way myself. I don't like to write about it; there are so many more interesting forces acting on human behavior; yet few are so powerful.

Active solutions to the problems of insecurity propel us toward life; they lead to positive reinforcement. There I go again, trivializing human accomplishment. Wouldn't it be better to speak of "creative achievement" or "benevolence" or "making a contribution"? Insecurity does drive worthwhile accomplishments. Unfortunately, pursuits motivated as compensation for insecurity rather than as natural expressions of our talents and ideals aren't likely to make us happy.

Most insecure people narrow their lives so as to concentrate on one, maybe two, pathways to happiness. Often, it's either love or work.

DRIVING AMBITION

It's yesterday's news that the compulsive pursuit of achievement doesn't guarantee happiness. Still, a lot of us keep at it.

A wise and gentle friend once told me how, at forty, he'd achieved a reasonable amount of success in his vocation and that now he was less driven and more interested in enjoying himself than in trying to be a superstar. He was having fun with his friends, reading more, getting out into the country on weekends. It sounded good. He's right, I thought. I should start taking time to enjoy life. And I will, I thought, just as soon as I finish this next book. Or maybe the one after that.

The search for self-respect through achievement is like following the yellow-brick road. As long as Success glimmers somewhere off in the distance, we're enthralled by its possibilities. We never discover that the Emerald City is a fraud, because we never quite get there.

Besides, on the road to the enchanted city of Success there are tremendous temporary boosts to self-esteem along the way. *Temporary*. And then there are the trappings of material success: a nice car, good-looking clothes, an attractive house, and a gorgeous array of consumer satisfactions.

Some people take refuge in their possessions the way turtles retreat into their shells. The possessions don't enhance life, they become a substitute for living fully. Is this beginning to sound like a familiar litany? "Money can't buy happiness." "Success doesn't make security." But wait, it isn't that simple. In fact, the relationship between insecurity and accomplishment is far from simple. Most of the really insecure people I've spoken to imagine that the solution to the problem of insecurity has to come from within themselves. Unless they can somehow make themselves more secure, no amount of acting on the world will make them more whole. Actually, the process is circular. We create more secure whole selves partly through insight, by uncovering some of the roots of insecurity, and partly through action, by achieving success and building a network of rewarding relationships. Confidence begets creative action *and* creative action begets confidence. Unfortunately, some apparently creative endeavors are merely compensatory—that is, instead of resolving a problem, they offer a defensive substitute as a counterbalance. Compensatory responses to insecurity are devoted to rearranging external circumstances; they involve activities that are pursued to excess and, if interrupted, leave the person intensely anxious.

Careerists who believe success will make them whole concentrate almost all of their energy on work, knowing full well that they are neglecting people they love, time for relaxation, and much more. They keep telling themselves that they'll get around to these other things once their achievement is securely in place. In this self-deception they are like the alcoholic who says, "I'll quit tomorrow." (Other people narrow down their lives to concentrate on a love relationship—the "most wonderful" husband or wife, the children, or perhaps a lover. If this love is everything, everything else is nothing.) When you put all your eggs in one basket, you can't risk dropping that basket.

There's nothing wrong with striving for success. Working hard is part of what makes life worthwhile. There are, of course, material rewards, and there is the pure pleasure of accomplishment. The trouble is, many insecure people become obsessed with achievement, as though it were a cure for feeling insignificant and unloved. There are many prizes for achievement, but love and self-fulfillment are not among them.

According to his daughter Susan, John Cheever was among those who pursue success hoping it will conquer self-doubt. After years of struggle, Cheever hit it big in the mid-1960s, winning the National Book Award, seeing his story "The Swimmer" made into a movie starring Burt Lancaster, and even landing on the cover of *Time* magazine. Cheever's sudden financial and critical success seemed better than winning the lottery. But, his daughter writes, "the high spirits never lasted. As the sixties waned and the euphoria began to fade, my father discovered the real secret of success: it doesn't make any difference. No amount of money or adulation or Hollywood deals could diminish his depression or his doubts. He was still alone."[4]

Cheever was a man who, despite his enormous talent, felt the need to put on patrician airs and invent an aristocratic New England background. He was ashamed of his family and he was ashamed of himself. He tried drinking, he tried love affairs, and he tried travel, but he couldn't escape his existential dread. As long as the dreams of accomplishment beckoned in the distance, he was not free of their sway. For Cheever, realizing his dreams turned out to be a cruel surprise. It was as though he'd been hiking up a mountain only to find upon reaching the peak that it afforded him no view, no sunrise.

The drive for success, like every other human endeavor, has several motivating forces. As much as we may mock the Protestant work ethic, it still works its claim on the imagination. In fact, recent political disenchantment and the shaky American economy have led to a resurgence of belief in the capitalist doctrine that thrift and industry hold the key not only to material success but also to spiritual fulfillment. "Greed," said the Michael Douglas character in the movie *Wall Street*, "is good." Not everyone shares this sentiment—at least not stated so shamelessly—and not everyone is in a position to seize wealth by acting ruthlessly. The average American may not get rich in an "'age of diminishing expectations," nevertheless achievement is still seen by many as the royal road to self-worth.

How can you tell if the pursuit of achievement is neurotic? Admiration, rather than the pure pleasure of doing things well, is what propels insecure people toward success. Achievement is likely to be an inadequate compensation for insecurity, especially if the achievement is not a creative expression of the self, but a substitute satisfaction of old needs for being seen and understood, and loved. If it's a substitute, the satisfaction doesn't last; it brings only momentary good feelings. Love won by achievement is aimed at the achievement, not at the person who achieves.

Thanks to the women's movement, contemporary women are now privileged to enjoy some of the problems that used to be male prerogatives. Workaholics are now as likely to be women as men. There's a difference though: Success for a man is more likely to mean personal achievement; success for a woman is often tied to acceptance. Successful women do things for themselves, but they're much more likely than their male counterparts to be concerned with doing things for other people.

*　　*　　*

People with low self-esteem often try to achieve security by making themselves appealing—If I were beautiful . . . , If I were a scintillating conversationalist . . .—rather than by revealing their vulnerability. Some people cannot imagine that their imperfections and needs might be endearing, and they are convinced that affection would be withdrawn if they were exposed. Afraid to just be who they are, such people hold back, or present only limited parts of themselves.

The search for self-respect through romance, motherhood, achievement, or making oneself useful to others produces a compelling, compulsive urge to keep busy. Some people must act to feel okay: If I'm really generous and nice and helpful, then everyone will like me. If I am beautiful, well-dressed, and sexy, then I'll never be alone. If I work really hard, no one will criticize me. It's easy to see the fallacy of this kind of thinking when it's spelled out in these oversimplified formulas. The reason these scripts keep driving us is that they aren't simple, they aren't spelled out—they aren't examined because they aren't conscious.

Most of us feel burdened and oppressed by the demands of living. Yet without busy routine we may feel empty, adrift. When we stop running, we're overtaken by a deep feeling that our lives are empty, and that underneath it all we are worthless. As long as the sense of identity is tied to doing, it falters when there is just being. Many of our activities are defenses against a deep sense of self-doubt and uncared-for worthlessness. We have an incessant hunger for response, a yearning for reassurance, and an acute vulnerability to criticism or rejection. If the right person gives the wrong response, we're suddenly deflated. Our egos get punctured like balloons. A sturdy self absorbs hurts; an insecure self is shaken by them.

One of my shortcomings as a psychotherapist is a propensity to tease my patients. Every once in a while I succumb to an irresistible urge to use sarcasm to make an interpretation. (If I were analyzing myself, I'd say it was a mild form of hostility: I get annoyed at my patients for clinging so tenaciously to self-defeating habits. Fortunately, I am not analyzing myself!) One thing I say from time to time is, "Oh, that would be *awful*, if you did that and somebody in this great big world didn't like it. That would mean not everybody loves you." I always expect patients to laugh with me at the folly of needing everyone's approval. They never laugh. They wince, they grimace, and they fall silent.

The truth is, we can't tolerate people not loving us and we can't take disapproval. Everyone hates criticism.

CRITICISM

All criticism hurts, but—to paraphrase George Orwell—some criticisms hurt more than others. Criticism stings the hardest when it's tied up with self-esteem. The critic expresses an opinion about something we've *done*, but we feel judged for who we *are*—judged and rejected. Why? The outer critic wounds us worst where the inner critic has already undermined our self-worth. The real pain of criticism is shame.

Criticism hurts more or less, depending upon who is doing the criticizing and about what. Sometimes it seems that criticism from certain people affects us so strongly because it has practical consequences. A bad book review means poor sales, a bawling out from the boss means more work, being dumped on by your spouse means no peace at home. This is all very true, but often, even where there are practical consequences, the real hurt is an attack on the self, a wounding of self-esteem. Who has the power to wound our self-esteem? A flippant answer is: Anyone we give that power to. A more understanding answer is: Those people who have the capacity to make us feel ashamed of ourselves. Obviously, we're most vulnerable to be shamed by those whose opinions we care about most. We care about certain people *and* we care very much about what aspect of ourselves is at stake in our relationship with them.

The "about what" that makes us most vulnerable to criticism are closely held ambitions. A teacher's teaching, a mother's mothering, a lover's loving—these things go to the heart of the self. Love rejected turns back upon the self as hatred—self-hatred and shame. We're most vulnerable to feeling shame in the face of criticism when we are most exposed. In order to be rejected we have to expose a need. And that's risky. It's when we dare to show off what we deeply care about that we are most deeply cut by criticism.

We can *feel* rejection even when it's neither intended nor apparent. Simple oversight, lack of sensitivity, or even well-intentioned "constructive criticism" can convey the sense that one isn't good enough as a person. Other people don't always know when we feel rejected because they don't always know what our hopes are.

At last year's graduation ceremony I knew I was going to get the distinguished teaching award. I'd won such awards several times in the past, but not recently. As a teacher in a medical school, I have so many competing claims on my time that sometimes I let my teaching slip. Not last year. I gave all my classes everything I've got, and they went terrifically. When it came time for them to announce my award, I tried to look unconcerned, but my heart was racing and I couldn't catch my breath. I wanted to get myself under control so I could say a few brief words of thanks. Then, finally, came the announcement. "And it will come as no surprise to you that this year's distinguished teaching award goes to Dr. T." My face went red. Sure, Dr. T. was a good teacher, and he was a friend, too, but I just couldn't believe they'd passed me by. When Dr. T. returned to his seat, I smiled and shook his hand. It wasn't easy. It's never easy to smile and eat shit at the same time.

One way we avoid the pain of criticism is to turn critic ourselves, attacking before we can be attacked. This strategy alienates other people and fools some of them about our own vulnerability. Another strategy to avoid the pain of disapproval is to submerge the self in pleasing others.

THE NEED TO PLEASE AND THE NEED FOR APPROVAL

The other side of intolerance of criticism is craving for praise. The same people who are deflated by criticism are inflated by praise. When the childhood need to be admired and confirmed is thwarted, it is intensified into a lasting craving. The unappreciated child grows to adulthood with an inordinate need to be loved and admired. These people may look like grown-ups, but the tenuous quality of their selfhood leaves them with a childlike dependency on others for reassurance and praise.

The secure person appreciates praise but does not live for it. The insecure person has an insatiable craving for reassurance, and needs praise to feel momentarily good about himself or herself. Feedback is important, but there's a difference between being open to other people's opinions and being entirely defined by them.

I'm sure you know people who are forever in search of guidance and approval. Sometimes it's obvious, sometimes not. Some of these people clamor actively for reassurance and advice; others, more controlled, go about their business independently but yearn for a special relationship. Once they find someone they can really respect, they become fixated on that relationship. Often with unhappy results.

Some people crave admiration to such a degree that they can't help but lie about their accomplishments. The lies may only be little ones—"embellishments"—still, it's sad. Some of us can't stop pretending.

Our dreams of glory often follow childhood scripts. Here's mine. (Now, *this* is embarrassing!) I daydream about being a professional basketball star. I don't conjure up this wish, it just comes to me. My fantasy has taken on a very particular shape, namely that nothing about my size or ability changes. (I'm a slightly overweight six-foot-four, and was a fair basketball player until my mid-thirties. I could dribble, pass, and rebound. Unfortunately, I couldn't shoot.) In my daydream, just one thing changes: I can shoot a hundred jump shots without missing. It's a version of having magic power for just a short time. In the fantasy, I convince an NBA coach to let me join a team during the playoffs and I have my moment of glory. Part of my pleasure is thinking about specific people who I hope will see me performing like a star. Embarrassing as telling this whole story is, the most acutely embarrassing part is—or would be—saying who those people are that I'm so desperate to impress.

What do *you* daydream about? Chances are that when the level of stress in your life rises, your fantasies will be about escape and relaxation. After all, wouldn't seven days of sleep set you right? Maybe you're one of those women who take a mental health day off from work, and then spend it doing laundry. The less hectic things are, the more likely your daydreams will reflect what you imagine would banish feelings of inadequacy and insecurity. Men dream of success and achievement; women more often dream of love and acceptance. As a result, most men are suckers for praise, as if praise were a drug and they got high on adulation. Women, on the other hand, like to be helpful and have great difficulty saying no.

People love to do favors. To be asked means that the other person likes you, needs you. But time is limited and we can't do everything. People with low self-respect feel they need to explain their reasons for saying no. What they aren't willing to do is to respect themselves enough to limit what they will do to please people.

My favorite lesson in saying no came from Salvador Minuchin, the world's leading family therapist—a very busy man. I called to invite him to speak, and I was giving him over a year's notice. His answer was short and sweet: "Oh, Dr. Nichols, I'd love to, but I can't." Period. That was that. Saying he *couldn't*, rather than *wouldn't*, left no room for argument. Saying he'd *love to* blocked any attempt on my part to tell him how important it was, how much we wanted him, how the sun might not rise if he didn't come, and so on. Now I sometimes use Minuchin's "I'd love to, but I can't" when I need to say no (I have a *terrible* time saying no), but I must admit that I have to prepare myself in advance, otherwise my instinct to please takes over.

Does this hint seem necessary or obvious to you? Well, perhaps you're one of the lucky ones who don't have to court other people's approval.

*   *   *

Life is tough enough without worrying about other people's approval. But it's really worrying, as much as hard work, that wears
us out. On top of all that we do, we carry the extra weight of
anxiety: anxiety about who we are and anxiety over the dreadful
possibility of being found out for what we're afraid we might be.
We recognize that our lives are unbalanced but cannot (or do not)
brave the insecurity that comes with breaking out of old habits. No
wonder the average person is worn out when the weekend comes.
As stress rises, so does the need for relaxation. Too much stress,
however, spoils leisure.

GUILTY PLEASURES

Plagued by anxiety, depression, vague discontent, and a sense of
inner emptiness, men and women seek solace in passive escapism.
Worn out at the end of the day, we surrender to self-indulgence.
On nights when we're too tired to read and fed up with regular TV
fare, we stop at the video store and pick up a movie. When plain
old popcorn doesn't seem sufficiently satisfying, we bring home
Ben and Jerry's ice cream. So what if the satisfaction is as nour-
ishing as cotton candy? It's sweet and it's safe.

In the decade of the couch potato, VCRs and designer ice creams
have become growth industries. There are big bucks to be made in
catering to the regressive attempts of unfulfilled people to find
some kind of pleasure in this world. As a matter of fact, there's
nothing wrong with controlled regression in the service of the ego.
Almost every form of joyful satisfaction involves some reversion to
childish modes of experience. If you can't let go, you can't relax,
have fun, joke, or play. Even if busy grown-ups need to relax by
giving in to passive self-indulgence, there's nothing wrong with
that. The problem comes when mature pursuits provide so little
satisfaction that regressive self-indulgence becomes the main
source of satisfaction—when we live to relax, rather than relax to

live. The result of dependency on immediate gratification is living in a state of restless, perpetually unsatisfied desire.

At the end of a dreary, lonely, and unsuccessful day we want release and escape. For some people passive relaxation is not enough; they hunger for more vivid experience in an attempt to revive jaded appetites. When they kick off their shoes to unwind from the pressures of the day, frustrated desires well up from the pressures of self-control. Some of these desires are *guilty pleasures*, shameful impulses we don't like to talk about. There's no secret about the popularity of compulsive shopping, escapist reading, junk food, and mindless television; but the extent of dependence on secret drinking, trashy books, eating binges, pornography, and kinky sex would surprise you. We lie a lot about what we do.

The more rigidly we control our onstage selves, the more tempted we are to indulge immoderate appetites offstage. The presence of roommates or other family members acts as a restraining influence, but when nobody's around we give in to guilty pleasures. Who knows what goes on behind closed doors?

Why are guilty pleasures sought in private, behind closed doors? Because we're ashamed of them. When pressure builds and other avenues of satisfaction are closed off, we become secret connoisseurs of our own decadence. We luxuriate in license. Guilty pleasures are a protest against regimentation, control, and deprivation. They are an outlet especially tempting to those people who are reluctant to stand up and fight openly for what they want: shy people, embarrassed people, people who are ashamed of their own natural desires.

Guilty pleasures are a rebellion against shame—or is it against guilt? The shame comes from the degrading sense that what we're doing is wrong *and* that we're too weak to stop. The guilt comes from the angry protest against all those people in our lives who frustrate us.

The married man who sneaks off to a pornographic movie justifies himself by blaming his wife for not satisfying his desires. The woman who indulges herself in eating binges is striking a blow against the cult of thinness, and against all those who control her life. The henpecked husband, the overburdened wife, and the dutiful son or daughter can soothe themselves and at the same time rebel against all those who keep them down. Never mind that it's a sneaky protest. At the same moment that they're reaching for the cookies or turning on the pornographic videotape, they are filled with almost as much righteous self-justification as excited pleasure: The hell with them! I deserve this. Shame sets in afterward.

The people most likely to indulge in shameful pleasures are those who haven't learned to satisfy their needs in company. Arising out of the frustrations of shame-sensitive individuals, greedy appetites for artificial and isolated satisfaction build up in public and take over in private. When we seek these forbidden satisfactions in secret, we do so in an all-or-none fashion. That's why sex with a stranger is so delicious. It has none of the predictability of habit, and none of the restraint that builds up with familiarity. When shameful desires slip their leash, we're helpless—we just say yes.

The shame of guilty pleasures inheres not in the actions themselves but in our attitude toward them. One person's secret vice is another person's harmless relaxation. It's when we're ashamed of our desires that we bottle them up. Shame creates a condition of denial and frustration that tempts us to give in—and let go—in private. Guilty pleasures are defined less by their content than by the dynamic of a *control phase* and a *release phase*. Control and release is the natural rhythm of desire, but when it is driven by shame it becomes an intense and destructive polarity.

Shame sets up a tension between self-control and self-indulgence, abstinence and satisfaction. Release brings momentary satisfaction but also self-loathing. When loss of control is equated to loss of dignity, release adds to the quota of shame, which intensifies the cycle of control and reform, thus re-creating the conditions for another fall. Each new surrender generates more shame. The additional shame drives the compulsive cycle even harder. Alcoholics call this cycle "the squirrel cage." After the ritualized acting out, shame sets in: *Oh, God, I did it again.* Acting out ends with drunkenness, orgasm, a bloated gut, or an empty wallet, and the person caught up in the squirrel cage feels additional shame for the hangover, the demeaning sex, the stomach-ache, or the lost money. In short order, cycles of control and release become stereotyped and ritualized.

That guilty pleasures involve indulgence of things normally pro-tected by shame is no accident. Take pornography, for example. Most pornography involves humiliation. The voyeur invades a woman's privacy, penetrating a barrier enforced by shame. Wom-en's pornography, which often takes form in romance novels, in-volves threats and triumphs over humiliation. In pornography, wish fulfillment triumphs over reality. Truth—disappointment, re-jection, inadequacy—never intrudes, at least not for long.

A central element often unnoticed in various forms of pornog-raphy is a totally gratifying object of desire, not really a separate person with a mind and a will but an extension of the self's wishes under absolute control. In pornography aimed at men, women worshipfully do all they can to please the man, thus relieving him of all performance anxiety.

Anthropologist Margaret Mead said that pornography involves the attempt "to stimulate sex feelings independent of the presence of another loved and chosen human being."[5] Yes, and it's safe from the possible shame of rejection as well. This guilty pleasures have in common: They are a regressive retreat into self-gratification, a renewable source of the illusion that one is loved.

Perhaps you're thinking, Okay, so shame and rigid self-control make some people prone to wallow in guilty pleasures, but isn't pornography a rather extreme example? Not really. The stereotyp-ical customer for pornography is a sleazy old man in a raincoat. This image is at once disgusting and comforting—comforting be-cause it's a way of distancing ourselves from something we'd rather not face, namely that the male sexual response is triggered pre-dominantly by visual stimulation. Men's fantasies are X-rated vid-eos, soundtrack optional. Tenderness highly optional. The average consumer of pornography differs from the average person not by being wicked but by being shy. Take, for example, sociologist Harold Nawy's portrait of the pornographic moviegoer. "Typically, he is white, middle aged, middle class, married, neatly dressed, college educated, and has a white-collar job. Maybe he is also unloved, unloving, and unwilling to take the risk of a truly close relationship."[6]

There is a part of most men that responds predictably to the bared breast or the flash of thigh, even if they're only images on a screen or in a magazine, unconnected to anyone they care about or even know. "But," writes Keith McWalter in the "About Men" column of the *New York Times Magazine*, "there is another part of us—of me, at least—that is not grateful for the traditional male sexual programming, not proud of the results. By a certain age, most modern men have been so surfeited with images of unattainably beautiful women in preposterously provocative contexts that we risk losing the capacity to respond to the ordinarily beautiful women we love in our ordinary bedrooms. There have been too many times when I have guiltily resorted to impersonal fantasy because the genuine love I felt for a woman wasn't enough to convert feeling into performance. And in those sorry, secret moments, I have resented deeply my lifelong indoctrination into the esthetic of the centerfold."[7] For "resented deeply" read ashamed.

The business of exploiting men's fantasies is big business. Hardcore pornographic films are now available in local video stores and on cable TV in hotel rooms. Titillated by exposure and tempted by widespread availability, more and more men turn to erotic outlets for their bottled-up emotions—*and* feel ashamed for doing so. Feminist enlightenment is no match for the unregenerate male libido. It doesn't prevent men from succumbing to the lure of pornography, but it does make them ashamed of having done so. Nor does feminist consciousness make women immune from the acceptable equivalent of pornography: trashy books.

Taught from an early age that their duty in life is to attract and please men, women in large numbers turn to romance novels for the fulfillment of their fantasies. As children, many of these women felt emotionally unresponded to and tried to overcome their loneliness and depression through erotic fantasies. They look to love to make them feel worthy and whole. In the average romance novel, the heroine doesn't have to do anything to overcome apathy and lack of initiative. She can be passive; men come to her. Intellectual enlightenment doesn't do away with the craving for male approval. Women who are addicted can find a harmless fix as near as the supermarket bookshelf.

The fact that our society has let pornography out of the closet raises an interesting paradox. Maybe "shameless paradox" is more like it. Take almost any appetite of which we are ashamed and you'll see a vigorous advertising industry promoting socially acceptable forms of it. We tell our children to say no to drugs but bombard them with the message that there is a pill for every ill. Compulsive gambling is a social disease that ruins people and destroys families, yet state-sponsored lotteries are not only legal but also advertised like toothpaste. Every vice has its own "want makers" on Madison Avenue.

America is a nation of consumers, a country in which the real talent is not making things but marketing them. Too pooped to drive down to the mall? You don't even have to leave the house anymore to commit shopping. The mailman delivers a never-ending stream of catalogues, and no less than three television channels are now devoted exclusively to selling. They sell us what we need and what we don't need: garden hoses, reclining chairs, jewelry, plush animals, porcelain flowers, commemorative coins, bird figurines, telephones shaped like tomatoes—ornaments, trifles, toys, geegaws, doodads, and knickknacks. Who buys that stuff? Don't kid yourself. As of 1988, one program alone, the "Home Shopping Club," was taking in over a billion dollars a year. "Taking in" seems particularly apt in this context, and none of us is immune: The culture of consumption encourages us to channel our restless dissatisfaction into shopping expeditions we know to be meaningless. It may be an exaggeration to say that advertising creates needs, but don't underestimate the capacity of the consumer culture to channel unconscious cravings into consumption. Sensitive men and women may disdain more obvious forms of conspicuous consumption, but most of us fall back on unnecessary purchases from time to time to bolster flagging self-respect. Nothing soothes the spirit like a new purchase.

Advertising plays upon our need for regressive indulgence and feeds our insatiable desire for impulse gratification. Facing a busy, stressful day? Go ahead, indulge yourself. Why not? "You deserve a break. . . ." I'm not suggesting that we outlaw junk food for break-fast. (If we did, only outlaws would eat junk food.) I'm not even trying to moralize. My point is that when our appetites for guilty pleasures are fanned by advertising, standards falter and we get caught up in shame-inducing control-and-release conflicts.

Compulsive overeating is one example of the control and re-lease cycle that almost anyone can relate to. Shame—about our gluttony and spreading waistlines—makes us control our eating. The more we control, the more we hunger. When frustration builds and we once again overindulge, we feel ashamed of ourselves and vow to be good—until next time. Overeating cycles vary from the harmless (weekend binges) to the pathological (bulimia). The peo-ple most likely to indulge in eating binges are compulsive dieters. The guilt and shame that follow spells of compulsive gorging be-come part of a ritual of "crime" and "punishment."

Dieting goes hand in hand with physical exercise. One of the unhappy side effects of the recent physical fitness craze is that compulsive runners and fitness addicts, male and female, often become obsessed with dieting. If a week's worth of workouts makes someone feel both virtuous and deprived, he or she may give in to bouts of overeating, often released by alcohol, on weekends. In some people, these gorging binges lead to extremely strong feel-ings of shame and disgust. Shame for their weakness and disgust over their oral cravings. More shame, more control. Cycles of compulsive overeating affect nearly everyone, whether in its more dramatic forms, such as bulimia, or just plain pigging out. The obvious solution—more control—only perpetuates the problem.

Working out is good for the heart and good for the soul, but it can also be a way of mortifying the flesh in an attempt to purge shame. If one is plagued by insecurity and filled with secret shame, then what better way to mortify and purify the self than to lift weights until every muscle is exhausted with the effort, or run until the body is bathed in purifying sweat and tension is replaced by heavy-limbed fatigue. Marathon runners feel exhausted but cleansed after completing 26.2 miles. They're proud of what they've made themselves do, as well they should be. But sometimes this pride is the only pride they have. When insecurity is rooted in unconscious shame, you can run but you can't hide.

It's plain to see that indulging in guilty pleasures can make us feel ashamed. What's less easy to see is that shame is behind them. Among the painful emotional truths we turn away from, none is closer to the bone than shame. We cannot bear to confront it because we cannot bear to scrape away the scar tissue over our self-esteem.

Facing shame is an act of courage, something not everyone has the stomach for. But with so many imponderables in life, doesn't it make sense to understand ourselves as fully as possible? Just remember this, what can't be seen is hard to change.

Now that we've seen how the denial of shame plays so large a role in the mature person's practiced self-deceit, and how it affects our everyday lives, it's time to take a more careful look at the dynamics of shame.

7

The Anatomy of Shame

If shame lies at the root of our insecurity, it seems obvious that someone must have made us ashamed. It's an easy assumption, and popular, too. If we're unhappy, our parents must have mistreated us. We are victims of their faults and failings; our shame is their shame. With this logic we're provided in one stroke with a rationale and a pair of scapegoats. It's comforting to be innocent. But the truth is a bit more complicated.

Shame takes us to the heart of human nature. Why? Because shame strikes at our essential identity. No other emotion cuts so deep into our experience of self that it can undermine our very worth as human beings. Shame is about who we are, deep down, our basic strivings and most fundamental conflicts. Therefore, to understand shame we must study the essential hopes and fears of human experience. Like shame itself, these elemental emotions are deeply repressed. To explore the depths of human nature, we need a psychology of depth, which does not end with Freud but certainly begins there.

THE PSYCHODYNAMICS OF SHAME

Although Freud himself had relatively little to say about shame, it was his structural theory and the concept of the superego that first made it possible to understand the dynamics of shame as a result of psychic conflict.[1,2]

The superego can be thought of as "the voice of conscience," but this equation falls short on two counts. First, although the superego does represent moral standards, many of its dictates are unconscious and often unreasonable and sadistically cruel. The superego hounds us with a sense of urgent oughtness, a categorical imperative predating any thoughtful consideration of right and wrong. It's this archaic, unconscious aspect of the superego that tortures us with guilt—even though the original reason for guilt ("bad" wishes and deeds from childhood) may be repressed and forgotten. The second complication is that the superego comprises not one but two agencies: the *conscience* and the *ego-ideal*.

The superego, then, is based on internalization of parental standards, both prohibitions (in the form of conscience) and ideals (in the form of an ego-ideal). The critical, punitive aspects of the superego are well known, because guilt is something we're all familiar with. But the superego, with its ego-ideal, also provides us with self-approval, self-love, and self-esteem.

It's important to realize that we do not form our superegos by identifying with our parents' conscious ethical standards; we form this moral agency by identifying with our parents' superegos, much of which are unconscious and irrational. The superego's approval and disapproval, self-esteem and self-criticism, is based on childish understanding, and misunderstanding, of what it means to be lovable and what it means to be bad. The ego-ideal is an unrealistic part of the superego, which has its origins in narcissistic overevaluation of the self and an idealized vision of parental power and perfection. Its goals are perfectionistic.

The ego behaves toward the superego as it once behaved toward a threatening parent whose affection and approval is needed (ego-ideal) and whose punishment and rejection is feared (conscience). The superego punishes us from within, delivering extremely painful blows to our self-esteem. Violations of conscience result in a sense of guilt; violations of the ego-ideal result in a sense of inferiority.

Once the superego is formed, the logical judgment of the ego about which impulses might be dangerous is now complicated by the possibility of illogical conflict with the superego. Remember, the superego is often harsh and not always rational. That's why we often feel too guilty to do something perfectly harmless like going to a movie in the middle of the afternoon. The same irrationality is true with respect to the superego's punishment. Consider, for example, a woman who feels guilty because she skidded on the ice and dented her car. Friends, realizing that she is being unfairly harsh on herself, might console her by telling her that it wasn't her fault. It doesn't work. It's nice to know your friends like you, but reason doesn't still the voice of the superego.

Being on good or bad terms with one's superego becomes as important as being on good or bad terms with one's parents once was. Self-esteem is no longer regulated solely by the approval of other people, but rather by the feeling of having done or not done the right thing. Complying with the superego's demands brings not only relief but also pleasure and security—the same blissful confidence little children get when they're good and feel well loved. ("Please love me; I'll be good.") The punishment for violating the superego's prohibitions is guilt. The punishment for failing to live up to the ego-ideal's standards is shame.

Freud believed that shame was related to sexuality, or rather one particular aspect of it, exhibitionism. In "Three Essays on the Theory of Sexuality," he described shame as one of the barriers against the sexual drive—a defense against the wish to see and be seen.[3] (Is this why we look away when we approach someone on the street?) In "Civilization and Its Discontents," he said that shame reflected danger from genital exposure, a vulnerability that human beings assumed when they adopted the upright posture.[4]

One reason Freud avoided the affect of shame may have been because Alfred Adler made such a point of "organ inferiority" and the "inferiority complex" as the basic motivating force driving a compensatory "striving for superiority."[5] Although Adler's claim that life is one long struggle to overcome feelings of inferiority fits the data of conscious experience, analytic studies of the child have since made it plain that the early infantile ego begins with a sense of omnipotence, not inferiority.[6] Feelings of inferiority come later, as the child is disillusioned about being limitlessly special. Actually, "shame" is probably more accurate than "inferiority feelings," because the latter implies comparison with external figures and does not quite capture the internal tension between the ego and the ego-ideal. Moreover, the concept of "inferiority feelings" does not accurately describe the shame and remorse that stems from failure to reach one's own potential.

Okay, let's take a minute to see where we are. Freud said this, Adler said that, but what is our understanding of shame thus far? Shame occurs when our (unconscious) ideals are violated. It results from conflict between the ego and the superego's ego-ideal. Remember, the ego-ideal is not merely a collection of abstract aspirations; it is the internalized voice of what our parents say is worthy of love. Shame is manifest when a goal of the ego-ideal is not attained, and therefore is the result of failure. The threat of shame for failure is abandonment and rejection.

Once the superego (conscience and ego-ideal) is firmly in place, we no longer have to be rebuked to feel bad. In fact, the level of internal guilt or shame may have an inverse relationship to the level of external censure. We know this intuitively in regard to guilt. How do you guilt-trip someone? Not by yelling at them. You expose someone to the mercy of their own guilt by deliberately refraining from criticism. Mention the infraction—forgetting a birthday, say— but then say it's okay (perhaps with a trace of irony): "That's okay that you didn't remember my birthday. . . ." *Zap!*

Behind the fear of shame stands the fear of contempt, which on a deeper level of the unconscious spells fear of abandonment: death by emotional starvation. The parent who uses shame to humiliate a child—saying, for example, "Look how clumsy you are!"—plays upon this fear. But even deeper rooted shame-anxiety is stirred up by the parent who walks away in disgust, because this even more strongly evokes separation anxiety.

Now let's get back to the development of psychoanalytic thinking and how it helps illuminate the dynamics of shame. Another reason Freud didn't have much to say about shame is because it relates directly to something that has only recently been emphasized in psychoanalysis: the self.

SHAME AND THE IDEAL SELF

The Freudian vision of humanness is simple, and simply devastating: At the heart of human nature is animal nature. Behind all our virtuous sublimations lie repressed desires, sexual and aggressive. It may not be a pretty picture, but it is undeniably true: We are driven by desire. Yet like many truths, Freud's has been overelaborated. Yes, we are physical beings with animal appetites, but we are also symbolic animals, the only ones capable of self-consciousness. Thus, the burden of being human takes two forms. One, the body, is standardized and given. The other, the self, is a personalized achievement, created partly out of the matrix of earliest relationships and partly from our own efforts.

Helen Block Lewis, author of *Shame and Guilt in Neurosis*, noted that Freud underestimated the concept of self, failing to differentiate it from ego and ego-ideal. She believed that the concept of self is central to an understanding of shame: "The self is, first of all, the experiential registration of the person's activities as his own."[7] Shame is about the whole self and its failure to live up to an ideal. Hostility against self is experienced in a passive mode, and therefore leaves the shame-prone individual subject to depression:

Shame of failure is for an involuntary event. It results from incapacity. Guilt for transgression is, by implication, guilt for a voluntary act or choice. The proximal stimulus to shame is thus deficiency of the self; while the proximal stimulus of guilt is some action (omission) by the self, which by implication is able. Shame thus feels involuntary; guilt feels as if it were more voluntary.[8]

The object of shame is the self, which is experienced as defective and having failed in its quest to attain a goal. These goals of the self relate to ideals, internalized through identification with the parents, especially the idealized parent as represented by the superego's ego-ideal.

The *ideal self* is a composite, enduring inner image of the self we want to be. In shame, the image of the ideal self is compared with the actions of the *experienced self*. It isn't just our actions that seem "bad"; it's what they reveal about us. Thus, it is primarily *qualities* of the self that make us feel ashamed, whereas it is our *actions* that make us feel guilty.

When someone questions our integrity and honesty, we're outraged. Why? In every one of us is a painful fear that we won't live up to our ideals of honor and integrity. We know that our actions haven't always been above reproach. And, at a deeper level, all of us struggle with self-doubt. The secret suspicion that we're afflicted with some profound personal flaw is a product not of real experience but of inevitable failure to live up to an inflated, unreachable ideal.

The ideal self is formed originally from our parents' expectations of cleanliness and self-control. But the ideal self may be complicated by conflicting parental models. A daughter's loyalty to her mother's image of strength and independence may spell betrayal of her father's image of her as helpless and dependent. Her shame, like ours, is a sad legacy of impossible conflicts about identity.

In *Childhood and Society*, Erik Erikson defined identity as the conscious and unconscious strivings for continuity and synthesis of personality, maintenance of congruence with ideals and identity of one's chosen social group, and a conscious awareness of who one is.[9] Identity is the self as subject and object.

Erikson went beyond the traditional psychoanalytic psychosexual stages by emphasizing social development and designating the critical psychosocial task of each phase, which the individual must surmount in order to be prepared for the next phase. In the second year of life (the anal stage) the psychosocial task is toilet training, but Erikson emphasized the attainment of muscular control in general rather than bowel control in particular. In learning self-control, the child properly gains a lasting sense of autonomy, whereas loss of self-esteem and shaming in the process leads to a pervasive sense of doubt and shame.

Instead of replacing the idea of structural conflict (ego vs. ego-ideal) with that of the self's identity, we can incorporate both: Shame and doubt relate to the development of self-esteem, and this implies a consciousness of the whole self. Shame reflects feelings about a defect in the self—originally, lack of mastery of the body—a lowering of self-esteem, a falling short of the values of the ego-ideal, and a flaw in one's identity representation. This brings us to the topic of narcissism.

NARCISSISM

"Narcissism" is a sticky word. So many negative connotations cling to it that our understanding is clouded with defensive anxiety. The dictionary says "self-love," and isn't that vain, egotistical . . . shameful?

To most people, narcissism means selfish preoccupation based on excessive admiration of the self. It conjures up the myth of Narcissus, the Greek youth who pined away for love of his own reflection. We disdain the narcissist for his strutting self-importance or pity him for his anxiety over other people's opinions. But how did "narcissism" become a dirty word? What's wrong with self-love? The answer is that we're ashamed of the weakness that this basic impulse implies.

In fact, narcissism is normal; it means investing the self with psychological interest. The tenacity with which negative connotations stick to it attests to the fact that self-love is close to the heart of the self—and heavy with conflict.

Narcissism pertains to self-esteem; it may be healthy or pathological, depending upon its compulsiveness and insatiability.

Normal narcissism—reflecting realistic goals and ambitions—is healthy self-esteem. Excessive narcissism—reflecting grandiose goals and ambitions—is based not on self-love but self-doubt. Such grandiose overestimation of one's own capabilities serves as a basic defense against underlying feelings of inferiority and self-hatred. There is no curse like extravagant expectations.

Because shame is felt in relationship to the self, it is closely tied to one's own narcissism. As we've seen, inherent in shame is a measuring of an image of the self as it is against an image of the self as it ought to be. When a defect or failure of the self is perceived, the resultant shame punctures narcissistic self-esteem, like sticking an ice pick into a tire. Shame is injured narcissism.

Since narcissism can be moderate or inflated, it takes a significant blow to make some people feel ashamed, while others feel shame merely for failing to achieve grand ambitions. Thus, for example, even a relatively secure woman whose husband has an affair may have trouble getting over the betrayal—not because she's still angry but because she's ashamed. Her anger over his transgression may be less painful than her shame over feeling rejected, and in some way inadequate. A man with grandiose ambitions may suffer equally devastating shame simply because he's been passed over for an award or promotion. In both cases, self-esteem is unexpectedly violated; both suffer narcissistic injury; one person's narcissism is simply more vulnerable.

Why is one person's narcissism moderate while another's is inflated? What is the genesis of a secure or fragile self? To answer this, I will introduce Heinz Kohut and the psychology of the self.

THE PSYCHOLOGY OF THE SELF

Kohut began his career as a classical analyst but later amended Freudian theory to emphasize interpersonal attachment as the most essential human need. By shifting attention from the drives to the self, Kohut deemphasized the mind in conflict and stressed instead the self in relation to others. Freudian theory is about drives and defenses: We're spurred on by drives but shackled by defenses; the result is anxiety and guilt. Psychology of the self is about a sense of who we are and our self-worth; we hunger for love and self-respect, but we're burdened by self-doubt and the torment of self-consciousness and, beneath that, shame.

When a child's need for affirmation is adequately met, the child gradually builds up a sense of worth and little by little becomes less dependent on the evaluations of others to maintain self-esteem. Shame is a traumatic disruption of this process, a narcissistic injury that drives the child into hiding. When this happens occasionally, the child is weaned from dependence and forced to develop his or her own resources. If it happens excessively, and the child is abruptly cut off from narcissistic supplies, the child's sense of self is damaged. Notice that I'm talking about a *need for affirmation*. That is not the same thing as a *need not to be abused.* Affirmation is a positive, active demonstration of love and acceptance.

The secure self is a product of feeling appreciated. Parents who criticize or ignore their child's healthy exhibitionism undermine that security. The unresponded-to self is not able to transform childish grandiosity into reliable self-esteem. When it comes to a child's self-worth, disinterest is as damaging as anger.

As I wrote in *Turning Forty in the Eighties:*

If the childhood need to be admired and confirmed is frustrated, it is intensified into a lasting craving. The child grows to adulthood with a piece close to the heart left behind. These people look like grown-ups, but the tenuous quality of their selfhood leaves them with child-like dependency on others for reassurance and praise. Exhibitionism is not sublimated, it is repressed. The child who hungered in vain for praise becomes an adult who alternately suppresses the craving for attention, then lets it break through in an all-or-none form in the presence of anyone who seems safe and receptive.

If selfishness means unconcern with others, these people are just the opposite. They are obsessed with the opinion of others and have an inordinate need to be loved and admired.[10]

When a child's grandiose fantasies are not responded to, they remain active in unmodified form. Unresponded-to children lack a firm sense of self and remain burdened by grandiose ambitions. They feel empty and worthless, subject to the shame of repeated failure to live up to aggrandized, wishful self-images. The shame over this emptiness and repeated failure is accompanied by depression.

The difference between Freud's vision and Kohut's is the difference between a creature driven by conflict with his own instincts and one dependent on his parents to build self-esteem—or forever after dependent on others to make up for its absence. If guilt is the dominant experience of men and women suffering structural conflict, shame is the major affect of those suffering from insecurity— the guiltless depression of the self who, deep down, feels unloved.

Shame is a reaction to failure in the self's quest to gain responsiveness and affirmation from the people who count most, the ones whose good opinion we crave. Shame is self-condemnation for falling short of inner goals, often rooted in extravagant (narcissistic) expectations. Shame is the pain of feeling unlovable. There is nothing worse, or more shameful, than feeling, "I am unlovable because I am weak, dirty, and defective."

Why must we suffer so?

If shame is such a driving force behind so many forms of insecurity, why don't we think more about it? And why don't we understand it better? Because the roots of shame are buried in the painful past.

In the next section I will examine the evolution of self-doubt as I explore the developmental progress of shame.

II
....
GROWING
UP
INSECURE

8

....

Love and Worth

The Foundations of Self-respect

Believe it or not, the natural human condition is confident enthusiasm, creative intelligence, zest, and loving appreciation of other people. The natural child is full of life and full of love. Unfortunately, in the process of teaching children rules for living, parents also teach them to be ashamed—ashamed of their feelings, ashamed of their needs, ashamed of themselves.

A common and painful sight on playgrounds and sidewalks and supermarkets, and in the homes of our friends or ourselves, is exuberant children bumping hard against parental scolding and rebuff. Look around and you'll see harassed parents losing control of their tempers and flailing out at sad-faced children. It's hard not to be moved by these little skirmishes of everyday life. It's annoying when parents let their children make too much noise in the movies or knock things down in stores, but watching parents berate and humiliate children in public really chills the heart. When parents say things like "How could you be so stupid!" or "You make me sick!" we wonder: Why do they have to be so mean? Can't they control their kids without humiliating them? (We're especially critical before we have children of our own.) Some of us are bothered more by lack of discipline, others by lack of sympathy. But regardless of which generation we identify with, it's painful to see so many sad hearts in the supermarket.

When little faces break, our hearts melt. Their pain is our pain. We remember what it feels like to be on the receiving end, and if we are parents ourselves, we feel guilty remembering the mean things we've done to our own little ones.

Once we begin to understand what's at stake—not just peace and quiet, but secure self-respect or shame and insecurity—the battles between parents and children take on added significance. As we become sensitized to the pervasiveness of shame, we begin to see mean-tempered scolding like sledgehammer blows, relentlessly pounding little children's self-esteem.

Parents make a lot of mistakes. Why not? Being a parent is an impossible job. The more we notice the mistakes, the more likely we are to think of successful child-rearing as a matter of avoiding mistakes. It's almost as though bringing up a healthy, self-respecting child were a negative accomplishment—*not* being too harsh, *not* being rejecting, *not* getting in the way of the child's natural unfolding.

There is ample support for the point of view that children are prodigies of nature, inherently confident creatures whose instincts propel them toward self-fulfillment—unless and until this innate vitality is subverted by adult codes and commands. The story of Adam and Eve reflects the general awareness that children of nature don't know shame; they have to be taught. Most of us get a little confused about exactly what Adam and Eve's sin was, but the idea of a Garden of Eden, a state of unspoiled childhood innocence, has always exerted a strong claim on the imagination.

Two of the giants of twentieth-century psychology—Sigmund Freud, founder of psychoanalysis, and Carl Rogers, founder of humanistic psychology—built theories of human unhappiness on the premise that shame and guilt and self-hatred are not part of the child's natural experience but are engendered by depriving parents.

Freud first indicted parents as seducers of innocent children, and later as agents of cultural repression, the source of all guilt and anxiety. If children grow up ashamed, unconsciously afraid of their own natural instincts, whom else do we blame except the parents?

According to Carl Rogers, children are born with a tendency toward *self-actualization*; left to their own devices, children tend to follow their own best interests.[1] No one has to teach them to be curious, or loving, or proud of their accomplishments. Unhappily, this healthy instinct toward actualization gets warped and subverted by the need to please. Children's hunger for affection and approval is fed by parents who respond conditionally, often more in terms of their own needs and values than what is necessarily good for the child. Consequently, children don't so much learn what's best for them as how to placate powerful but capricious parents.

Another idea that reinforces the belief that children will prosper if parents don't interfere is the concept of good-enough mothering. According to British psychoanalyst Donald Winnicott,[2] the quality of care children receive is important, but it need not be some unattainable ideal. Good-enough is good enough. This benign outlook is a reassuring antidote to the enormous burden of frustration and guilt many perfectly adequate parents carry around because they aren't perfect; but it unintentionally contributes to the idea that a parent's main concern should be to avoid being abusive.

For further evidence of the harm parents do, we need look no farther than the daily newspaper. Widespread accounts of child abuse—let's call it what it is: beating and sexual molestation—make it clear that childhood is a mine field of destructive influence. Moreover, as children of alcoholic parents know, destructive influence takes many forms. A bad example can hurt as much as bad treatment.

All this evidence of bad parenting strengthens the conviction that cruelty and neglect are to blame for shame and insecurity. If naturally sweet children grow up sour, it must be because their parents poisoned their self-confident attitude toward life. If only parents would stand back and not block natural developmental urges, then children would not be subject to morbid anxiety, self-hatred, guilt, and shame. As I said, it's almost as though bringing up a self-respecting child were a negative accomplishment— *almost*.

THE PSYCHOLOGICAL BIRTH OF SELF-RESPECT

While it *is* true that parents needn't be perfect to raise healthy children, it is *not* true that children will grow up happy and secure if only their parents would leave them alone and not undermine their spontaneous progress. Quite the contrary: Secure self-respect is an interpersonal achievement, one that must be actively nurtured.

The idea that good parenting means not disrupting the child's healthy progress assumes that a basic sense of connectedness, attachment, and security are givens. In fact, however, infant research shows this is not so. The process of connectedness that fosters interpersonal well-being is neither passive nor given. It's an active accomplishment.

Babies are not the completely helpless creatures we once thought, nor do they begin life in some kind of undifferentiated fusion with their mothers, as the theories of Margaret Mahler, Donald Winnicott, and Harry Guntrip would have us believe.[3] Another image of infancy that has been repudiated is the Freudian conception of the infant as a relatively solitary collection of reflexes, instincts, and sensory capacities.

Infants are more than little eating and crying and wetting machines. They do not discharge instincts in a vacuum; they express their basic needs in relationship with other people. Moreover, these other people are more than convenient providers, "objects" of sexual and aggressive drives; they and the infant's relationship to them are essential to the child's very nature. The infant approaches these relationships with a distinct sense of self, formed very early in life.

*   *   *

According to the acclaimed work of infant researcher and psychoanalyst Daniel Stern, the infant's emergent sense of self begins in the first two months of life: as a sense of physical cohesion with a continuity in time; as having intentions in mind; a single, distinct integrated body; an agent of actions; an experiencer of feelings; an architect of plans; and a communicator.[4]

Somewhere between two and three months, an infant can smile responsively, gaze into the parent's eyes, and coo. These interactive accomplishments create a very real social feel. The infant appears to have a new sense of who he or she is and who you are.[5] From two to six months, infants consolidate the sense of a *core self* as a separate, cohesive, bounded physical unit, with a sense of their own agency, effectance, and worth.[6]

At first, the sense of self is a physical self: a coherent, willful, physical entity. Then somewhere between the seventh and ninth month, infants start to develop a second organizing perspective, *intersubjective relatedness*. They discover that there are other minds out there. Self and other are no longer merely physical entities. They now include subjective mental states: feelings, motives, and intentions. These mental states become the subject matter of relating. Mental states can now be read, matched, aligned with, and attuned to—or misread, mismatched, misaligned with, and misattuned to.

Attunement, a parent's ability to read and share the child's affective state, is a pervasive feature of parent-child interactions and one with profound consequences. It is the forerunner of empathy, and it is what is meant when clinicians speak of "mirroring," meaning reflecting another's internal state. The powerful effect of attunement is related to the child's basic security and need for attachment.

As child psychologist Jerome Kagan explains, the concept of *attachment* "conveys the idea that the infant has acquired a special emotional relation with those who care for him, and experiences pleasure or serenity in their presence but anxiety and distress when they are gone."[7] The original function of attachment was protection from predators. Mother's presence meant safety; separation meant overwhelming fear and loneliness. Attunement is the psychological equivalent of being present, "being with" the child.

Through attunement parents demonstrate their understanding and acceptance of the child's feeling state, which in turn exerts a prepotent influence on the child's sense of worth. Obviously, the people who care for the child have the greatest power to alter his or her emotional state. If the child's sense of self is formed through interaction with care-giving adults, then the nature of the self-image should vary depending on the nature of the interaction. When care givers are attuned, the child feels loved and secure; misattunements are felt as ruptures in relationship and are extremely unsettling. Attunement, the parents' acknowledging and validating the child's internal state, then, is the primary mechanism that shapes the sense of self. Let's see how this process works and how by their active efforts parents can nurture a secure sense of self-respect.

THE CONDITIONS OF WORTH

Self-esteem is not at first an abstract, psychological problem but a concrete, physical one. It takes root in the elemental physical experience of the infant, when the reliable satisfaction of biological needs builds basic trust. There is no security, no possibility of self-respect, without physical safety and satisfaction. But, from the start, physical well-being is a product of relationship. When care givers tend to the baby's needs, the baby experiences having an effect, receiving a response, being real, being understandable, and being important.

Parents create a trustworthy and dependable environment by being attuned to the baby's rhythm and needs; they create a secure and cohesive self by providing *empathy*—understanding plus acceptance—and serving as adequate models for *identification*.

Empathy is transmitted to the very young child, almost automatically, by *emotional attunement*. Later, mirroring is a more active expression of acceptance. Attentive parents convey their appreciation of the child's healthy strivings and thus help to solidify a sense of self and confirm a sense of worth. "Look at me! Look at what I can do!" says the child. The parent's enthusiastic response—"Yes, I see!" —conveys acceptance, not only of the performance but of the developing self.

Parents also offer a model of identification. The little child who can believe "My parents are terrific and I am part of them" has an extra source of self-esteem. Ideally, the child, already basically secure from adequate mirroring, draws additional strength from identifying with the apparently enormous power of the parents. Even undemonstrative parents, who offer little praise or reassurance, can help compensate for missing self-confidence by providing worthy models for identification. If a little child were able to verbalize this experience, he or she might say, "Maybe Mommy didn't tell me that I am already fine just the way I am, but I am going to grow up to be just as big and smart as she is." Later I will explain more about how identification works and how it can go awry, but now I want to describe the developmental progress of empathy and clarify its impact on self-esteem.

Emotional Attunement

The vast majority of parents' time during the infant's first two months is spent in regulating and stabilizing sleep and feeding cycles. As young parents (and those with good memories) know, the infant's needs and rhythms are all-powerful. Nature designs things so that parents *have to* take care of their babies. They holler to be fed and whine when they're wet—and somehow always seem to be either one or the other. Their demands are intense and unrelenting, and impossible to ignore. The parents may be powerful in the wide world, but at home everything depends upon whether the baby is crying, fretting, eating, smiling, gazing, or sleeping. Heaven is a happy baby.

During this time of wailing and wetting, and pervasive fatigue, parents may feel like unpaid hospital orderlies. All they do is minister to the biological demands of their imperious little patient. But even these earliest interactions are laying the foundations of interpersonal relatedness. From day one, parents and child are engaged in a mutual exchange of social behavior. While parents are preoccupied with feeding and changing dirty diapers, they are at the same time rocking, touching, talking, singing, jiggling, and making faces. Babies are relieved when their wet diapers are changed and their hunger is sated; but in addition, when their moods are responded to with regularity and dependability, they are soothed. Contentment is attentive parents.

This reliable parental responsiveness is what Donald Winnicott called the holding environment. [8] It's an apt metaphor. The mother who is there to gratify the child's need makes the need and its gratification part of the child's relationship to her, holding the child in the arms of her safety, protecting him from being alone with his need. Safety and security mean more than need-gratification; they mean being connected to caretakers. Infants panic when their needs aren't met by reliable gratification, and they suffer primitive agonies when the bond with care givers is disrupted. Self-esteem, which grows out of the child's secure knowledge that he is loved as a person in his own right and wanted for himself, is a product of this bond, this reliable holding environment. It's not enough for parents to love their children or even to say that they love them; they must demonstrate that love: ministering to physical needs and being attuned to the child's emotional experience. Love is a verb.

Attunement begins before language and is shared largely through matching affects. Parents share the moods of their young infants and let them know through a kind of imitative gestural dialogue. When baby giggles with delight while shaking a rattle, mother matches the mood with an excited shimmy, a big smile, and an exuberant "Yes!" With the advent of language, attunement takes a quantum leap. Verbalized versions of experience vastly increase the capacity for understanding and validation, as well as misunderstanding and invalidation. Prior to language, parents are attuned or not attuned only in a very global way. After language, parents can respond to much more highly differentiated categories of experience, and the child begins to learn that certain actions and feelings are "bad," while others are "good."

With words comes a powerful channel for communicating approval and understanding. Parents point to and name familiar objects, and count, and tell what the kitty says and what the doggie says—and children imitate. Parents teach, children learn. But running through all the many things parents teach is a powerful subtext: right and wrong, good and bad, acceptable and unacceptable, understood and misunderstood. It's nice to know what the kitty says, but it's much more important to know that you are loved and accepted.

At the same time that parents are expressing understanding and acceptance in words, they continue to express themselves nonverbally, often revealing what they'd rather conceal. We can praise our children even when our hearts aren't in it, but our faces—smiling and gazing, or looking away in disgust—often betray what we really feel. Children see right through phoniness. I'll have more to say about this later, but first let me reemphasize a point I will make again and again: The critical contribution to a young child's sense of worth is not approval, not praise, and not permissiveness. It's empathy: understanding and acknowledgment.

Empathy

Little children love to hear, "You're a good boy (or girl)!" and hate it when their parents say, "You are a bad boy (or girl)!" But what really counts is whether or not parents understand children *and* let them know it. Too often parents try to control their children's actions by denying their feelings. ("Oh, you don't want that! That's not good for you.") When they express feelings, children are asking both to be understood and to be allowed to do something. It's a nice distinction, I know, but it's true, and it's important.

An effective parent communicates understanding first and then responds selectively to the child's requests. The form of this two-stage process is: "I understand, you feel like . . ." followed by a "yes," a "no," or a "maybe later." In principle it's simple. Here's how it works:

Say a little girl runs to her mother shouting, "The Popsicle man's here! I want a Popsicle!" Maybe the mother is taking her ease, sitting with her feet propped up, eating bonbons and sipping a tall cool drink, having spent a leisurely afternoon perusing popular psychology books. When her importunate daughter runs to her, she's overjoyed: Oh, goody, now I get to try out this wonderful two-stage response to feelings. So she says, "Oh, gee, sweetheart, I sure know how you love Popsicles and, yes, one probably would taste great right now, but I'm afraid that Jeeves is just about to serve dinner, so you can't have a Popsicle just now. Maybe tomorrow." She's well-rewarded by her daughter's response, "Gosh, Mummy, I am a little disappointed, but the main thing, the really important thing, is that you understood my feelings. That's what *really* counts." What a warm sense of satisfaction mother feels. And to think, just yesterday, before she had a chance to read about empathy, she had said to a similar request, "Leave me alone, you greedy, rotten, spoiled brat. Can't you see I'm taking my ease and eating bonbons!"

See how easy it is to do things right? Why is it that some parents seem to get a little tired of their children's constant demands? Or maybe come home from work drained by the stresses of the day, too frazzled to be paragons of patience? "Yes, dear, I understand, Fluffy does look funny swimming underwater . . . but [ever-so-gently] kitties don't belong in the aquarium. Come on now, Mommy will help you fish Fluffy out."

The point of view I'm trying to parody is that it's easy to be understanding. It isn't. Oh, it may start out that way. When new parents first bring baby home from the hospital they are overcome with love for that smiling miracle of their own creation. True, babies are a handful, but such an adorable handful! Loving them is easy. Empathy, too, is easy at first. Attunement between mother and child, feeling the same thing at the same time, is the beginning of empathy. It's not hard to look pleased when baby smiles or explodes in gleeful laughter; it's hard *not* to look pleased. But there's a second ingredient necessary for empathy.

Empathy also depends upon the parents' ability to allow their children tc *differentiate*, to have their own wishes, their own interests, and their own feelings. This is the hard part: to love them not only because they are kindred, in flesh and in spirit, but also despite differences. To love them because, while they are of us, they are also separate persons in their own right. This is mature parental love, and it is this love that allows children to begin life safe and secure, and to solidify that secure sense of self as worthwhile even as they begin to experiment with going their own way. To enable children to grow up secure and independent, parents must subordinate the narcissistic love for the child who is part of them to the higher love for the child who is a separate self.

Parents help children feel good about themselves by paying attention to them and admiring them. They build self-respect not only by admiring but also respecting the child's separate self, which includes the right to be different.

At one time or another, we've all heard someone ask, "How would you feel if your son (or daughter) married someone of a different race, or dropped out of school, or in some other way radically deviated from your hopes and expectations?" The "correct" answer, I suppose, is that, regardless of what you'd feel, you'd try to be understanding and supportive. Well, you don't have to wait for these adult trials of understanding. The need to accept children—not only for what you want them to be, not only for what they are, but even for what they wish they were—begins early.

What children show off for their parent's approval is not simply who they are and what they can do, it is also grandiose fantasies of who they wish they were and what they dream of doing. Children don't merely say, "Look at me, see what I can do." They also say, "I'm Superman, I can fly," or "I'm Wonderwoman and this is my magic lasso." They're comic book heroes. They're not little and weak—oh, no—they're big and strong! They can climb up skyscrapers, fly with a cape, transform themselves into powerful robots, wear masks, see through walls. They can kill bad guys. People love them.

I remember the parents of one little boy telling me that their son liked to pretend that he's the parent, that he's in charge. They knew it was just a game, but they weren't sure what to do. Shouldn't they gently discourage this wish to be the boss? Shouldn't they say, "No, honey, you be the little boy, we'll be the parents"? No.

If parents accept and admire this inflated, pretend self, the child is reassured and gradually modifies his hopes and ambitions. How-

ever, if this grandiose self, this normal stage of narcissistic development, is ignored or punished, the grandiose ambitions remain
unmodified in fantasy.

If the child's need for affirmation is adequately met, he or she
will gradually build up a sense of worth, and slowly become less
dependent on the opinions of others to feel worthwhile. In time,
the well-reassured child develops self-assurance.

Identification

It's easy to understand how paying attention to children and
admiring them, accepting both their childish showing off and their
developing independence, works to build up a feeling of being
loved and lovable—and therefore worthwhile. But it's also important for parents to provide adequate models of identification and
to tolerate the young child's hero-worshiping idealization of them.

Identification is a major source of identity. To a small child,
parents are gods who set the standard for life's highest possibilities. The more unambiguously parents embody such possibilities,
the more secure the child's budding identity. This doesn't mean
that parents have to be perfect (only a few of us are). It means that
parents shouldn't disrupt the natural process of identification by
overburdening children with parental faults and failings, by allowing self-conscious embarrassment to make them shun the child's
hero-worship, or by taking cowardly revenge on spouses by mocking them in front of the children who identify with them. I'll have
more to say about practical steps to support the child's need for
models of identification later, right now I simply want to explain
how identifying with parents contributes to self-worth.

Identification builds self-worth by forecasting a future of
strength and by providing an ideal to aim for. The first of these two
sources of self-esteem is easy to understand. Little children draw
confidence from being like a powerful parent, someone who knows
how to navigate the wide world. This aspect of identification is,
however, more than conscious imitation. It's a form of psychological merger with another person who is experienced as being part
of the self—and a projection of the self into the future.

Although identification is largely an unconscious process, you can get a sense of the reassurance it offers by remembering an ordeal you wondered how you would ever get through. I imagine childbirth must be like this—such a strange and frightening prospect. By the way, an ordeal doesn't have to be noble or heroic to be threatening. When I was drafted into the army, I felt profoundly isolated, cut off from friends and family, and cut off from the world of books and ideas on which I depended to maintain my self-esteem. I'm not proud of it, but I was deeply shaken by being uprooted from the university and transplanted to Fort Bragg, North Carolina. One thing that helps us get through these uncertain and threatening situations is the knowledge that others have done it before us. I took comfort from thinking: Millions of men and boys have done this; so can I. To a small child, life itself is uncertain and threatening. Thinking that Mommy and Daddy have mastered life gives the child courage.

Identification builds confidence, and it builds self-respect by instilling ideals. Little children feel good when they feel like their parents, not just the real parents but a childish idealized version of them. Children are not shy about hero worship. Just as the admir-*ing* parent pays attention both to the child's real accomplishments and grandiose ambitions, the admir*able* parent accepts the child's identification with both real and idealized attributes. As children grow and gradually detach themselves from idealized others, they build up their own internalized goals and ideals. Young children feel good when they live up to their parents' images; older children and adults feel good when they live up to their own ideals.

Self-confidence means "I can do many things." Self-respect means "I can do many things, and my life has meaning and purpose because I have goals and ideals."

COMES THE JUDGE

Contrasts make for awareness. The possibility of self-approval implies its opposite: disapproval. Disapproval, in turn, implies judgment, and therefore a judge. Saint Augustine said that God is our judge, while Ralph Waldo Emerson preferred to believe that judgment rests with each person's private conscience. Students of child development place the judge in the nursery.

Here, for example, is John Bowlby, author of the classic studies on attachment: "In the working model of the self that anyone builds, a key feature is his notion of how acceptable or unacceptable he himself is in the eyes of his attachment figures."[9]

The interactions of very young infancy are primarily spontaneous, playful, and relatively unorganized. But when the infant begins to walk and talk, his mother reorients him toward fulfilling social expectations. She smiles her approval when baby gets his own toy, begins to feed himself, and behaves well (not throwing his cup), and so on. This introduces pressure to perform in order to win approval. What begins to be gained is enormous; what begins to be lost is also enormous: Acceptance is forever after conditional.

Parents shape children's behavior by responding selectively. Before they even consider teaching rules and controlling behavior, parents automatically convey their attitudes about what is shareable through *selective attunement*. Their smiling attention or look of annoyance effectively announces which subjective experiences are within and which beyond the pale of mutual consideration and acceptance. In this way the parents' fears and aspirations shape what the child does and how he feels about himself. Is it all right to throw toys? Is it all right to masturbate? To get dirty? To laugh loudly? To show preferences for different people?

This selective bias in the parents' response to their children is the perfectly normal first step in the process of socialization. As the child grows, our expectations grow; and as the child grows, parents deliberately teach rules of acceptable behavior. Mother may shriek with delight when baby first pulls her hair. Later on, she may not be so delighted. All parents respond selectively, and clearly withdraw approval in specific situations. "No, no, don't touch that!" The gradual selectivity of parental response and the gradual withholding of approval for certain kinds of behavior leads to the gradual taking over by the child's psyche of functions formerly performed by others. Parental control fosters self-control.

That parents respond selectively and later teach right and wrong is obvious and familiar. The good parent is more teacher than judge. Let's see how this process miscarries and leads to insecurity and shame.

The natural child seeks self-expression, to feel the full satisfaction offered by the body and to derive the most comfort and pleasure from others. But as this kind of limitless expansion is not possible in the world, the child must be checked for his own good. Parents are the checkers. When their restraining influence is gradual and gentle, the child learns what is and what isn't okay with them, and gradually adopts these lessons as internal standards. When disapproval is linked to specific behavior, and not too harsh, the child learns to modify his behavior.

Trouble comes when parental disapproval is too severe or too frequent. When criticism is traumatic the child is frightened; he feels judged: It's not just the behavior but he himself who is bad. If such things could be reduced to a formula it might resemble the difference between "No, no, don't touch that" and "You're a bad boy!"

Children can adjust their behavior to conform to whatever rules their parents enforce. A child can feel lovable and worthwhile as long as the rules are reasonably predictable. Whether the rules are strict or lenient, the child can control what he does. Feelings, on the other hand, are something that a small child cannot control. Parents don't have to be actively cruel to foster shame and they don't have to be harsh to foster insecurity. Insecurity results from a lack of acceptance. Understanding and tolerance of what children feel has such profound consequences because children cannot control who they are. They are who they are and they feel what they feel. What does vary, in light of their parents' response, is whether they grow up feeling basically okay—lovable and secure—or not okay—unaccepted, flawed, unlovable.

The strongest adults, people with secure self-respect, have a sense of self-worth and a set of ideals that are more important to them than external approval. These rare and lucky ones don't need awards or admiring approval to bolster their self-respect; it's already solid. They are less vulnerable to shame because they are secure in their own worth. As children, they built up this inner security as their parents were generous with acceptance and gentle with lessons about appropriate behavior.

The most insecure adults suffered the opposite fate. Their parents failed to fill their need for appreciation, made them feel that acceptance was conditional, and showed disapproval in such a way that the children felt as though they were in some way dirty, weak, or defective. Insecurity is a product of inadequate demonstrations of admiring acceptance. Shame is a product of sudden, painful, critical shocks to self-esteem.

In boxing, it's the blow a fighter doesn't see coming that knocks him out. It's the same with traumatic blows to a child's trusting, open and vulnerable self.

It may not be pleasant to grow up with parents who yell at you all the time, but children get used to it. They may not be secure, but they aren't necessarily ashamed. A trusting child who proudly shows off something special about himself or herself is like a boxer leading with his chin. At that vulnerable moment, sharp criticism, turning away, *or even an inadequate show of appreciation* strikes deep shame right to the heart. Self-esteem collapses as if felled by a hammer.

Shame is an acute collapse of self-esteem, developmentally linked to parental failures to respond with adequate attention and appreciation to the child as a whole and worthwhile human being.

Now that we've seen how growing up secure depends largely on understanding and acceptance, and insecurity comes about not so much from active cruelty as from a failure to admire children and take them seriously, let's examine in more detail the process by which inadequate empathy creates disturbances in self-esteem— chronic disturbances, in the form of insecurity, and acute disturbances, in the form of shame.

9

·······

Why We're Insecure
The Introduction of Shame

EMPATHIC FAILURE

It's so hard to be a parent. We're asked to be selfless enough to respond to our children's needs—care and feeding, attunement and empathy, and all the rest—but what about the child in us? What about our needs? We try to set aside our needs and respond to theirs, but the effort is costly. Parental guilt isn't just foolish self-reproach. Children *do* drive us crazy, and we *do* yell at them. Every parent has felt that terrible blind fury, and most of us have yelled at our children, screamed at them, blistered them, withered them . . . and seen them stricken, with sad faces and eyes full of tears. When memory stabs us with our failures, we think of traumas—acute episodes of unkindness, times when we really lost our tempers and really let them have it. We're filled with remorse, imagining the hurt we caused. In fact, single episodes are far less important than general patterns. Here's why. General rituals get named; specific episodes do not. Events as lived get coded and stored as generalized interactions—going to bed, eating, dinner, bathtime, playing with Mommy, playing with Daddy, feeling loved. It's the general quality of these interactions that counts.

Insecurity, like security itself, is a matter of slow manufacture, not sudden breakage. Shame, however, is acute and sudden.

*   *   *

Shame is a traumatic and punishing discrepancy between what the child wants to feel—admirable, lovable—and what the parent's judgment reflects—that the child is annoying, even obnoxious. This is a narcissistic injury, a sharp blow to the child's healthy exhibitionism, a blow that hurts so bad that the child wants to hide, and a blow that momentarily severs the sustaining emotional link between parent and child. If this happens occasionally, the child is weaned from dependence and forced to rely on himself or herself as the source of self-esteem. If it happens excessively and at a young age, the child is cut off from sustaining narcissistic supplies while the self is still tender and undeveloped. The result is a damaged sense of self, permanent insecurity, and a lasting vulnerability to shame.

Insecurity from lack of acceptance and appreciation creates oversensitivity and leads to the accumulation of strong hidden feelings. Thus, self-doubt is doubled: Basic insecurity breeds oversensitivity to exposure of so much that is hidden. This makes the child acutely vulnerable to shame. Shame comes when the child exposes sensitive, intimate, vulnerable aspects of the self and is met with disinterest, disgust, or contempt.

Shame stems not from punishment, but from rejection and contempt. Hatred and anger are "hot" affects; they lead to guilt. The guilt-ridden child feels beaten, fears attack. Shame, on the other hand, is a "cold" affect, an acute feeling of rejection. Angry, guilt-inducing parents say, "Why did you do that?" or "How could you do this to me?" emphasizing the injury to the other person. Shame-inducing parents say, "Don't be such a big baby," "Stop showing off," or "Leave me alone," emphasizing inadequacy or burdensomeness. Shame is more common in "disengaged" families, who pride themselves on independence and self-reliance and value their privacy. In shame, the parent-child relationship is acutely disrupted, the child feels cut off and rejected and wants to hide.

Anger and guilt are more common in "enmeshed" families, who prize togetherness. These families don't reject; rejection is beyond the pale.

Parents often generate shame in their children for the same aspects of self that they themselves are ashamed of. We all have our hang-ups.

If a father is ashamed of strong emotion, he may show annoyance, even contempt, at his daughter's natural spontaneous exuberance, her squeals of delight and her shrieks of laughter. In response, she will likely learn to be ashamed of, and even disown, that expressive emotional part of herself. In time she may relegate emotionality to what psychiatrist Harry Stack Sullivan called the realm of "Not-Me."[1] She may grow up to be a woman who lacks either awareness or expression of feeling. Or she might become aggressively self-sufficient, someone who appears contemptuous of others, especially others who aren't ashamed of showing their feelings. We hate in others what we fear in ourselves.

A father who is ashamed of his own dependency may shame his son for being dependent: "Why are you always hanging around your mother?" A mother who is ashamed of her own sexuality may shame her daughter for showing signs of sexuality: "Look at how you're dressed! You should be ashamed of yourself." Thus is the legacy of shame passed down from one generation to the next.

Children tend to stop doing whatever makes their parents uncomfortable, or embarrassed, or disgusted. Unfortunately, some things can't be helped. For example, all infants go through a period of mouthing and teething on everything they can get their hands on. If a mother finds the mouthing of objects disgusting, she may instill a feeling of shame by signaling her disgust. She might flash a disgusted look or wrinkle her nose and say, "Yeuch, that's icky!" This introduces a bad feeling in the child for something that he does, something he can't help doing, something that is part of him.

Lack of acceptance doesn't have to take the form of disgust to make a child ashamed. The same thing happens if the mother looks sad and unhappy whenever her one-year-old drops a toy or does something ineptly. And the same thing happens if a father shows disinterest when the baby shows off. Listen as Daniel Stern describes how a parent's lack of empathic acceptance generates a feeling of badness in a small child.

In a similar fashion, another mother used "depressive-signals" just as the previous mother used "disgust-signals." Whenever her son did something maladroit, as is expectable in a one-year-old, so that something got knocked over or a toy was disarranged, the mother would let out a multi-modal depressive signal. This consisted of long expirations, falling intonations, slightly collapsing postures, furrowing the brows, tilting and drooping the head, and "Oh, Johnnys" that could be interpreted as "Look what you've done to your mother again," if not "What a tragedy that your clumsiness with that toy train has caused the death of another dozen people."[2]

Parents respond—accepting, rejecting, or disregarding—to a self that seeks confirmation. The child experiences joyful, prideful appreciation or lack of interest, not only as the acceptance or rejection of specific offerings but also as acceptance or rejection of his tentatively established and still vulnerable self. Once children become basically secure in their own self-esteem, they can withstand frustration, rejection, even shame. But when there are insufficient mirroring responses, there is no adequate basis to withstand frustration, and there is exquisite vulnerability to shame.

You only have to look to see children express their yearning for mirroring: "*Please* tell me you like it. Say it was good." A failed response—"Not now, can't you see I'm busy?" "Stop showing off"—leaves them empty, longing, ashamed.

You might get a sense of this tremendous yearning for acclaim if you've ever felt like crying at the Academy Awards. As the presenter reads off the names of the nominees, you're busy guessing who will win; maybe rooting for your favorite. At the same time, you feel a certain tension, an edge of anxiety. Then the lucky one's name is read and the camera catches the face of the winner in the audience. A magic moment, frozen in time. Then the shock breaks and there's that excited rush up to the stage to claim the golden Oscar. Then a giddy struggle to find words, an outpouring of honest joy and gratitude. It's that moment, a moment of tearful, happy dreams-come-true, that every one of us shares. For an instant, we, too, are winners, bathed in appreciation. We, too, are wonderful. We, too, are special. We, too, are loved. That's why we watch; that's what we need; that's what we've always needed.

The emotion of vicariously sharing an Academy Award is a useful reminder that children crave appreciation not only for who they are, but also for their grand dreams—dreams that for them are very real possibilities.

Among the most important aspects of the developing self that parents respond to is the baby's exhibitionism—that wonderful wish to make an impression. Showing off produces pleasure in the parents and makes the baby feel good. If, however, there is no response when the baby shows off, the result is an acute disturbance of self-esteem. (You can test this. The next time you're around a little child who is showing off for your approval, keep your face absolutely expressionless and watch the result.) It's as if the baby said, "Look at me!," and the parents responded with, "Who cares?"

Grand fantasies are as important to little children as real accomplishments. On the road to mature self-respect, children pass through a stage of believing in their own omnipotence, their own perfection, their own absolute acceptedness. What they need is a grown-up's appreciation to maintain and validate this image of the self, long enough to consolidate the feeling of being lovable and special. The child must have this grandiose state of mind before he can give it up. When a child's inflated fantasies about the self are crushed by a scornful parent, the child feels not merely insecurity but shame, because it's an acute rejection of a vulnerable part of the self, a traumatic shock. Shame is most crushing under conditions of narcissistic vulnerability.

Does the child get mad at this mean treatment? No, not at first anyway. He hates himself for the demented pride that deluded him into thinking he was worthy, special. One minute his heart is pounding with joy, joy in doing and pride in being. Then comes the cruelly indifferent response, or worse, blatant rejection: "Leave me alone!"

People who were deprived of an admiring mother go through life looking for mothers to admire them, continuously hungry for the oohing and ahhing they need to feel worthwhile. But if they were made to feel ashamed as well as insecure, they're in a double fix: craving attention but acutely vulnerable to rejection.

The adult fear of being exposed as foolishly proud or ambitious is an outgrowth of the childhood experience of being made to feel ashamed of wanting to be special. Which of us hasn't been stung at one time or another by those awful words: *"Who do you think you are?"* Some people show anger in retaliation, but it is a defense against the bitterly shameful feelings of self-blame and self-hatred for the stupid, blind, insatiable need for acclaim that makes us pant after appreciation. ("Oh, what a fool I was for imagining that I could be special!") It's the terrible sin of hubris, punishable by the gods.

Children who hunger in vain for appreciation can at least hope to become powerful and successful grown-ups—unless, of course, what they see in their parents makes them despair about what they will become when they grow up.

PARENTS AS HEROES WITH CLAY FEET

In addition to providing empathy, parents contribute to their children's self-respect by serving as models of identification. If the child feels intimately connected to the parents, their strength feels like his or her own, and it serves as a strong protection against the shame of weakness and inadequacy.

Identification is almost automatic, but parents must be worthy of respect and must allow their children to tag along and look up to them. Parents must permit and enjoy the child's idealization and merger. This means letting them hang around you, letting them imitate you, letting them dress up in your clothes, letting them play at sewing or cooking or mowing the lawn, and it means not letting your own embarrassed self-consciousness lead you to disabuse them of thinking that you are wonderful. It also means not mocking the other parent. Divorced parents are often tempted to get even by disparaging each other. Don't! Married parents do the same. ("You're just like your father!") Most parents try not to be blatant about such attacks, but the message comes through. Parents who are overly critical or withdrawn, or who rebuff the child's attempts to imitate them, impair identification, and gradually undermine security.

Shame comes from traumatic shocks to identification. Suddenly, once-great parents turn out to be great disappointments. The parents become distant and unreachable, or suffer a sudden loss of prestige in the child's eyes. Tremendous admiration gives way to tremendous disillusionment. Notice that I said *traumatic* shocks. In the normal process of growing up, children outgrow identification with their parents. When children gradually outgrow idealization and gradually give up identifications, they become a thing of the past, but they leave behind a residue—self-reliance—built up from successfully resolved reliance on parents.

There is a decisive difference between a gradual loosening of the strong infantile tie to a parent, which allows a child to build up an internal structure, and a sudden interruption of the process. When idealization is aborted, when the child is pushed away or prematurely exposed to serious flaws in the idealized parent, the parent is shunned as a protector and a model. This child will forever search for a mother to love him or a father to admire. The result is shame and insecurity.

As children grow they discover that their parents are less than perfect, less than ideal. Disillusionment accelerates in adolescence. Parents of teenagers are hopelessly naive, they can't do anything right, and they are terrible hypocrites—at least in the eyes of their critical offspring. This adolescent rebellion is only the most visible stage of a process of disillusion and differentiation by which children graduate from hero-worship to self-reliance. As is the case with failed acceptance, it is sudden and traumatic disappointments in parents that produce shame. A child who grows up with alcoholic parents or parents on welfare is not necessarily ashamed of them—or himself. But if a little boy opens his eyes in astonishment to see the big strong father he loves come home drunk, staggering, knocking things over, and cursing in anger, he may suffer a traumatic blow to his sense of identity. Likewise, a daughter who sees her competent mother stand by submissively while her husband berates and belittles her, may suffer a similarly shameful disillusionment—in her mother *and* about herself. If the child were to put this experience into words, it might be: "I am a part of him, and he is a drunken slob"; "My mother is a helpless pawn of men, and I will be the same." Some people vow *not* to be like their parents, but the shame is the same.

One form of revenge for the disappointment we suffer in our own parents is a readiness to criticize and condemn all parents. When inevitably they trace problems back to childhood, psychological critics always seem to end up blaming parents. So much of psychotherapy turns out to be a conspiracy between therapist and patient to turn shame and guilt into anger against heartless parents: The uncovered emotional "truth" is that we were victims of cruel or inadequate parents. In these self-serving reinventions of the past, anger is resurrected and manufactured.

Heinz Kohut, the doyen of compassionate psychoanalysts, blames wounded egos on parents who sound like cardboard villains: One patient's problems were said to have arisen in response to "his oddly unempathic, unpredictable, emotionally shallow mother." Further, she damaged his self-esteem "by grossly and grotesquely misunderstanding his needs and wishes." In this instance, unlike most, the father doesn't escape the analyst's censure: "He was a self-absorbed, vain man, and he rebuffed his son's attempt to be close to him."[3]

The only place I've ever encountered such selfishly cruel parents is in secondhand descriptions by someone with an axe to grind. All the parents I've met in many years of clinical practice, including some very disturbed people, were busy doing the best job they could. Even those unhappy few who were locked in a sad struggle for control with their children were still trying to do what they thought was right.

When it comes to doling out blame, mothers get more than their share. If a child grows up insecure, who else do we blame except the mother? This is unfair for two reasons: It overlooks the fact that the mother-child interaction is *circular*—mother reacts to baby's temperament and baby reacts to mother's reaction, and so on—and that the mother-child relationship is *triangular*—mother's response to baby is profoundly affected by the quality of mother's relationship to father.

Babies are not blank slates on which mothers write out their own scripts. Infants are born with wide variations in temperament. Some are easy, and life is rosy; some are difficult, and life is the reverse of rosy. The unquietable irritability of some colicky babies and the insatiable demands of others will overtax even the most devoted and resourceful parents. Worn down by an infant's voracious appetite, quick retreat, stiff unyielding posture, rageful outbursts, or apathy, a mother is soon exhausted and discouraged. It will be hard, maybe impossible, for her to stay tuned to the baby's needs, much less mirror and affirm the baby's emotions. When parents are overburdened (for whatever reason), any of the child's needs or strong emotions can be an unwelcome additional burden. Parents may show intolerance directly—yelling, hitting—or indirectly—ignoring, looking annoyed. Who could blame a mother for getting sick and tired of excessive demands, hypersensitivity, or constant rejection? (Answer: children when they grow up, husbands, psychotherapists, authors of self-help books, sociological critics, and, most of all, mothers themselves.)

Among the most common criticisms of mothers is that they hover over their children, exerting too little discipline and allowing too little independence. They are "enmeshed," or "intrusive," and their children are "mother-smothered." Why would a woman be so overinvolved with her children that she couldn't exert effective discipline, and neither she nor they would have a sense of separateness and autonomy? Because her need for intimacy and affection is not fulfilled in her marriage. In her book, *Women and Love,* Shere Hite said that married women have affairs because they're starved for affection by husbands who are unable to give them what they most desire, intimate connection.[4] It's this emotional hunger that drives them into the arms of other men. The same longing drives mothers into emotional affairs with their children.

The cooperativeness necessary to nurture and discipline children tests even the best marriages. Some couples lock into polarized struggles: the stricter one parent is, the more lenient the other. Other couples, unable to cooperate or compromise, divide the child-rearing chores, but all too often the father leaves the field: "If she doesn't want my opinion, she doesn't want my help." This is the beginning of a long, slow rift, like some great block of ice that breaks in two and drifts apart on a vast wintry sea.

At this time, I want to clarify a very important point. I've said that active shaming isn't necessary to make a child feel ashamed, and all the explanation of the gradual building up of self-worth reinforces that. Still, common sense tells us that parents may hurt their children with active attacks on their self-esteem. So, which is it: traumatic failure to provide empathy and ideal models, or active shaming? It's both.

ACTIVE SHAMING

Parents sometimes deliberately shame their children to shape their behavior. It's mean but effective. It works like a slap in the face that leaves no mark—no visible mark, that is.

Parents who don't learn early how to control their children's behavior soon become caught up in an unhappy cycle of disobedience and criticism. It's hard to show appreciation for children who don't obey, and it's hard for children to obey when they don't feel appreciated. Say a little girl doesn't clean her room when she's told, continues to throw wet clothes down the laundry chute even after she's been told countless times not to, and argues with her mother almost constantly. Her mother's tried everything—making the girl sit in her room, praising positive behavior, awarding stars for completion of chores—but nothing seems to work. She's exasperated, and she's angry. Her constant criticism has long since blurred the distinction between disapproving of behavior and con-

demning the child's self. In the process of a never-ending struggle
for control, her nagging hammers away at the child's self-esteem:
"You *never* . . ." "Why must you *always* . . ?" "What's *wrong* with
you?"

When blaming produces intolerable shame, the child may learn
to deny responsibility or find ways of excusing it. While the parents
are desperately trying to teach some responsibility, the child is
desperately trying to preserve some dignity and self-respect. The
parents say, "I can't believe you did that!" The child learns to
answer with, "I didn't" or, more ominously, "I don't care."

Parents often resort to shaming their children in public when
the children do something that makes the parents ashamed. "Stop
that! You're embarrassing me." Part of what the child hears is:
"*You* are embarrassing."

Parents induce shame by letting the child know that he or she is
a disappointment: "Crybaby." "Why can't you be more quiet!" "You
pig! Don't eat with your mouth open." We do need to control
children, but the perpetual critic induces more shame than control. The expression "finding fault with someone" conveys what
children feel when they are constantly criticized: They are faulty.

Another thing children hate is when their parents mock them
with knowing winks in public. The child behaves ineptly or shows
off and the parent makes a show of tolerance, but the child catches
the mocking look exchanged between grown-ups. Why do parents
do this? As I write this, memory, that traitor, zaps me. I used to do
this when my kids were little. We'd be out to dinner with friends,
and the kids would be rattling on about what they were doing or
else making too much noise. They wouldn't quite cross the double
line, but they were hogging all the attention. I'd cast knowing looks
at my men friends. What was I trying to say? I don't know, but I can
see now what the children must have felt: Daddy was embarrassed
by them.

As I noted earlier, parents project their own shame onto their
children, mocking them for failings they cannot tolerate in themselves and showing disgust for whatever they are ashamed of.
Take, for example, exuberant play, getting dirty, or masturbating.

Even psychologically enlightened parents, determined not to shame their children for these activities, often betray disgust in their expressions. When words lie, the eyes show it.

Some parents berate their children openly for these normal childish activities. There are even parents who actually enjoy humiliating their children. This occurs among parents with pathological narcissism who overvalue their children and therefore compete with them. These parents are particularly likely to humiliate children they feel fail them as narcissistic objects. Some husbands whose wives adulate the children strike out jealously at the weakest member of the triangle and cruelly humiliate their children. When children are loved not for themselves but as objects to show off or as pawns in a marital struggle, they're trapped in shame, victims of parents who don't love each other or themselves. If we don't love ourselves, how can we love our children?

One of my patients remembers that whenever she did something wrong around the house her father would scream at her, "I can't believe you could be so goddamned stupid!" Imagine being a little girl looking up at your father screaming at you like that. Horrible scenes such as this may become deeply embedded in the memory, or blocked out as too painful. In either case, examples of active shaming are so compelling, so painfully evocative, and so easy to identify with that they reinforce our intuitive sense that shame is indeed a product of active abuse and not simply the frustrating failure to meet the child's need for admiration, as I've said. But active shaming is also a form of withdrawal, sharp withdrawal, of approval. Even when parents scream mean things at their children, the result depends upon the state of the child's self-esteem. A relatively firm, cohesive sense of self decreases the propensity to react with shame. Getting yelled at is never fun, but the relatively secure child realizes: It's them, not me. The insecure child is much less able to make this distinction.

The most painful and damaging experiences of shame depend not only on the child's degree of security, but also on what the child is being shamed for. Remember, shame is an unexpected blow, like driving into a tree in the fog. When the child is proudly showing off and meets with shame, the impact is doubled. It's a head-on collision.

There are some things children have to depend on, to know for sure. If there was nothing at all they could depend on, they'd be totally lost. Maybe that's why some people spend so much time contemplating trees and plants and the sky. These things change, but slowly, predictably, dependably. For the shamed child, it's people you can't depend on.

Shame plays its most prominent role during childhood and adolescence, the time when we're discovering and creating our own identities and our own place in the world. Sadly, the same mechanism that nurtures a certain reticence concerning personal privacy also conditions a deep and pervasive anxiety about the very worth of the self.

Much of growing up, learning to trust, learning to make friends, and learning to love is a process of learning to shift the boundary lines of the domain of the private—learning when it's safe to be open, and when it isn't. The shamed child begins this process with the handicap of oversensitivity. It's a problem for life.

10
·······
The Humiliations of Childhood
School, Church, and Play

THE FORMATIVE YEARS

Psychological critics have always been generous in crediting parents with responsibility for the origins of unhappy emotions. Because most parents are anxious and guilt-ridden already, this works out fine. In the process, however, we've come to exaggerate the importance of the so-called formative years and underestimate the enormous influence of teachers and friends on personality development. This oversight is particularly significant with respect to shame, which is not laid down once and for all in some critical period of early childhood, but continues to be an important developmental issue throughout childhood and adolescence.

In the previous two chapters I described the foundations of the self: how security is a function of acceptance, and how shame comes about when the child exposes vulnerable aspects of the self and is met with rejection. You may not have noticed, but this description rests on a particular way of describing self and others: The self is a separate whole entity, formed in relationship to others but existing apart from them. We are selves with personalities. This is a familiar and legitimate way of thinking, but in a very real sense there is no self, no personality, without others.

Alone or in company, we experience ourselves in relation to

other people. Self-consciousness, pride, and shame—these are meaningless concepts without relationships: past, present, and future possibility. "Personality" and "self" turn out to be a set of expectations, formed from past relationships and having an impact on all those to come.

When school-age children expand the context of their lives, they bring with them from home a set of expectations that influence but do not determine the result. In the years from five to twelve, the experience of self is shaped and reshaped: In these crucial years, children develop pride or shame about themselves in relation to academic, social, and physical skills; and they develop habits that harden shame by hiding it, or heal shame by finding friends with whom they can be open and find acceptance.

CONFORMITY: THE CULTURAL IMPERATIVE

When I graduated from school in 1973, I landed a job in the one part of the country most unfamiliar to me, the Deep South. I remember driving my old blue Volvo from Rochester, New York, to Tucker, Georgia, in the dog days of summer. It was so hot that my eighteen-pound cat, Malcolm, just lay under the back window with her tongue hanging out, panting. I was hot, too, but also excited to be seeing for the first time a whole new part of the country. Coming down out of the north Georgia mountains, I left the main highway to drive through some of the small towns in this, the farthest south I'd ever been. I still remember what I saw: shopping malls, car dealers, and McDonald's. What began as a big disappointment turned into a game, the object of which was to find something different, something distinctive about the South. Grits for breakfast—that was it. The new South is not visibly different from the Midwest, or the East, or even the far West. Ours is a big country, but television and franchised chain stores have leveled regional differences.

Because we are such a large and relatively homogeneous country, it is easy to overlook the influence of culture on American children. It's easier to see the impact of culture on personality when subcultures collide. A boy from an orthodox Jewish family who enters public school wearing a skullcap will be confronted with large questions about who he is, what's right, and what's wrong. But even when it's too constant to notice, culture is there, sitting on our lives like the unchanging climate in the desert. The imperative of life in the desert is to cope with the heat, to horde water and avoid getting scorched in the sun. The imperative of culture is to conform, to avoid rejection or, worse, banishment.

Culture shapes self-respect negatively by defining what is shameful (taboo), and positively by molding goals and ideals. As adults, we don't often see culture; it's everywhere around us, invisible, and we long ago learned to avoid breaking the rules that might remind us of its existence. It's different for children. They aren't conditioned yet and they don't know the rules. They have to learn the hard way.

Children must learn to conform to the expectations of teachers and principals and lunch ladies and bus drivers and coaches and scout leaders and Sunday school teachers. And they must conform to the expectations of other children. By the time they're ready for school, children have already learned about pleasing their parents, to win approval and avoid criticism. There's nothing trivial about feeling loved or unloved by your parents. But there's something different and dangerous at stake in pleasing friends and adult authorities outside your family: acceptance or rejection. If you break the rules at home, you can be punished; if you break the rules on the playground or at school, you can be expelled, banished.

Children start learning early how to fit in, how to maintain the link to those around them by conforming to their codes. Nobody wants to be alone.

So strong are social codes that even misreading them can be a source of great embarrassment. A kindergartner who uses a word that's okay at home but not at school, like "crap," runs into reproach: "We don't say that here!" The teacher may be teaching politeness, but the child may be learning shame. The problem isn't what the teacher says, but how she says it. When children feel rebuked, "yelled at," that's what they remember, not what somebody was trying to teach them.

From ages five to twelve, children are busy learning rules and codes that call them away from their pleasure in the straightforward expression of their natural energies. They must learn to master the body and the real self. Every child must learn to act like a "little man" or a "young lady." Character is a face that one shows to the world, but it hides an inner defeat. The child emerges from these years with an approved role, all clearly cut out, but his or her insides will be filled with nightmarish memories of impossible battles, being laughed at and left out, terrifying anxieties of darkness, pain, rejection, failure, inadequacy, aloneness—mixed with limitless desires. If this sounds overwrought it's because, after each one of us goes through the awful anxieties of childhood, merciful memory muffles much of the pain.

The difference between learning the rules and learning to be ashamed of the ungoverned self is the difference between growing up socialized and growing up insecure. It's not a question of one or the other. Every child learns a little of both—how to get along easily, and uneasily.

SCHOOL DAYS

School is a big place when you're five. Scary, too. Your parents have prepared you for the first day of school with a mixture of excitement and apprehension. If you have a big brother or sister, you feel grown-up; you know everything will be okay. If you're the oldest, you're more scared. You could get lost. The teachers could be bossy. Other kids might tease you. Over the next few weeks you'll get to know the place, find your way from one room to another, and learn the routines. But now everything is new, unknown and uncertain.

Lining up outside the door, you notice all the other kids. So many! And because there are so many, you start to notice the differences. Most of them are bigger than you. They're first-graders now, or second, or even third. Laughing and poking each other, they seem right at home. They could beat you up

*if they wanted. You see a lot of ordinary kids, but also kids
who stick out: fat kids, kids wearing nerdy clothes, bullies, and
some kids who are real little. All these differences! You hope
nobody will be mean to you. You hope you'll be accepted, and
you hope you'll find somebody to be your friend.*

*Standing in line, you become aware of yourself. If you're
looking at other kids, they must be looking at you. What will
they think? You only wonder about this once in a while, and
only for the rest of your life.*

School is a whole new world whose imperatives, as yet unknown, children must learn to fathom. What they learn and how
they learn it will affect not only their education and careers but
also how they get along with people and what they think about
themselves. As Walker Percy said in *The Second Coming*, it's possible to "get all A's, and flunk life." When children move from home
to preschool to the larger, more competitive world of elementary
school, they begin to make judgments about their own abilities.
Demonstrating competence becomes critical to self-esteem.

To be successful, children must overcome hurdles, from when
things are easy to when they get hard. In today's schools, this
comes early. Small children must learn to do something very unnatural, sit at their desks all day. (What comes naturally is intense
physical exploration.) By the second grade, homework is common. After-school assignments extend the hours of learning and
begin to instill self-discipline. But some children, and their parents, aren't ready for this hurdle so young. Some of these children
become rebellious and defiant, alienated kids, future dropouts.
Other children, bright enough to get by without doing their homework, or lacking in self-confidence and afraid of exposing their
work, tell their parents they don't have any homework and then
make excuses to their teachers.

When it comes to homework, school and family are like two
parents who must coordinate their efforts to enforce the rules or,
without (necessarily) meaning to, subvert each other's efforts.
Schoolwork and homework are not just tasks to be learned, they
are also challenges to the child's sense of self. When the tasks are

too hard or come too early, the child's budding sense of competence comes under attack. Children need to be pushed over the hurdles of learning but supported in the process. We must lend them our confidence in them, our enthusiasm, and our own discipline.

Education experts are well aware of the need to support self-esteem, and most schools have a variety of programs (with names like "I'm Special") to build self-confidence while teaching the three R's. Today's teachers try very hard to help children feel good about themselves. I observed a gym class, for example, in which the teacher was introducing the hurdles during the track and field segment of the curriculum. Before demonstrating the correct form for hurdling, the teacher talked with the kids about how exposed they might feel in gym class, and encouraged them with the idea that "everybody is pretty good in some things, not so good in others." He urged them not to tease kids who didn't do so well in a particular event, "It's okay to laugh with each other. But if you laugh too much, you know what happens? You kind of make that person feel bad."

Physical education programs are now designed to minimize competitive anxieties by deemphasizing sports that demand complex skills and focus on winning and losing. Instead of choosing up teams for football and baseball and basketball, elementary school children are taught running and throwing games where everyone can participate and no one keeps score. Later they'll have programs with names like "Project Adventure" to teach them self-confidence and cooperation. Although many children (mostly boys) still elect to play competitive baseball or football, these activities are no longer the commanding standard of achievement they once were. Soccer, which in many suburbs has supplanted football and baseball in popularity, allows most children to participate and feel good about themselves regardless of whether or not they are particularly skillful or athletic.

Similar efforts to instill confidence and minimize competitive anxiety are practiced throughout the school curriculum. Teachers write encouraging comments on tests and pass them back privately to avoid embarrassing children who don't do well. Two kids who get into a fight are now as likely to be sent to the school counselor as to a disciplinary vice principal. There is an increased emphasis on teamwork and getting along, rather than on individual striving. And when the results of contests are posted, they're apt to be accompanied by inscriptions like "Congratulations to all participants." None of these efforts, however, can repeal the realities of childhood.

Special programs and compassionate teachers cannot do away with the many and inherent sources of shame in school. While this wise and gentle gym teacher was speaking so reassuringly to his class lined up in front of the hurdles, the heavyset kids drifted to the back of the line, hoping to postpone as long as possible the awkward moment.

Gym class can be a trial. Here, more than almost anyplace else, kids are exposed to the scrutiny of their peers. Everybody can see which kids are graceful and adept, and which are not. "Loser" is still one of the meanest things kids call each other. It isn't only maladroit children who are insecure about their performance. Even the most apparently proficient children can feel ashamed of themselves if they don't live up to their own high expectations or if they are extremely sensitive to any sign of failure or criticism.

In one of the schools I visited, a popular sixth-grader had just broken the all-time school record for the hundred-meter dash. The same boy refused to enter "The Road Runner," a school-wide cross-country race, because he was afraid he might come in second. Self-esteem based on superiority is bound to be shaky.

If it's hard to hide on the playing field, it's harder still to hide in the shower. Boys embarrassed by small muscles or big stomachs must, nevertheless, stand revealed. Those slow to reach puberty may be acutely embarrassed by their lack of pubic hair, which can make a boy feel deficient and inadequate. Girls have even more trouble than boys. Most of them think they're too fat or too thin. In junior high or middle school, they worry that their breasts are too large or too small. And many of them ask to be excused because they're having their period—two or three times a month.

When a child is called to the blackboard and doesn't know how to work a problem, a teacher's gentle reassurance can't do away with the fact that the child may feel stupid and exposed. Grade inflation and tracking haven't helped. High praise for success imparts unrealistically high standards in children. No matter how well a child does, he or she could have done better. Getting a C may be as bad as getting an F once was, and bright children who don't win awards or earn honors may be as ashamed as poor students who fail a grade. Tracking, which is a logical attempt to group children by ability, marks some children as "slow," inferior.

Those children who are highly successful but with fragile self-esteem suffer acute disappointment in themselves when they stumble over something they aren't the best at. Some kids who have always been excellent students just can't seem to master a foreign language or grasp geometry. Those who have always been athletic discover that although they can run fast, they can't catch a softball or aren't flexible enough to do gymnastics. And even the most nimble child may hit a growth spurt when legs, suddenly long, no longer move the way they once did.

The meaning that inevitable failures and disappointments will have for a particular child depends to a large extent on the child's self-respect. For example, a little girl who suddenly discovers that she's one of the slowest runners in school may continue to feel okay about herself if she's secure in her parents' love and her own self-esteem. The very same discovery may have a devastating impact on a little boy who depends very much on successful performance to shore up his shaky self-respect. Of course, not every failure makes children feel insecure, and not every inadequacy makes them feel ashamed. For shame, you need a witness. In school, the witnesses that count are other children and the teachers.

Teacher, Teacher

Teachers teach. They teach math and science and English and social studies, and they teach the complex penalties for breaking the rules. The official rules are clear and known to all. Thou shalt not be late, run in the halls, say the F word within earshot of adults, or fight and get caught doing so. Good and bad means obedient and disobedient. But there is another rule, one that is invisible, rarely broken, and more harshly enforced: Thou shalt not challenge the teacher's moral authority with provocative questions, disregard, or outright defiance.

It is now commonplace to bemoan the lack of discipline in contemporary American schools. Teachers seem powerless to demand quiet and attention in the classroom. Today's children are said to be growing up with little respect for adult authority. I happen to agree. Visit a public school and you'll wonder who's in charge.

Just like parents, teachers who are not in charge fight back with whatever means are available. Concurrent with the decline of effective discipline, there is an increase in attempts to control through shame. This is true of weak parents, who threaten and attack children's self-respect, and it's true of teachers who can't control their students.

Shaming has always been an integral part of the school system. Teachers no longer sit students in the corner with dunce caps, but they have their ways. One conversation I happened to overhear took place in a fifth-grade social studies class. The teacher was explaining election procedures and one student was obviously not paying attention. After a few minutes the child did tune in and asked why voting was done by secret ballot. The teacher responded by saying, "What do you think I've been doing for the last ten minutes [fool]?" This mildly contemptuous remark had nothing to do with the question. It was revenge for the previous mocking of the teacher's authority.

It turns out that this sarcastic teacher was one of the most liked and respected teachers in the school. I must have caught him on an off day or a weak moment. The point is this: It isn't only mean teachers who shame their students. Shaming usually isn't something we do deliberately. We do it when we ourselves feel vulnerable. Teachers often react emotionally, and respond by ridiculing children, when one child is being mean to another. (Do as I say, not as I do.) And teachers make a lot of sarcastic cracks on days when they come in feeling angry or upset. But by far the most common reason teachers use shame on their students is when the kids make the teachers look bad.

Teasing

Nobody likes to look bad—not teachers, not students. Looking bad is one thing kids fear most when they come to school, and one of the most common ways they deal with their anxiety is by teasing other kids. Teasing is an anxiety-relieving discharge of shameful fears accomplished by ascribing flaws to someone else: *I'm not a baby, you are!*

Verbal teasing among children begins around age five. A boy might, for example, call a girl a forbidden word, like "doo-doo." The girl might laugh as long as she knows it's a game, but if the boy persists, the girl might get upset and cry. An older child might tease back or decide the game is stupid. The little boy who says "doo-doo" probably doesn't intend to be mean, just silly. It's a form of aggressive bravado—"Look at me, I can talk tough"—usually with no intent to hurt.

This verbal sparring is like play-fighting. It helps define hierarchies of power and belonging. You can see the beginnings of this in toddlers, as one holds out a toy to another only to pull it back. This is not simply selfishness; it's a test of relative power. Kids soon learn who you can say what to. You can say "dummy" to a classmate but not to a teacher and not to a big kid. Learning to tease and to cope with being teased is a test of social skills.

Teasing serves two apparently contradictory functions. Mutual teasing helps define the boundaries of a social group or clique. It's about exclusion; friends tease as a way of threatening or rejecting outsiders. Yet teasing can also be a signal of acceptance.

As with animals crowded into one another's territory, children feel a little exposed, a little threatened, in large groups. Therefore, large groups of unsupervised children often engage in a great deal of teasing. Derisive laughter and ridicule are self-protective reflexes. Children are aware of their own insecurity and weakness. If your mockery can make someone else feel weak and ashamed, you don't have to feel that way (or recognize that feeling) yourself. And you're likely to be applauded by your friends.

Elementary schoolers are cute and small only to adults. To one another they are not cute. They are life-sized.

On the playground, girls begin to stand off by themselves in little groups. Small groups of friends are safe with each other. Each little cluster of whispering girls excludes some other girls and all boys. Boys pride themselves on being rough and tough. (If you horse around, you aren't a scaredy-cat.) Boys work at acting like boys. At recess, they hit, poke, play-fight, pile on, chase each other, wrestle, and shove. Indoors, there always seem to be more of them than there actually are.

By about age ten, when teasing has reached its peak, it takes on a different form. The comments become sharp, pointed. They hurt. Children who look or act different are frequent targets. The fat child or the one with glasses is often singled out and picked on. They get as much notice but less sympathy than kids with an obvious deformity, such as a withered arm, say, or a port-wine stain splashed across the cheek.

Children come to school relatively secure, ready to make friends and resist teasing, or relatively insecure, shy, sensitive, and easily hurt. Their personalities have already begun to jell, but they aren't set. Much depends on what happens at school. Here's an example.

A mother called me recently, worried about her daughter Andrea, age ten: "She's not doing so well. She seems very unhappy about school." I agreed to a consultation and asked to see the whole family. (As a family therapist, my perspective is that the problem, the one I can treat, is how the family handles the dilemmas of its members.) Apparently this was a close-knit family, for the mother readily agreed to the appointment and wasn't surprised that I asked her to bring everyone.

Contrary to what I expected, this did not turn out to be an anxious mother worried over nothing, or parents magnifying a child's problems in order to mask their own. Andrea was indeed very unhappy. She was suffering a great deal of teasing at school. According to her, the other kids picked on her because she was heavy. I was puzzled. She was overweight, but not very, and besides, I happened to know several girls in the same school, as heavy and heavier, who were never teased about their weight.

*So I decided to consult an expert on the social life of chil-
dren, my daughter Sandy. When I asked Sandy why the kids
didn't tease her friend who was overweight, Sandy said, "She
feels good about herself, and she has a lot of friends. Who
cares if you get teased, as long as you have friends."*

*Putting this together with what I already knew helped me
make sense of Andrea's dilemma. This was her first year in a
suburban middle school. Unlike most of the kids, who were
from a nearby elementary school, Andrea came from a distant, rural school. She had entered a new environment, where
most of the kids already had friends, and she was a shy, sensitive, and insecure child who had trouble breaking in to the
established cliques.*

*When I asked Andrea what her friends said when the other
kids teased her, she said with tears in her eyes, "I don't know;
I don't have any friends."*

*Fortunately, I was able to help Andrea by encouraging her
parents to be understanding without trying to solve a problem
she had to solve herself; and after I met with Andrea twice to
discuss how she was going about making friends, she was on
her way to fitting in.*

Few things tug at a parent's heart as much as hearing that their
child is being teased by other children. Unfortunately, some of the
ways parents respond only make matters worse. The biggest mistake parents make when dealing with quarrels between siblings or
peers is failing to respect the boundary between the children's
world and that of the parents.

Parents love their children and want to be helpful, but trying to
solve their problems for them isn't helpful, it's intrusive. Like quarrels between siblings, teasing teaches social skills. Sure it hurts,
but getting hurt is something children have to learn to handle.

The usual advice parents offer about teasing is not only intrusive, trying to solve their problems for them, it's also wrong. Trying to help, Andrea's parents told her what parents always tell their
children, "If you ignore them, they'll stop bothering you." By the
time teasing has gotten bad enough for a child to complain, ignor-

ing it usually won't work. Not responding will often cause the teaser to raise the ante by flinging more painful taunts. If the remarks are cruel enough and the child cries, the battle is lost, and the child will be an easy target next time.

Belittling the incident doesn't help either. ("Sticks and stones may break my bones, but names will never hurt me.") It *is* important to a child what other children say; teasing *does* hurt. It hurts a lot. Children want to know that their parents understand the feeling.

A parent can understand more about the teasing by paying close attention to what a child focuses on. If the child focuses on the person doing the teasing, it may be that the child is afraid of a bully or afraid of losing a friend. If the child focuses on the content of the teasing, it's a sign of something the child is ashamed of. To be exposed and laughed at for something that feels trivial—say, braces—is not as bad as being teased about something you consider part of yourself, such as your skin color or physique.

What children eventually learn on their own is to tease back. It's their way of saying, "I'm not a victim. I can play this game, too."

Not all children are as fortunate as Andrea, who eventually did make friends in her new school. Between 5 and 10 percent of the children in elementary school have no friends. Many of these children are actively disliked. These are the rejected ones. They are lonely and have low self-esteem. Many of these children mask their shame, but if pressed they will reveal that they're hurting.

Rejected children are more likely to have trouble in school, to be truant, and eventually to drop out.

Some of these children are rejected because of the way they behave—being a bully, for example. Others simply behave inappropriately, acting silly, showing conspicuously bad manners, or talking nonsense. Sometimes this is a clumsy attempt to join in the play of others. Some children have good social skills but erupt on those occasions when something they're ashamed of is touched upon. Finally, there are those children who behave appropriately but are shunned by the others because they have serious liabilities, such as a low IQ, a physical disability, or they are extremely unattractive.

The presence of rejected children serves as a reminder to all the others: If you are too conspicuous, if you fail to conform to expectations, you're likely to get teased, and if you make a habit of it, you can become a pariah, without friends.

When they come to school, children still want attention. Now, however, it's dangerous to stand out. There are highly prized awards for conspicuous success, but equally powerful punishments for getting caught in the act of trying to be special. By the time they reach the fifth grade, children have learned how to fit in: what to wear and, more important, what not to wear; not to appear stupid; not to be too eager or too cooperative; not to be a scaredy-cat; not to mess up when you have to perform in front of other kids; not to hang back—a lot of *nots* to worry about! In the face of all this anxiety, healthy pride and assertiveness give way to a more powerful pressure to avoid mockery or ostracism.

By middle school, children's behavior is hedged in by the fear of shame, which keeps them well inside invisible boundaries. If you hang around the halls of a middle school or junior high, you'll notice that the vast majority of interactions among children are friendly: chatting, joking, copying each other's homework—the whispering of girls, the boisterous enthusiasm of boys. The adolescent dress code permits enough variation that you may not immediately notice that nobody breaks it. Kids can choose the preppie look, the I-don't-care look, or the heavy-metal look. These choices balkanize them into subgroups, each one demanding conformity and punishing deviation with ridicule.

Kids know the rules by this time. You have to look close to see the effects of shame. Mean, aggressive teasing is no longer common. Casual teasing has lost its punch because by this age children's defenses are pretty much in order. Also, they've learned some empathy. Teasing now takes on its adult form. Kids tease their friends as a way of demonstrating closeness. Friends accept teasing from each other as a playful way of acknowledging insecurity. They are experimenting with intimacy and vulnerability. You'll see few incidents of active shaming; what you will see is constant banter about the possibility of suffering embarrassment. Kids joke constantly about failing, getting picked on, being weird, screwing up, and getting laughed at. Standing out and making a mistake is now considered funny, like all other things that are in reality frightening and profoundly shameful.

The issue of how parents respond to their children being teased underscores an important point. Childhood is not a linear progression from family to school and beyond. A child's ongoing relationship with his or her family plays a vital role in how the child will deal with challenges posed by the world beyond the family.

For most children, it's only the parents' sympathetic understanding of what happens at school that matters; the school experience itself is not within the family's control. It's a different story with religion, where the family's beliefs determine not only how they will respond to the child but also what experiences he or she will be exposed to.

CHURCH

In *The Future of an Illusion*, Freud described religion as a system of wishful thinking, big lies that resolve tensions and make it easy to act with the convenient rationalizations people need—the psychoanalytic analogue of the Marxian formula, the "opiate of the people." Since then, religion has often been the whipping boy of popular psychology: Religion is repressive and irrational, denying the body and condemning natural human passions; psychology is humanistic, liberating, rational, permission-giving. Nonsense.

The image of religion as a repressive force is a false stereotype kept alive by critics and skeptics who reject their own repression, and reinforced by the excesses of certain sects and cults. The existence of dogmatic and authoritarian denominations proves only that some people need and want to submerge themselves in obedience, to simplify their own confusion and abdicate the awful responsibility for struggling with internal conflict. Religion doesn't impose anything on us; we create and select the religions we need.

To provide a set of rules for living and serve as a source of spiritual meaning is the dilemma of religion in our time.

Religion and Self-respect

Religion offers doctrines of philosophy and theology—visions of ultimate truth—that help us get a grip on what is happening to us. It also provides systems of moral precepts, satisfying the adult urge to know and do what is right, and shaping the lives of children: building self-worth or undermining it, as these vital truths are interpreted and understood, or misinterpreted and misunderstood. Religion is culture, a pluralistic definer of identity, a commitment that joins like-minded groups together and separates them from others, a source of pride in belonging or shame in being excluded. Whether or not we explicitly identify ourselves with religious practices, we're all affected by the values that religious tradition introduces into our culture, values that help us understand our dilemmas and show us how to earn our own self-respect.

Religion, which shares with humanistic psychology the image of the perfectibility of the human spirit, can be a beacon for self-respect by giving us something to strive for. But even at its best, religion may offer a vision of righteousness that remains forever out of reach. Self-respect implies standards, but for self-respect to be realized, standards must be set in such a way that it's possible to get a passing grade.

At one time, religion, with its promise of reward for good deeds and punishment for evil, helped maintain the structure of society. Today, we no longer have secure communal ideologies of redemption. When there is a decline in the doctrinaire allegiance to religion, there is less from the outside to strive for and define the good. We no longer have a larger worldview. Stripped of collective ideologies, men and women have become psychological beings who have to justify themselves from within. The result is an intensified self-consciousness and a greater pressure on the self, less guilt for breaking faith with God and more shame for breaking faith with ourselves.

The more we separate ourselves from external authority and

inflate our own private, inner worlds, the more anxious we become. The individual who can be everything can also be nothing. The tortured shame of the modern neurotic (unlike the classic sinner) only points to hiding and shrinking, which in turn only aggravates separateness and hyperself-consciousness. Religion offers a way to overcome bad feelings of loneliness and imperfection in order for people to come out of their isolation and embrace a larger and higher wholeness.

In recent years, many religions have translated the relatively impersonal and abstract notion of a community of the elect into concrete terms in the form of communal services, classes in marriage and family life, and social functions. The image of the stern, crabbed, and sour-natured Cotton Mather cleric is outmoded. Today's clergy are often more attuned to humanistic concerns than most psychiatrists. Pastors speak out about healthy self-esteem, telling us that our worth is not determined by success or wealth or even by religious devotion, but simply on the basis of who we are. You wouldn't have heard this twenty years ago. Where once they quoted scripture on the evils of the flesh, priests and rabbis and ministers now give sermons about wellness and wholism, recognizing and endorsing the equal claims of physical and spiritual concerns.

Many people, of course, continue to seek spiritual meaning in religion. Still others turn to religion not so much for spiritual inspiration as for a sense of belonging, a way to subdue selfishness, and a link to the traditions of the past—to be good, to feel good. Some do this through mortification of the flesh, through praying, fasting, meditating, or reading scripture. These disciplines are cleansing, banishing despair by purging guilt and shame. And perhaps this burden of shame is one reason for the dynamic resurgence of conservative approaches to religion—fundamentalism, evangelicalism, and pentacostalism. Fundamentalism offers great security in dividing the world into black and white, sinner and saved. To be born again is to be saved, from many things, not the least of which is shame.

In most religions, Christianity certainly, there is a sense in which salvation begins with accepting one's sinfulness or, if you prefer, human weakness. One reason we're ready to accept ourselves as sinful is that we're burdened with guilt and shame. What, then, does accepting one's self as sinful do? Does it confirm shameful unworthiness, or does it signal the beginning of realistic self-acceptance? It depends, of course, on how this message is translated to the child.

Much of what is written about the impact of religion on psychological well-being is abstract intellectualism—from the Freudian debunking to the Jungian flight into mysticism to humanistic critiques, all neatly ordered and rationalized. But if we consider the actual lessons learned by boys and girls when they attend Sunday school or Hebrew school and sit through services, we will see that religion satisfies a variety of unconscious needs. In this, religion is no different from any other product of human ingenuity—art, science, or literature. They all contain versions of truth and distortion of the immortal desires of the human heart.

Religious devotion offers children an idealistic structure for the transformation of narcissism. Remember, narcissism, self-interest, is a universal fact of human experience. Although it is neither good nor bad, it does cause conflict for children, like any basic drive that may pit the child's interests in conflict with others. Children can use religious teaching to help them check selfish behavior, of which they may be ashamed, and subdue exaggerated strivings for personal superiority. A child who feels shameful and guilty may derive a heightened self-esteem from feeling at one with the religious community. In addition to reinforcing self-control, a religious affiliation serves as a source of identification, enhancing self-respect by strengthening the child's ego-ideal.

Christianity offers Christ as an idealized image of rectitude, someone to emulate, something to aim for. But whether it is Buddha, Confucius, The Prophet, or the saintly men and women of the Old Testament, every religion offers models of the pious and good life, figures to identify with in the struggle to overcome insecurity and enhance self-respect. Sophisticated thinkers like Dietrich Bonhoeffer argue that it is not necessary to "become like Jesus" to be worthy in the eyes of God. "The real man is not an object either for contempt or for deification, but an object for the love of God. . . . The real man is at liberty to be his Creator's creature. To be conformed with the Incarnate is to have the right to be the man one really is. Now there is no more pretense, no more hypocrisy or self-violence, no more compulsion to be something other, better and more ideal than what one is. God loves the real man."[1] But does the real child know this?

The Sin of Pride

One of the first things children learn in Sunday school is that the Bible is filled with stories about good and bad. Biblical characters are sensitive, modest, and dutiful. They are followers. They accept authority. The child learns that pride is haughty—the sin of hubris. We are "servants" of God, or "children" of God. Pride might lead to disobedience.

One of the most troubling elements in many religions is a discouragement of independent thought. Jews turn to the Talmud to settle disagreements about how men and women should live, and Christians, especially Roman Catholics, have tended to emphasize authority in such a way that individuals may feel disqualified to decide ethical dilemmas for themselves. Children are taught not so much to think about moral matters as to observe the rules. This message is especially likely to be transmitted by insecure authority—Sunday school teachers with no more than rudimentary training, and ministers who preach rather than inspire.

Religious authoritarianism does serve a socializing function, but as one Catholic priest told me:

Religious educators should have some regard for the natural, instinctive aspects of the child. They should not discourage curiosity and questioning. They should not simply say "Obey," because this makes children feel bad about themselves. I was lucky. My father encouraged my questions. My mother was different. She disapproved of questioning, and many times she'd end a discussion by saying, "Are you too proud to have faith?"

How this authoritarian element in religion is handled helps determine whether young children are proud or ashamed of their own curiosity and independence. When religious educators are heavy-handed, children feel devalued. It's not them that matter, only obedience. This creates a brittle, blind allegiance—comforting to a young child but impossible for a questioning adolescent to sustain. This is one of the main reasons people abandon the religion of their childhood: They think of it only in a rigid and doctrinaire way. They remember with resentment being made to feel ashamed of questioning, and they feel they must reject religion in order to achieve self-respect.

You Can't Hide from God

Religion can help satisfy the two most powerful narcissistic needs of the child: mirroring and idealization. God loves you (mirroring) and God is great (idealization). But God sees everything, and this heightened sense of scrutiny brings with it a heightened sense of shame, especially if children think of certain aspects of themselves as bad.

One of the first things children learn about God is that He is all-powerful and all-knowing. You can't hide from God. This is a frightening prospect for a child (who may be ashamed of certain thoughts and certain deeds). If there's no hiding, there's no privacy. You're always exposed.

Nietzsche was acutely aware of God's invasiveness, and for this reason felt that God had to be overthrown. In *Thus Spake Zarathustra*, Nietzsche wrote: "But he has to die: he saw with eyes that saw everything; he saw man's depths and ultimate grounds, all his concealed disgrace and ugliness. His pity knew no shame; he crawled into my dirtiest nooks. This most curious, overobtrusive, overpitying one had to die."[2]

Surely a religious person could argue that Nietzsche's reaction to God's omniscience is based on his own deep shame. The same God who is all-knowing can be thought of as loving and forgiving. (This is the position that the deeply devout Charles Darwin took when he wrote about God's watchfulness.[3]) However, regardless of what a mature religious position might be, small children are uneasy about God knowing everything about them. Never mind that the God of the New Testament is a kinder sort than the stern and retributive God of the Hebrews. To a child, no place to hide means no place to hide.

A playful parallel of God's omniscience is contained in the Christmas carol about Santa Claus coming to town: "He knows if you've been bad or good, so be good for goodness sake!" It's meant to be cute, but the line, and the warning behind it, gently remind small children of the ever-present danger of guilt and shame.

The Evils of the Flesh

If God knows everything, including your sins and innermost thoughts, what pressures does this set up for young children? Many religions teach that children are born stained with original sin. Somehow, I don't think this mean doctrine has any real impact on a child's mind. What does have an impact, however, is the idea that one's creaturely instincts are wicked.

While today's enlightened ministers and rabbis are preaching a humanistic acceptance of the self and the body, children are still learning, as children do, oversimplified messages about right and wrong, good and bad, virtuous and shameful. This is very important to understand. Children want to be loved so badly that they overreact to some of what we try to teach them. Even when we're simply trying to teach them what's right, our words may frighten them.

God is love. If God is all-loving, you can trust Him—and yourself in relationship to His love. He knows but understands, even your faults. This promise of understanding and forgiveness tempts children to open themselves up to God's representatives, hoping for acceptance. But since religious teachers are, after all, only human, their responses are sometimes sharp and cruel. And as we've seen, when a child exposes the vulnerable self and is met with harsh criticism, the result is traumatic shame.

An orthodox rabbi told me about overhearing a Hebrew school teacher ask the class before the High Holy Days to talk about the things they'd done wrong and should atone for. When one student opened up and said that he went to the movies with friends on the Sabbath, the teacher said, "I can't believe you said that!" As in the family, it is precisely such unexpectedly sharp rebukes that cut deepest. A relatively secure child might simply learn not to trust this particular teacher. But the teacher's response, though insensitive, is related to the idea that God's punishment is distancing Himself from us. You think such and such thoughts, or do such and such things, and God's punishment is to withdraw, leaving you alone with your shame.

The purging of guilt and shame, institutionalized in the sacrament of confession, has always been one of the great appeals of religious devotion. Confession offers the promise of instant release from anxiety. But what could possibly prepare a child to feel totally accepted?

Priests who hear confession are usually accepting, but not always. In the confessional, a child is extremely vulnerable. A priest who says something mean or simply fails to show compassion may confirm a child's shame. And what about what cannot be, or at least is not, confessed? It's too shameful, and so is the child.

One of the worst aspects of religious judgment and punishment is that you can be punished for things you can't help—the evils of the flesh.

St. Augustine, one of the most influential teachers in Christianity, derived from the story of Adam and Eve the curious lesson that sexual desire is sinful, that infants are born with original sin, and that Adam's sin corrupted the whole of nature itself. Even those who think of Genesis only as literature and those who are not Christian live in a culture shaped by this interpretation.

No one intends to teach children that sex is dirty. Unfortunately, many adults suffer so much pain and confusion about sexuality, and are so worried about threats to their children's innocence, that they overemphasize the risks and dangers of sexuality. In an effort to shield children from corrupt influences everywhere, parents and religious leaders alike plant little seeds of poison in children's minds, little seeds of fear and mistrust, later to bear the bitter fruit of sexual conflict and frustration.

If children grow up ashamed of sex, repressive religious teaching may be partly to blame. When it comes to sex, religion is equivocal, but when it comes to divorce, religion is unequivocal: Divorce is bad.

Religion and Divorce

According to the New Testament, when Jesus was asked by the Pharisees about the legitimate grounds for divorce, He replied, "What God has joined together, let no one put asunder." Divorce, which had been accepted in Jewish tradition (as a male prerogative in cases of a wife's infertility), now became sinful and forbidden. Modern law and custom have done away with the forbidden but not the shameful. Where does this leave children of divorce? Not only must they cope with having their families torn apart, they're also burdened with a cruel and unnecessary sense of shame for something that isn't their fault.

Adults tend to forget that children worry so much that they can blame themselves for anything that happens. Recently I heard about a ten-year-old daughter of divorced parents who told her father that her mother still loved him and wished they were still together. The father didn't pay much attention. It was obviously untrue, just something a kid might make up. His new wife, however, felt threatened and wondered what the child was up to. "Why would she say such a thing?" Simple: to erase the pain of divorce.

Being Religious Means Being Different

Religious codes can be hard, but for some people nothing is harder than ambiguity. For the very religious, religion offers a comprehensive set of rules for living and entrance into a community of the faithful. Religious affiliation helps some children shore up self-respect in the face of adolescent pressure to conform to self-destructive expectations. This can invigorate the child for healthier participation in school and social life, or it can serve as a substitute, a place where the child can withdraw from the pressures of the adolescent world. It's the difference between religion as a guiding ideal—calling attention to what's important, what matters—and religion as a haven and an escape.

As I've mentioned, religious education can fortify the ego-ideal, pointing the way to self-respect, or it can reinforce the self-condemnation of the dogmatic superego, fueling the quota of self-criticism, or both. Either way, religious education can put children in conflict, not only with their own natural predilections but also with the larger culture, other children, and institutions.

Children from very religious homes may be marked as different, and may have to run a gauntlet of ridicule from their nonreligious peers, especially when they move into a new neighborhood or start a new school. When a new kid shows up wearing a skullcap and sidelocks or ashes on his forehead, or has very conservative attitudes, the other kids will pick on him. All children have potentially competing loyalties to church and family versus friends and school. For most children, such conflicts are minimal because these various sources of identification are in harmony. But a child from an orthodox family may be subject to the family's decision to segregate themselves in order to reinforce their own beliefs and to protect their children from divided loyalties.

Children vary in their response to being different, depending upon their self-esteem and the strength of their family identity. Some Jewish children, for example, are embarrassed to have to say, "I'm sorry, I can't be there, I have to stay home because it's a Jewish holiday." Very insecure children may lie about their religious affiliation (like anything else they're ashamed to admit). On the other hand, some children are proud of their religious traditions and say, "I am a Jew. Let me tell you how we celebrate this holiday." The strength of the family's religious identity and the extent to which they have built self-esteem determine how the child will handle such trials. Some parents who have not been religious themselves nevertheless want their children to be. When they first start learning the new rules, these children are vulnerable to feeling ashamed. One child came home from Hebrew school in tears. When his mother asked him what happened, he said, "I told them that we went to the zoo on Saturday, and all the other kids laughed at me."

Among religious children, in whom devotion to ritual is a major source of pride, those more observant may shame those who are not: "Stupid, how could you not know the stations of the cross!" "What do you mean, you don't light Shabbas candles?" Such remarks may be a natural expression of the initiate's own anxiety, but they hurt nonetheless. Wherever there is religious fervor, there is the potential to shame that which is natural, uninitiated: "How can you dare eat bread before washing and praying!" It's not the religion, it's how it is presented. A zealous, demanding parent or teacher can use religion to shame a child: "How can you start your day without prayer?" An older child, with a firmer sense of identity, can think about this question and answer it. A young child, unsure of himself or herself, is intimidated and able only to comply or rebel. In either case, the potential for feeling ashamed of the spontaneous self is great.

Intermarriage can also undermine a child's identity. What often happens is that two young people, very much in love and more or less alienated from the religion of their parents, marry thinking the religious difference is unimportant. Later, they often change their minds, adding (or recognizing) another source of conflict. A child of parents in conflict over religion may wonder: Who am I? What am I? Where do I fit in? And if the conflict is severe enough for one parent to undermine the child's respect for the other parent, then the child is cheated out of an important part of his or her own self-respect.

It isn't intermarriage that's the problem, any more than religious upbringing necessarily fosters shame. The fact is that every institution with a governing role in children's lives has the potential to enhance self-respect by fostering mature goals and aspirations— or to reinforce shame by exposing the child to harsh criticism and severe judgment.

When we talk about the institutions that shape children's lives, we must not forget their own, or what was once their own, play.

THE GAMES CHILDREN PLAY

In play, children can release their full natures, not just the sanitized versions they allow to surface during the many hours that their lives are shaped and controlled by adults. Spirited play releases physical tension and generates excitement; it's a chance to cut loose and have fun. But the greatest thing about the games children play is freedom—freedom from adult constraint, freedom for imagination to raise its wings. A little girl may be trapped at a small school desk all day, but in play she can run and romp as free as her heart desires. A little boy who was such a fool as to imagine that he could be special and was humiliated by a teacher who said, "Who do you think you are?" can heal his hurt pride playing heroic games. Pure play is pure release, childhood's natural antidote to shame.

The Structuralization of Play

In play, children learn to define themselves as competent (but only as long as they are free to choose what games to play). They are free to be children—a stage of life you must have before you can give it up. And whether we like it or not, in play, children also learn to be boys or girls. Boys learn to be more concerned with winning, girls with relationships. Boys become more competitive, proud of winning but ashamed of losing. In the world of boys, a good loser is still a "loser."

Girls have a different agenda. While boys judge themselves in terms of their ability to win, girls judge themselves in terms of their ability to care. Traditional girls' games like jump rope and hopscotch are taking-turns games in which competition is indirect, since one person's success doesn't necessarily signal another's failure. Whereas boys are ashamed of being inept, girls are more ashamed of social rejection and fracturing relationships. So girls strive to avoid being mean or selfish, or even shy. Theirs is a world that coheres through human connectedness rather than a system of rules. Girls see each other not as opponents in a contest for winning and losing but as members of a network of relationships on whose continuation they all depend. When boys choose competitive games and girls choose cooperative games, they are expressing the selves they want to be. This freedom to shape their games to fit their needs is lost when adults take over.

Today, children's leisure time has come, more and more, to be structured by adults. Instead of going outside to play in informal groups, children now take lessons and participate in organized sports leagues. We love our children and want them to have all the advantages, so we enroll them in gymnastics and ballet and swimming and skiing and karate. And then we drive them to lessons and practice and games. Driving the kids to soccer and karate and dance reflects a parental commitment to providing children all the advantages of overcontrolling and overmanaging their lives for them.

It starts early. Trying to give their children an edge, parents enroll them in sports and classes and lessons before the children are really ready to master complex skills. Pushing children, gently or otherwise, to be superkids cheats them out of childhood. Fixing so many of our hopes and anxieties onto our children, we've crossed the boundary between our world and theirs and taken over their games.

Children in the early school years enjoy a sense of mastery from learning new skills, including sports, which give them a chance to feel acceptably competent in the exercise of their bodies. Swimming from one end of the pool to the other or shooting a ball into a basket are rewards in themselves. It doesn't matter if they do it slowly or it takes them three tries. Young children who play among themselves show little interest in competition. Somewhere around nine or ten, however, there is a change. Children begin to judge themselves on the basis of how well they do compared with someone else. Simply participating is no longer enough. Now they have to be good. Many children drop out.

From age twelve to sixteen, between 80 and 90 percent of children drop out of organized sports. A similar pattern holds true for those teenagers who drop out of music. They drop out because there's too much emphasis on performance, too much pressure to excel, too much shame for not being a "winner."

When children play among themselves, they feel successful by demonstrating competence: by simply participating and mastering the basic skills of the game. This is true whether the game is playing tag or hopscotch or dodge ball, or sandlot sports. In sand-lot sports, a group of kids get together to play ball. They make up teams and play until it's time to go home. They do keep score and they do play hard, but if one team consistently wins, it's cause to swap players, not celebrate. The object is playing, not winning. These games have—had—all the physical energy and emotional passion that sport has to offer, with much less of the pressure found in today's organized baseball and soccer leagues. The main difference? There weren't any adults around.

Coaches and parents try to minimize competitiveness and with it the idea that only by winning can a child succeed in sports. Nobody likes to see angry parents screaming at Little League games, but it happens.

I recently watched a Little League game. It was the first year after the kids hit the ball off a tee, the first year children pitch. They are now old enough to throw hard but too young to throw accurately. One little boy was afraid to stand up close to the plate. When it was his turn to bat, he'd shy away from the plate, hoping for a walk. The coach, meaning well, encouraged the boy to stand closer—"Don't be afraid." Then his father got into the act—it must have been the A word. The boy moved closer, but he started to cry, and his father yelled at him, "Don't be a sissy, stand in there!" The more the father yelled, the more the boy cried. It was pitiful.

Few parents are this blatant and this mean. And yet even if parents could control themselves, there are still certain aspects of organized sport that create unnecessary pressure. As long as children play for one team and against others, they will be aware of the won-lost record and, inevitably, measure their self-esteem by how many points are scored and how many games are won. (I've always made a point of asking my children after a game, "Did you have fun?" And they've always answered by saying whether they won or lost.) Another source of pressure in suburban sports leagues is the presence of a large audience of adults. Parents, grandparents, and friends line the field shouting encouragement. Some of these adults are there to enjoy watching the contest, but many more attend out of a sense of obligation to support their children. This "support" is a mixed blessing. Parents are there to witness their children playing, but for many kids, what they witness is the child's (real or imagined) failure.

Sports would be far healthier with two changes: do away with fixed teams, and stop encouraging parents to attend. On election day, there are barriers to prevent electioneering within so many feet of the voting booth. When kids play sports, adults shouldn't be allowed within a mile.

Many parents are careful to avoid criticizing their children for striking out or missing a shot on goal. They deliberately try to avoid putting pressure on their kids. But then they overdo their cheering for success. If success is so wonderful, what does that make failure? It's hard to legislate feelings, including your own, but if you watch your child participate in sports, it's probably best to be appreciative without making too big a deal out of getting a hit or scoring a goal.

As I write this, guilt makes me wince. I remember watching my wonderful daughter, Sandy, on the soccer field doing a very respectable imitation of Ferdinand the Bull. While other kids were running up and down the field, charging after the ball, Sandy would be making observations meteorological, or examining the grass for bare spots. Daddy, meanwhile, was sitting on the sidelines screaming "encouragement." After a while, I learned to keep my mouth shut—but only with great effort. Then came number two, my boy, Paul. He was a star. I used to root like crazy for him. Every save was a miracle, every goal was cause for major celebration. I didn't realize it at first, but my excessive enthusiasm was reinforcing impossible expectations. When time proved him to be good but not quite the greatest athlete who ever walked the face of the earth, he was terribly disappointed in himself. I was disappointed in myself. In both cases, I was projecting my own anxiety onto my kids. It wasn't fair.

Video Kids

With their own play increasingly taken over and structured by adults, today's children long for the escape and release play is supposed to provide. Besides structuring children's games, well-meaning adults have also sanitized them, expanding their control and contracting children's freedom to express sexual and aggressive impulses. Longing for cathartic release, more and more children seek escape in television and movies. If they can't play out their own expressive impulses, at least they can watch others doing so.

Elementary school children love to watch cartoons, especially those featuring powerful superheroes who triumph over their enemies. Even a vulnerable fellow like Popeye can, by eating spinach, overcome those more powerful than himself. As children get older (somewhere between eight and twelve), their preferences switch to television sitcoms and movies featuring clever, wisecracking adolescents outwitting repressive adults. In the movies, young adult actors playing slick teenagers do what kids wish they could do: take off their clothes, break things, and make fools of grown-ups.

The minute they get home from school, children turn on the boob tube and sit down to be diverted, amused, entranced. They're offered suspense, catharsis of fear and pity and loathing, erotic arousal (take a look at those steamy soap operas), and an outlet for every fear and passion. When they go to the movies, they'll watch whatever's showing (never mind the ratings), and temporarily get out of the boredom and confusion of their lives.

At the movies, they find a release from drudgery and adult authority, and the persistence of human capacities for decency and malice, for good deeds and bad. They seek escape from the limitations of themselves in the darkness of the movie theater. Here, for a while, they're free to experience vicariously the pleasure of breaking down restraints and overcoming inadequacies. Just like adults, they love blockbuster adventures like *Indiana Jones* and *Star Wars*, but they also flock to grade-B comedies featuring teen-agers triumphing over everyday obstacles, in the form of adult restrictions (*Ferris Bueller's Day Off* was a schlock masterpiece of this genre), or the tyranny of popularity (*Heathers*), or just plain being little (*The Karate Kid*). Outside, at home and at school, children sometimes feel helpless in a hostile world. But there in the dark, their hearts can cheer for the heroes, root for the under-dogs, and laugh at the fools. They are, themselves, not without some of these qualities—cowardice and heroism, unattractiveness and attractiveness, rejection and popularity, shame and pride. Movies show them what they want, what they feel, and what they fear. Movies allow them, for a little while, to dream of living with-out shame.

Now that we've seen how the forces of socialization shape pride and shame in young children, let's go on to see how these forces intensify as we explore the adolescent experience, when character begins to coalesce.

11
· · · · · · ·

Adolescence
That Awful, Awkward Age

Freud called the years between the time children enter school and the time they reach adolescence *latency*, not because they are uneventful, but because they have a slow, steady sameness. Relations in the family are relatively stable. Kids at this age do more for themselves around the house and spend as much time as possible outside it with friends. Meanwhile, their parents, facing middle age, are rediscovering their own lives: reevaluating careers, trying to find time for friends, worrying about money, and dreaming of vacations. Preteens need their parents less, and parents have more time to themselves. It's the calm before a storm.

The storm is called adolescence: a time of unequaled turbulence, when anguished parents watch good-natured little children turn into hulking, sullen, brooding, adolescents. For teenagers, life is simple. All they have to do is stand by while their bodies, raging with hormones, shoot up, change shape, and sprout hair in the most unlikely places. Well, not exactly stand by—just finish school and figure out what they want to do with the rest of their lives; fall in love and have their hearts broken, at least once; shed old friends and make new ones; and transform themselves from the children they were into the adults they want to be.

We think of adolescence as one long, chaotic and undifferentiated period between childhood and adulthood. It starts at about age thirteen and ends around eighteen, or nineteen, or twenty-one, or thirty, depending upon who's counting. In fact, even if we confine ourselves to the period from age thirteen to nineteen, adolescence is a stage with several subphases, each with tasks to accomplish. Each one a step toward consolidation of identity and self-respect, each one mined with insecurity and shame.

Early adolescence begins when the growth spurt initiates the onset of puberty. The major challenge of this period is adjusting to a new self-image, and children may suffer shame if the changes occur particularly early or late. For example, a girl who develops precociously may worry about becoming too tall to be accepted, and may become acutely embarrassed at being so different from friends and classmates, as well as by sexual feelings for which she has had little time to prepare. Early or late, body changes have the potential to alienate a child from the familiar self, and to isolate him or her from friends.

Mid-adolescence begins a year or so after pubescence. Now movement toward the opposite sex begins to break up friendships. This is a time of revolt and conformity: revolt against parental dictates and conformity to peer group standards. Children are vulnerable to shame because when they repudiate parents they are also repudiating part of their own identity. And, of course, sensitive adolescents must struggle to find acceptance by their peer group at the same time they are suffering through teenage crushes and sexual experimentation—several sources of shame.

Late adolescence is the time when identity is consolidated, a time for intimacy and love, and a time to come to grips with the future. Although boys and girls must liberate themselves, to some extent, from their families in order to become persons in their own right, they must find a way to achieve self-respect as individuals without becoming ashamed of their families. Moreover, the twin tasks of achieving identity and intimacy, often described as separate, are, in fact, coordinate achievements. Independence (not isolation) is a prerequisite to real intimacy, and the answer to the question "Who am I?" depends, in part, on knowing that one can love and be loved.

Adolescence is a pivotal time for consolidating self-respect as the self begins to emerge from the family. It is also a pivotal time for shame, because it's not just an emerging self but a changing self that is vulnerable to acceptance or rejection, and because habits of hiding or openness, formed in adolescence, are carried into adulthood.

"WHAT'S THE MATTER WITH KIDS TODAY?"

"Why can't they be like we were, perfect in every way?" These lines from *Bye Bye Birdie* capture the sentiments of many parents. (The older we get, the more creative our memories of what we were really like.) Our view of adolescents is, quite naturally, filtered through the lens of adult concerns: When I was a kid . . . Why do they have to be so snotty? What in God's name are they doing out so late? As long as we think of teenagers as objects in relationship to ourselves—rude or polite, cooperative or uncooperative—instead of as independent persons in their own right, it's easy to forget how much pressure they live with.

Adolescents, those spoiled, arrogant, noisy teenagers who prowl the shopping malls, wearing outrageous clothes and thumbing their noses at convention, live under terrific stress. Imagine growing up with the knowledge that acid rain is poisoning every lake and stream east of the Mississippi, chemical pollution is burning away the ozone layer of the atmosphere, your uncle Harry or your gym teacher might turn out to be a child molester, drug dealers control the streets and a significant part of the economy of American cities, eating apples and sunbathing can cause cancer, and making love can lead to the fatal AIDS virus. Which of us can look back on the worst of our high school years and say that we ever faced anything as bad as crack, or urine tests, or AIDS? In the old days, *bad* meant getting caught smoking cigarettes in the bathroom or drinking beer in the parking lot. These crimes were *serious*, at the time, but not serious enough to get you expelled from the system for life.

It's a grim time to be growing up. Today's teenagers are preparing to take their place in the adult world, secure in the knowledge that sex is death and rain kills fish. These are terrifying things to contemplate when you are fifteen or sixteen. In addition to the dramatic hazards that plague this generation, teenage ambivalence over dependence and independence must be resolved in a world in which both parents are probably away at work, and in which, in many cases, Mom and Dad live under separate roofs. Today's children also live with incredible pressure to succeed, and it starts early. Competition for admission to the best schools begins with preschool and doesn't let up. By the time they reach high school, most middle-class children are subject to enormous pressures to get A's, do well on achievement tests, even cultivate extracurricular activities—whether they want to or not—in order to get into the right colleges.

Given all this pressure, adolescents need a great deal of support. Unfortunately, they don't get enough, especially at home.

The family is relinquishing the socialization of children earlier and earlier. Even when they're little, Big Bird is likely to be the one who teaches them their ABCs. The schools, mass media, and peer groups are taking over the guidance and education of older children from parents who are too busy working to exert much influence. Our society has never had clearly differentiated functions for adolescents. Now we give them more material advantages but also more pressure and less support. All that's on the outside. On the inside, today's adolescents have something familiar: the torment of self-consciousness.

BOYS AND GIRLS APART

The first commandment of the juvenile era, Boys and Girls Apart, prepares the way for the tremendous biological divergence of puberty. The adolescent growth spurt starts between ages ten and eleven for most girls and between twelve and thirteen for most boys. As a result, in the sixth through eighth grades, girls tower over boys, some beginning to look like young women, while most of the boys are still immature. When girls are around, boys show off and brag. They strut and posture, and they talk dirty. *Asshole, shithead*—these words are another version of *I dare you*. They're prove-it words that boys use to show they're strong. This is the little-boy version of male bravado, a way to deny anxiety rather than attempt to establish relationships.

At puberty, girls' breasts enlarge, their hips get round, and their legs lengthen. They grow pubic hair and axillary (underarm) hair; the labia and the clitoris develop, and the clitoris becomes erectile. Female adolescence is a time of budding promise when girls can feel proud of their emerging womanliness. But as Simon de Beauvoir has observed, physical changes bring a heightened self-consciousness, and with it a heightened vulnerability to shame:

> When the breasts and the body hair are developing, a sentiment is born which sometimes becomes pride but which is originally shame; all of a sudden the child becomes modest, she will not expose herself naked even to her sisters or her mother.... [Her body] becomes an object that others see and pay attention to.... The young girl feels that ... she becomes for others a thing.... She would like to be invisible.[1]

Pride or shame? Much depends on the attitudes of parents and friends. Other kids are going through similar changes to varying degrees and at various rates. Thus, a girl with pimples can take comfort from knowing she's not alone, and a girl whose period hasn't started yet won't worry so much if some of her friends haven't yet reached menarche either.

Most girls are prepared for puberty by their mothers and by health teachers at school. Still, most girls await the changes somewhat anxiously and are relieved at the onset of menses. Occasionally, despite preparation and precaution, a girl will be seriously embarrassed when her first period stains her dress at school or when she drips blood on the floor at a party. They still call it "the curse," a symbol of woman's burden and her inferior status.

Most parents say all the right things: "It's just a natural part of growing up." "We're proud of you." But in this, as in many things, it's what parents do, far more than what they say, that counts.

Parents' reactions—to adolescent developments, and to themselves—play a critical role in shaping children's gender identity.

A father who is jealous and competitive with his son can make the boy ashamed of his masculinity or inhibit his aggressiveness. The boy feels a sense of shame for being "bad," without knowing why.

A mother who is anxious and critical of her daughter's makeup and short skirts may create conflict in the girl over sexuality, or may drive her into a precocious promiscuity. The girl feels something is wrong and feels shame because of her own wish to be a sexual being. If her yearning or her experimenting with makeup is attacked—"You look trashy!"—she'll learn that sexuality is something to be ashamed of. Years later, when she has an anxiety attack over feelings of attraction for the boss, she may wonder why. But if a mother enjoys her own life and has a husband who appreciates her, a daughter is most likely to feel good about becoming a woman.

And, of course, siblings have a polarizing effect on each other. A boy who is jealous of his sister's easy affectionate ways may stiffen his resolve to be tough, *muy macho*. If he's embarrassed by his own dependency wishes, he may cut himself off from the emotional refueling he still needs from his parents, and later have trouble being open enough to achieve intimacy. If a girl is frightened by an older sibling's aggressive outgoingness and the attendant noisy struggles with parents, she may stifle her own assertive nature and swear a secret vow always to be agreeable.

To a pubescent girl concerned with her attractiveness, her father's response is particularly significant. Fathers, already uneasy about their daughters' budding breasts and developing curves, are likely to be even more anxious in today's climate of hyperawareness of sex abuse. If a father draws away from his daughter because he feels he should no longer be physically close, the girl may feel that her father finds her unattractive or is repelled by something about her. Because her conclusion is unlikely to be well thought out, it has abundant unconscious self-doubt to feed upon. Teenage girls have plenty to worry about.

Skin secretions are changing and becoming more sebaceous, contributing to the bane of adolescence, acne. Sweat glands are becoming hyperactive and creating an odor that may embarrass the girl. She feels herself becoming a woman; she may or may not feel that's a good thing to be.

Despite changing times, many girls still regret, from time to time, being female. Although such self-doubts are perfectly natural, in today's climate of energetic feminine pride, a girl who is ambivalent about becoming a woman may be ashamed of herself for being retrograde, unfeminine, or both. Boys, too, occasionally wish they belonged to the opposite sex. Why not? It's natural to envy the attributes and advantages of the other. But for boys, such wishes are even more shameful, associated as they are with castration and perversity. Here, as so often, shame flourishes when ordinary but troubling sentiments are kept secret.

The most obvious changes in the pubertal boy are increased size and muscular strength. At age twelve or thirteen, the testes begin to increase in size and the scrotal skin to toughen and harden. The penis gets larger, and the boy develops pubic hair and axillary hair. The beard and body hair appear about four years after the first pubertal changes. After an embarrassing period of uncontrollable cracking, the boy's voice deepens and he is no longer mistaken for his mother when he answers the phone. Most boys are physically mature at seventeen or eighteen, but some complete maturation at fifteen and others not until twenty.[2]

Many boys (and girls) begin masturbating before adolescence, but the activity generally increases after puberty. According to Kinsey's data, the percentage of boys who masturbate increases from 45 percent at thirteen years to 71 percent at fifteen years.[3] Those who don't masturbate are likely to have nocturnal emissions. A boy's first ejaculation can be disturbing. One minute he's playing with himself and feeling good, then unexpectedly his penis starts throbbing spasmodically and a strange milky fluid squirts out in irregular pulses. The boy may worry that he's damaged something. He's certain that he's bad. He's never going to do that again!

Shameful but irresistible, masturbation falls into a control and release cycle. It's embarrassing and shameful, so the child renounces the practice. Later, every time he or she gives in, there is an incremental loss of self-respect.

Masturbation is usually accompanied by fantasies that relieve the emptiness and loneliness of the act. Today's children are bombarded by images to agitate their ardor and fuel their fantasies. Check out MTV. Look at the ads in *Rolling Stone* (which are only a slightly more explicit version of ads in tamer publications): You'll see shirtless young hunks, locked in smoldering eye combat with pouty-faced seductresses wearing tight blue jeans and undershirts with their nipples poking out. Sheepish stares and wolfy grins, glittering eyes and lewd smiles. What are they selling? Who cares.

Adolescents are preoccupied with sex. Sex as a promise of ecstasy, sex as a game, sex as maybe, sex as someday, sex as no. Later, alone in their rooms, they dream of sex as yes, sex as now. In fantasy, sex can be romantic and lyrical: billowy linens and heaving chests, soft kisses and gentle caresses. Or sex can be lewd and lascivious: wet, red lips and hot, pink tongues—as you wish.

Then there's afterward. Is she a ridiculous romantic? Is he a dirty-minded sex freak? Can people see it on their faces? Could be.

Sex is the chief attraction and chief affliction of adolescence. Teenagers live in a state of constant, oppressive horniness. For some kids it's delicious; for others it's dirty.

In over twenty years of hearing anguished patients confess secret shame, I've heard some painful revelations, including infidelity, rape, and serial murder. But in all those years the two most agonizing confessions, the two people most profoundly tormented by what they had done, were a nineteen-year-old boy who masturbated "as often as once a week" (it took him three weeks to tell me what was on his mind), and an eighteen-year-old girl who had engaged in some minor sex play with another girl (it was two months before she could bear to reveal her shameful secret). There are no words for how deeply ashamed these two were for what they had done.

Exposed and trapped in their own bodies, preoccupied with and troubled by sex, adolescents feel conspicuous and vulnerable. In response to this heightened feeling of exposure, they turn inward. When you ask them what they're thinking and feeling, they say, "Nothing." They retreat from too much visibility. They long for privacy.

PRIVACY

We all need privacy at times. The reason adolescents need it so badly is that revolutionary changes in their physical and psychic selves make them feel so terribly vulnerable. Their minds are much in conflict. What's acceptably erotic and what's dirty? Is it okay to daydream about someone, or would people laugh if they knew? Do I look good in this outfit, or is it too showy? Fragile egos in formation need protection.

Every teenager is plagued by pressure that at times is too much. Every teenager needs escape, needs privacy.

Teenagers retreat to the privacy of their rooms to soothe themselves and heal their hurts. In the morning they wake up, exiled from their dreams, into the raw world. In the evening they want to relax, they want to escape from anxious pressures. They check frustration and rejection at the door, and retreat to the sanctity of their privacy. They release themselves from vexation and vulnerability by getting away from the eyes of others, by getting lost in their music, and by entering the world of dreams, endless dreams.

Self-indulgence—Self-denial

In real life nothing much happens, although everything is considered. In fantasy, everything is possible. Sexual fantasies and masturbation can, obviously, be a cause of shame. But they are also a seductive way to relieve it. We think of sex as a drive that we "give in to" or "gratify." But it can also be an attempt to heal the self from hurt. Nothing soothes the spirit like sexy pleasure.

But frank sexual fantasies can make teenagers anxious (just as R-rated movies can give rise not to pleasure, but to embarrassment or disgust). One minute they're transfixed, gaping at the latest video of Madonna, all wet-lipped and tarty, writhing orgiastically in a black silk slip. The next minute they feel guilty, ashamed, and disgusted with themselves for being such slaves to sexuality. (This is the reason for the timeless appeal of the vampire legend: Yielding to the suave seducer can turn you into a sunlight-fearing bloodsucker, a creature of darkness damned for all eternity.) One week they are voluptuaries, the next week they're monastic.

Asceticism holds tremendous power over the adolescent imagination. It's the power to block out guilt and shame; the power of the ego-ideal to make them feel pure, good. They want to make the world a better place, and they want to purge themselves of unholy appetites. They become concerned about injustice. And with a new interest in ideals and ideologies they begin to take an interest in religion (or some esoteric equivalent), although it may have only bored them previously. They renounce the bad and extol what they consider good—often abnegation, self-sacrifice, and self-denial. They're seeking reasons and meaning in life, and they're strengthening their superegos, controlling the unruly upsurge of sexual and aggressive impulses.

Some dream of entering the priesthood or becoming missionaries, some take refuge in books with idealistic heroes (like Holden Caulfield or Anne Frank or Alyosha Karamazov), some stop eating meat ("the flesh of animals"), some stop eating almost everything.

Most teenagers are anxious and uncertain about their bodies, but in our culture girls and women (still) suffer the most over how they look. When the fashion-model aesthetic compounds anxious self-doubt about budding sexuality, many girls turn from picky eaters into compulsive dieters. Fasting serves many purposes. It's an expression of piety, a victory over greedy appetites, and a quest for perfect thinness. Parents may try to argue—"You look fine!"— but reasoning is at best irrelevant, at worst counterproductive. If the latent agenda for fasting is not attractiveness but self-denial, then what good is rational argument? In households that equate food with maternal affection and goodness with obedience, self-starvation may be the last desperate measure for a girl to gain power to resist her parents. If eating is equated with compliance, she can rebel simply by refusing to eat. When parents of a budding anorexic become concerned, her rejection of their entreaties— "eat, eat!"—makes her the center of attention.

Teenagers are bombarded by contradictory messages about eating. On the one hand, they're admonished to take responsibility for control and mastery of their bodies—mastery that will be theirs, they're told, if they diet and exercise. Some girls dutifully take on both commandments as twin obsessions.

Teenage boys, subject to similar pressure but a different aesthetic, can mortify and improve themselves at the same time by lifting weights, running, and doing chin-ups. (Dirty, weak, defective? Not me, boy, I'm going to be strong and pure, like Sir Galahad, or maybe Arnold Schwarzenegger.) In the popular (with adolescents, anyway) movie *Brewster McCloud*, a teenage boy who wants to fly (literally) away from his problems, tries to transform the skinny body of a weakling into a powerful physique by eating health food and doing chin-ups by the hour.

Teenagers, absorbed in self-examination, can withdraw socially to escape anxiety and pressure. Alone in their rooms, they lose themselves in reverie. One of the things they dream of is being popular.

CONFORMITY AND THE WISH TO BE POPULAR

Longing for popularity and fearful of rejection, adolescents are conditioned to conform. Caught between need and fear, they do what they have to—*anything*—to fit in. It's wonderful to stand out and be admired, wonderful but risky. The risk is ridicule.

When she was in the eighth grade, my daughter invited me during "Career Week" to speak on how to become a psychologist. I was proud to be asked. As soon as I walked into the school building, a group of boys made some comments about my aftershave lotion: "Hey-hey, heavy smell of Polo." "Who's wearing that cologne?" The remarks weren't exactly hostile, but they had a certain edge, and, just for an instant, I remembered what it was like to be an adolescent. If I had to return the next day, I can assure you I would not have put on after-shave. Some people probably respond differently than I. Still, there it is, something about the adolescent subculture that zeros in on anything that stands out, like a heat-seeking missile.

It's mean, but it isn't meanness that makes some kids "bust on" others; it's shame-anxiety, projected outward. Hazing is shaming, as are teasing, staring, debagging, or forcing someone to behave in an undignified manner. And just as Eskimos have a rich vocabulary for snow, adolescents have a wealth of shaming words: *weird, wimp, nerd, loser, geek, dork,* and the ever-popular *asshole.* The sharp edge of these words is almost always blunted by a joking, teasing tone. Together with their friends, teenagers sit around making witty, sarcastic remarks—about other kids, about the teachers. The object is to prove yourself an advanced guard in the war on stupidity, clever enough to spot the shortcomings of other people. *They* are dumb. *They* are stupid.

In many cultures, a person is born into a personal community, a group of intimates linked by kinship and tradition. But in contemporary America each person must create his or her own personal community. Every child must learn to attract friends and fit in as a member of the group. To do so, children work at being appealing—agreeable or interesting—and avoid doing anything that might result in ostracism. Social failure is the number-one fear of adolescence.

The anxious self-scrutiny of adolescence reflects an almost unbearable need to fit in and be accepted. Teenagers long to look like their idols—professional teenagers—film actors and rock stars, adults masquerading as youngsters. The most admired teenage icons have always been adults: James Dean, Marlon Brando, Debbie Reynolds, Elizabeth Taylor, Pat Boone, Elvis Presley. These stars were what teenagers wanted to be: sexy, tough, independent. Even now, when it seems most movies cater to and are about teenagers, most of the actors are way over twenty-one: Madonna, Tom Cruise, Michael J. Fox, Martin Sheen. Patrick Swayze was in his mid-thirties when he played the muscular young dance instructor in *Dirty Dancing.*

Beginning as young as twelve or thirteen, children are drawn toward a bogus maturity. Makeup, designer clothes, cigarettes, the "Miami Vice"–look—these things are popular because they seem grown-up. Kids want to be older and more sophisticated. They want to be cool. They want to be someone other than themselves.

But when teenagers search their mirrors, they are far more alert to any sign of something they would be ashamed of than they are hopeful of finding something to feel good about. They don't want to look bad, and they don't want to screw up.

Somewhere between childhood and adolescence we learn to be ashamed of betraying our ignorance. Remember squirming in embarrassment when your innocent enthusiasm made you uncool? It may have been a little thing, like clapping between movements of a symphony, and then feeling the silent censure of the audience. You learned two things: Don't applaud at the wrong time and don't give way to spontaneous delight. Be cool.

It's sad how soon we learn to be ashamed of naïveté—the very quality that allows for wonder and curiosity and asking questions. But, no, asking questions isn't cool. Cool is being complete, and so adolescents begin early to surround themselves with a thin screen of sophistication (adolescent insouciance), behind which they appear to be knowing, imperturbable, self-confident—everything they're not.

Conformity is driven by shame-avoidance. When individual idiosyncracies feel dangerous, kids cauterize their uniqueness: They burn away anything that sticks out far enough to be ridiculed. Conformity buys acceptance by mortgaging individuality. If children are afraid to deviate for fear of rejection, they won't think about what they like, what looks good and what feels good, they'll think about what is accepted. Instead of a fun hairdo or a pretty shirt, a young adolescent will choose the right shirt or hairdo.

When they get to be about fifteen, some teenagers, only some, will risk affectations and mannerisms that mark them as unique, special. Something to make them stand out from the crowd. Others, maybe most, are too concerned with being sufficiently armored to risk standing out. They follow the crowd. Most kids would die before wearing the wrong stuff to school and kill for a pair of status sneakers or the right logo on a polo shirt. Hyperbole? Maybe. But certainly the metaphor is an apt reflection of what is at stake: self-respect. Children who stand in front of their closets wondering what to put on aren't really vain and egotistical; they're insecure. In the process of developing a self, we all need props.

Wearing the wrong thing is bad, looking foolish is worse. Humiliation is a highly sensitive social product, calculated by multiplying the intrinsic value of what is exposed by the value of the person before whom it is exposed. Using a five-point scale, dropping a fly ball (3) in front of a schoolyard full of kids (5) may be more upsetting to most adolescents than flunking a test (4) and telling their parents (2). Adolescents have a tremendous need of a safe place where they can confide problems and reveal concerns. Diary sales are high in this age group.

Everyone can be chosen or rejected, and kids may never know why they are rejected. This makes for enormous uncertainty in personal relations and exquisite sensitivity to looks, stares, smiles, wisecracks, and criticism. Some day they'll ask such questions as, "What is the meaning of life?" But now, all they want to know is, "Do people really like me?"

Some kids, who for one reason or another don't fit in with the majority and are squeezed out of the conforming cliques, join forces with each other, reinforcing their differences and gaining strength to set themselves off from the majority. The enormous popularity of movies like *Porky's* and *Revenge of the Nerds* is due to more than the sight gags. Steve Martin's successful updating of the Cyrano de Bergerac story in *Roxanne* proves that the humiliation and then triumph of social outcasts moves audiences as much today as it did in 1897 when Edmond Rostand first wrote the story.

Some teenagers are like Cyrano, exhibiting themselves counterphobically, bringing about the danger of disapproval in order to master it. They break the rules or play the fool, as if to say, "I don't care what anybody thinks!" It isn't true.

The jokester strikes a common but bad compromise between wanting to show off and be admired versus the fear of being criticized where vulnerable. Instead of revealing his real feelings—for possible approval or criticism—he shows off only his cleverness. Others may laugh, but when they do so they are appreciating only the jokes, not the person. The real person isn't even showing.

Adolescent behavior is a compromise between the wish to be appreciated and the fear of humiliation. If a wish arouses too much anxiety or shame, the mind erects defenses to block it; if not, the mind opens up to it. The balance between wish and fear is mobile, and complicated. In reverie, for example, a teenager may indulge in fantasies of being special, a desire to be savored in private only to be forgotten or repudiated moments later. Adopting the attitude that showing off is only make-believe—just clowning, not to be taken seriously—can reduce anxiety. All of us seek the fullest expression of satisfaction compatible with a tolerable degree of anxiety or shame. For teenagers, the guiding questions are: What would win other people's approval? What would make them disapprove—rebuke or ridicule?

By mid-adolescence the peer group changes into a youth culture, with something of an anti-adult orientation and becoming heterosexual. It's an age-appropriate subculture in which children try out adult behavior. Once they made themselves feel big by engaging in clever commentaries on the stupid world and its stupid people; now they're becoming more open. Affectations begin to drop away when teenagers become easy and trustful with certain people they care about and who seem to care about them.

BOYS AND GIRLS TOGETHER

The passions of first love are as subtle and gently lyrical as getting run over by a truck. In emotional and sexual intimacy we undress ourselves and are exposed as nowhere else. The joy of intimate acceptance is enormous, as is the pain of rejection.

The road to falling in love is a long one, and achieving real sexual intimacy takes even longer. The first steps are taken when boys and girls start hanging out together and calling each other on the phone. Meanwhile, children experiment with the idea of being attached to someone in the form of early adolescent crushes.

Puppy love may seem silly and cute, but to the child it's a serious prelude to falling in love. The objects of early adolescent affection are often clearly unattainable. Children of this age are looking for ways to try out new forms of intimacy. Rather than rushing into face-to-face intimate relationships, adolescents search for ways to take half steps. A twelve-year-old girl may spend hours daydreaming of an older boy she admires from afar and about whom she constructs a wealth of fantasies. A thirteen-year-old boy may fantasize about the prettiest girl in school. Watching her secretly, all goggle-eyed and mute, he's filled with urgent longing, a longing he doesn't fully understand and wouldn't dare describe. Embarrassing emotions are hard to share. If a child does feel comfortable enough to share the crush, it should be regarded as a privileged communication.

Early adolescent crushes are most usually on an older person, either of the same or opposite sex. The object of the adoration is often very much like the love-struck adolescent, or someone he or she would like to be. At this age, the distinction between objects of identification and love is as blurry as it will ever be.

Melanie, age thirteen, developed a fascination with a local television newscaster. Because the newscaster was a woman, some kids thought Melanie was odd; her teachers wondered if she was looking for a mother substitute. Melanie watched the news every night (at 6:00 and 11:00), entered every contest the station offered, went to local fund drives, and toured the station—five times. Instead of simply accepting and acknowledging the obvious ("You really like her, don't you?" "You really think she's neat."), Melanie's parents wanted to know, "What's the big attraction?" and "Why do you like her so much?" Melanie could only mumble, "She's *so* cool." In fact, there was nothing unusual about Melanie's crush on a woman she admired, a woman she'd like to emulate. Nothing unusual except perhaps Melanie's openness. Too bad her friends and family couldn't have been more sympathetic.

The essence of a crush is that the relationship is fantasy. Children control both halves of the relationship within their imaginations. They're safe. Life in the real world isn't so safe. Actions have consequences.

By the eighth grade, boys and girls may be sitting together in the lunchroom; at about the same time they begin to mingle in public places—at the mall, at the skating rink. They develop attractions, which when shared can lead to embarrassing revelations. The great challenge of adolescent pairing off is to fall "in like" with someone sufficiently attractive to be appealing yet not so popular as to be beyond one's reach. ("You like her? Yeuch!" "Bobbie? Who do you think you are?") A child who risks opening up vulnerable feelings, liking or not liking someone, can get burned if these secrets become the subject of conversation (sharp gossip designed to knife friendships other kids envy). That's why the phone is so popular. It's safer.

Boys and girls begin calling each other on the phone as early as sixth grade. By fifteen, phone conversations become a major preoccupation. It's easier to express new and difficult emotions with the safety and privacy of distance.

Up close, boys and girls start making contact by teasing and flirting. The first physical contact often takes place during rough-and-tumble play. Seventh- and eighth-grade parties are likely to include boys and girls, and some of the games they play, like football and tackle Frisbee, permit tentative exploration of the mysteries of the other sex in a very nonthreatening way. By the ninth grade or so, teenagers no longer play boisterous games at parties. They're too cool for that. If there are any games, they're likely to be kissing games. Boys and girls pair off, and they begin necking and petting—tentatively at first.

Tentatively. Every step toward new and awkward experience is tentative, most especially the first step. A girl may first overcome her inhibitions on a date with an older boy. A boy is likely to gain his first experience with a blind date or a girl from another community who's older and will take the initiative. Getting started is the hard part, remember? After that it gets easier.

How far do they go? A whole new world of physical sensation is opening up to them. They're drawn toward it, and scared of it. Because sex is private, parents don't know what their kids are really doing. Some parents are naïve enough to think their kids aren't doing much of anything; others, scared (and jealous) of the vast opportunities open to adolescents, imagine their kids are going all the way. Most aren't. It's still not usual for middle-class kids to have intercourse before college. Young girls wanting to be touched but fearing to be penetrated aren't often pushed all the way by young boys eager for satisfaction but anxious about performance (and its consequences). After they've been dating for a while, they are likely to engage in mutual masturbation, which provides some relief and usually plenty of guilt. It varies quite a bit, but most teenagers who date engage in a greater or lesser amount of sex play, which is likely to heighten tension rather than relieve it. No wonder their minds are filled with sex.

Another institution for boys and girls getting together is the school dance. All the ingredients for a good time are available here: music, decorations, refreshments, lust, hate, panic, and embarrassment. Dances promise a good time, and some kids with the sweet ease of the self-assured really enjoy themselves. The rest are waiting patiently to be admired, wishing but fearing to make the first move, or joking around to distract themselves from the main event. For most teenagers, the high school dance is one of life's first glimpses into The Inferno. Too many witnesses to one's awkwardness.

Boys and girls are scared and awkward about getting together. Some of this is simply inexperience. They don't know what to do, and they don't know what's expected. But that doesn't really explain the enormous anxiety about adolescent relationships. The reason there is so much shame-anxiety about young love is that love, the ultimate acceptance, calls for the maximum amount of openness. Love lures the shy self out of hiding and draws it to the soothing caress of another person's affection. But when you're exposed, you can get bruised.

Shame, like other hurts, is most traumatic when it's least expected. If a boy walks up to a girl and asks her to go to the movies, he knows she might say no. Knowing he could be turned down prepares him and cushions the shock. The same boy is likely to feel more ashamed by rejection if a girl he has been dating says she has too much homework to go to the movies, and he later finds out she went with someone else. Our egos are most exposed when we least expect attacks on our self-worth.

The fonder you are of someone and the closer you've been, the more rejection hurts. It feels like: This is the person who knows me, really *knows* me. If he or she doesn't want me, then something is definitely wrong with me. Life holds few hurts as bad as being rejected by someone you love.

Teenagers are alternately warmed by the approval and burned by the criticism of their peers. Shame-sensitive children who cannot tolerate burning rejection pull away from the group, avoiding the heat but losing the warmth. Some children give up social involvement because it's too costly. Some seek refuge with a steady. "Going with" somebody can be a natural outgrowth of self-respect and pride—two relatively secure people joining together in search of intimacy as part of the culmination of their development. Going steady can also be a safe haven—two shy people clinging together, giving and getting reassurance, lost in their own little world.

Despite what anxious parents think, movement toward the opposite sex does not arise from the sex drive alone. The narcissistic supplies needed to maintain and increase self-esteem are not as likely to come from friends as from the opposite sex. Friends accept you but take you for granted. And with friends there's always an undercurrent of rivalry. At a certain point in adolescence, children are expected to start dating, and prestige with friends of the same sex requires success with the opposite sex. So whether it is a culmination of self-respect or compensation for insecurity, or a little of both, in late adolescence children seek someone to complete them and admire them. It's called intimacy, a complex achievement, tied up in complex ways with identity.

ADOLESCENT REBELLION AND THE SEARCH FOR A SELF

According to Erik Erikson, "identity precedes intimacy."[4] That always made sense to me. After all, as Erich Fromm put it, in *The Art of Loving*, you have to love yourself before you can love someone else. Perhaps, but this truth, like many, also reflects unexamined male bias.

A boy's path to success was and is through the development of skills to accomplish and achieve. A girl's traditional path was preparing to attract the man by whose name she will be known and by whose status she will be defined. Today's girls are encouraged to develop their own skills and their own sense of self. Still, for girls, identity and intimacy are fused, whereas for boys identity—self-definition—comes first.

For young men, more so than for young women, adolescence is a struggle for identity in the sense of differentiation and autonomy. For men, *generativity* (Erikson's term meaning concern for and involvement with other people) is a mature accomplishment of mid-life (which is pretty late in the game considering that child-rearing comes earlier). Women don't have to learn generativity, it's steeped in their souls.

There has been a shift. The women's movement has successfully challenged our narrow view of the proper roles for men and women, but it hasn't altered the fact that women's lives, more so than men's, are embedded in relationships. Women have careers, but their identities are still tied up with attachment, care, and relationships; their integrity is tied up in an ethic of care.

The concept of *identity formation* suggests an active search for the creation of a self. Unfortunately, insecure children are often driven more by negative avoidance. They're too concerned with rejecting those aspects of themselves that they're ashamed of to discover who they are and want to be.

The search for a self—the famous *identity crisis*—comes from the effort to find harmony and integration among the many and diverse strivings that we've been considering, and not from the effort to create something new (a self). The self we know and show to the world is an amalgam of all that we are, our likes and dislikes, hopes and fears, talents and inhibitions, drives and defenses, pride and shame. The lucky ones forge selves dedicated to maximizing satisfaction and self-respect. The unlucky ones are more worried about minimizing shame and insecurity. (What they can't do well immediately, they won't do at all. Anything to avoid exposing gracelessness and ineptitude, painful frailties best kept hidden.)

Most teenagers go through a period of rebelliousness, defining themselves as independent through opposition to their parents.

(Parents trying to cope with teenagers are hereby forgiven for confusing self-assertion with insolence, and teenagers trying to cope with parents are likewise excused for mistaking their parents' worry for total lack of trust, but only until they get to be thirty.) Actually, adolescent rebellion serves a dual purpose: readjusting family boundaries and creating self-respect for teenagers as independent people. Rebellious adolescents are redefining themselves and redefining the family structure.

Most people understand that adolescent rebellion is normal and that it serves a purpose, but, as adults, we tend to misunderstand the child's experience by seeing it primarily in relation to ourselves. In the process, we exaggerate the "rebelliousness" and underestimate the inner turmoil of adolescents.

If we look at the family as a system in transformation, we can see teenagers as the vanguard for change. In pushing for autonomy they are attempting to loosen their ties to the family and redefine the rules of their relationship to their parents. Parents are reasonable. They understand the need for change, *slow* change. Teenagers are impatient. One minute they're reasonable, the next minute they're high-strung and hysterical. Their push for autonomy polarizes their parents into pulling harder to maintain family cohesion and to enforce the old rules, and vice versa. Conflict is almost certain because parents want to slow the transition ("If only they'd be responsible") and teenagers want to speed it up ("If only they'd respect me").

Early signs of "defiance" begin to occur at age twelve or thirteen. Preadolescents begin to argue about anything and everything—eating habits, clothes, chores, messy rooms, homework, and grades. The predictable battles take place over whatever the parents are most anxious and insistent about. A mother with few friends may nag her daughter about inviting other kids to do something together; a father who didn't get much education may pester his son into defiance over homework. The problem isn't really friends or homework or clothes or eating habits; the problem is that teenagers are challenging the rules that govern family relationships. Unfortunately, many parents overlook the circularity of these struggles: More control only produces more rebellion.

Parents who think of their teenagers as defiant confuse autonomous strivings with stubbornness. Most teenagers are strong-willed, not oppositional. They struggle, not to defy their parents but to achieve a measure of self-determination, and they struggle however hard it takes. How far they carry that struggle, how extreme their behavior, is determined largely by how tenaciously parents resist in an effort to retain control. A girl who cannot win control over how to dress for school may seek to express herself by putting on dramatic makeup after she leaves the house. If she cannot win that battle, she may escalate the conflict further, deliberately coming home late or getting into shouting matches with her mother. Or she may defy her parents by smoking cigarettes or shoplifting or experimenting with drugs. Reckless experiments, chancy relationships—all for the honor of taking defiant risks. So many dangerous attractions, and such ignorance!

Potentially destructive excesses of behavior are only the most obvious consequence of parental failure to accept their children and give them room to grow. Parents who hold on too tight too long force their children to develop negative identities. The more inflexible their parents are, the more defiant teenagers will be. Too many put-downs wear away at children's self-esteem and prompt them to reject everything about their parents. This can lead to a negative, shame-based identity. Some people are so ashamed of their parents that they spend their whole lives trying not to be like them. They're so busy *not being* their parents that there's no room left to be themselves.

It's doubly sad when people squander their youth resisting family ties and parental traits, and then in mid-life discover that they're becoming just like their parents. It feels as if you're trapped in your genes: "My God, I'm getting to be just like my father!"

Parents who are unfulfilled themselves, and with each other, have trouble letting go. They're too insecure to accept the child's growing autonomy and too self-doubting to realize that values instilled earlier will win out against the child's perplexing and disturbing experimentation. Parents who try too hard to control and protect their children may provoke them to rebel and reject out of hand family values they otherwise might only question.

Parents who need their children too much to let go exert an intrusive force that is impossible to ignore. Their children are so overwhelmed by their parents' attempts to control them that they have only two choices: submit or rebel.

The conflict between generations is complicated by turmoil within the parents and conflict between them. The dialectics of adolescent rebellion are not simply dyadic—between parents and child—but triadic. A mother who needs her children too much to let go is likely to be alienated from her husband. A father who insists that his children spend their spare time with him is unlikely to be enjoying the company of his wife.

Adolescence can be a second chance for self-respect. Teenagers can correct the narrow reality of the family, discovering dormant potentials in themselves and winning the esteem of their peers and the respect of their teachers. But for this to happen the child must venture far enough to be exposed to wider realities. Children must be secure enough in their parents' love that they neither try to please them by doing whatever they want, nor try to defy them by doing exactly the opposite.

Young children idealize their parents and draw close in order to draw strength from them. Adolescents repudiate their parents—or at least blind allegiance to them—and pull away in order to find strength in themselves. Teenagers don't want to be like Mommy and Daddy anymore; they want to be themselves. Self-respect demands that they prove to themselves that they are capable and do not need their parents to direct their lives. ("Please, Mother! I can do it myself!")

The sudden reversal of adolescent feelings toward parents is a measure of how urgent the need to create distance where once there was closeness. This withdrawal—repudiation, really—is still felt as a loss by teenagers. It causes them considerable sadness and pain.

The child's contradictory needs for distance and closeness are reflected in repetitive cycles of emotional withdrawal and emotional hunger. The same teenagers who reject their parents as

hopelessly out of step—hypocritical, selfish, and incompetent—
still need them. One minute they're stubbornly set on doing things
their own way, the next minute they're all uncertainty and doubt.
(*"Mom*, what should I wear?") Attunement—matching their
moods—is easy at this stage, like following behind a drunk driver
on an icy road.

When you're an adolescent, home may not necessarily be where
the heart is; still, it's important: a place to eat and sleep and soak
up strength and love. Unfortunately, many adolescents, struggling
to break out of the illusory self nurtured by their families through
latency, come under additional attack by parents who can't tolerate their teenagers' need to experiment with becoming their own
person. Struggling to maintain self-control and to achieve self-
expression, beset by conflicting emotions and under the impact of
insistent impulses, teenagers need a great deal of understanding,
at least tolerance. Parents who demand too much control and
deliver too many put-downs drive their children to war, with the
family and with themselves.

Fortunately, there is life after high school. In the years of young
adulthood we come into ourselves and learn to do a pretty good
imitation of being a grown-up. We leave home, make a start on
love and work, and learn to negotiate the world with some skill and
some ease. And yet we haven't resolved adolescent insecurity,
only submerged it. While we're wading through the preliminary
business of adulthood, our insecurity sits like a rock not too far
below the surface. I don't have to tell you how often we stumble
into it, sometimes bruising, sometimes bloodying, our toes.

We leave adolescence with a constructed self—a tentative self,
perhaps, but a self nonetheless. We've seen how that tentative self
is plagued by insecurity and haunted by shame. Now that I've
explained the dynamics of shame and its role in development, let's
see what parents can do to minimize shame and build self-respect
in their children.

12

....

Positive Parenting

Many perfectly normal, average, unhappy people have no memories of special injuries suffered from abusive parents on which to hang the blame for their insecurity. And so they're puzzled: If their parents didn't criticize or belittle or abuse them, why are they so insecure?

It's true that the heart's memory softens the bad and enhances the good, but it isn't true that well-being is merely the absence of abuse. And it isn't true that good parents are simply not bad parents. Self-respect requires positive parenting.

BUILDING YOUR CHILD'S SELF-RESPECT

Nobody has to tell parents that children need love; it comes naturally. When they smile, or splash in the bath, or run to your arms, how could you not love them? Their accomplishments are amazing, and so is their hunger for appreciation. We shower them with attention and applause, and they soak it up like thirsty flowers.

Raising a new human being is such a wonderful thing that parents can be forgiven if they are so smitten with their sweet darlings that they succumb to adoration. Baby worshipers begin with giggling and cooing, but once enraptured they cannot resist the laying on of hands. They tickle and poke and jiggle and shake, all the while chanting in a special high-pitched language. Finally, in the full throes of rapture, they bury their faces in the little one's fleshy folds and kiss them all over. Sometimes it appears to the uninitiated that the worshipers are hungry and determined to eat the objects of their idolatry, but it's only a regular service of baby worship.

We've all seen grown-ups at it. The fulsome tone of voice, the honey-sweet words, endlessly marveling and exclaiming. When babies are little, it's almost automatic. They're so animated themselves that they drive up the intensity of our response. Maybe our enthusiasm gets a little gooey, but at least it's sincere. Loving parents share the moods of their infants, and show it. Often this means exuberance. But it isn't exuberance, or any other emotion, that conveys loving appreciation; it's being noticed, understood, and taken seriously.

Baby worship is a sign of love, but its impact depends upon whether or not the parents' show of emotion matches the baby's rhythm. As you'll recall from Chapter 8, attunement, which is the foundation of attachment and security, means matching the baby's mood, not imposing your own giddy enthusiasm. Tenderness can't be forced. The mother open to loving the child-who-is lays her own sensibility aside and takes in and holds the child's, like a mirror or a twin. The child responded to is a self. The child whose feeling state is understood and responded to is a self respected.

Most parents know intuitively that a child's self-esteem needs all the support a parent can give. So until they lose their cool, parents make a point of praising their children's accomplishments: "Oh, Becky, that's a wonderful drawing! Can I hang it up?" And of course the child beams with pleasure. When a little boy or girl says, "Look at me! See what I can do!," the parent's "Yes, I see!" validates not only the performance but the developing self. The parent's witness is the self's nurture.

When they've been too busy or annoyed to respond warmly to

their children, most parents later feel guilty and attempt to make up for distraction and disinterest with forced enthusiasm and lavish shows of praise. But real love is based on acceptance, not praise.

Children need to be appreciated for who they are, not flattered or fawned over. Appreciation means acceptance. It's not cheerleading, rah-rah speeches that children need, it's acceptance—tolerance and appreciation and respect for the child's rights as an individual.

The way to demonstrate tolerance and acceptance is through empathy—putting yourself in the child's shoes, comprehending the child's momentary psychological state. It's easy when the child is cheerful, or when the two of you are sharing the same experience. For example, when you wake up to the first snowfall of the season and your child exclaims, "Oh, look at the snow!" it's easy to share the child's delight, "Yes, isn't it pretty!" putting aside any annoyance you might have about having to drive to work in the white stuff. Empathy is achieved by remaining open and receptive to the child's inner experience. It's hard when we're threatened, as most parents are by their children's hurt and anger.

Several years ago I was supervising a young therapist's play therapy with a depressed five-year-old. Week after week the little girl came in and played listlessly with the toys, and week after week the therapist came to supervision and complained that his little patient never expressed any feelings—no joy, no anger. And week after week I could think of little more to say than "Be patient." Finally, after about two months of treatment, the therapist called for an emergency supervisory session with me. It seems that he showed up late for a session, and the little girl got mad. She demanded to know why she always had to be on time, even if she didn't want to come, and complained that all the therapist ever did was pester her about what she was feeling. Instead of realizing that this was a breakthrough—the little girl finally got angry at something and trusted the therapist enough to show him—the therapist wor-

ried that the relationship had been ruptured, as though honest
anger would break a good relationship.
   If a therapist, trained to welcome any expression of feeling,
can lose perspective the instant a child turns her anger on
him, imagine how hard it is for parents to tolerate their own
children's expressions of anger.

Small children are fierce little engines of upset. When they get
going, it gets us going. And since it's natural to want to stop our
upset, we respond by denying theirs: "Don't cry." "It'll be all right."
"Don't worry."

Here is the writer Harold Brodkey describing a thirteen-year-old
boy's awareness that his mother cannot tolerate his upset.

If at any time restlessness showed in me or if I was unhappy even
about something very minor at school she would be upset. . . .
   I'd never brought up in conversation with her matters that had to do
with feelings of mine that were unclear or difficult: what good would
it have done? She would not have made the effort to understand; she
did not know how; she would only have felt lousy and been upset.[1]

The voice is, of course, Brodkey's. This thought could not be so
clearly articulated by a thirteen-year-old, who would feel only
anxiety and shame if his moody moments so aggravated his
mother. In the same passage, Brodkey has the boy saying, "All
right, her happiness rested on me." What a weight!

The parent who loves egoistically cannot bear the child's suffering. "Egoistically" is a cold word for it; the point is not that
some parents are selfish and unloving, rather that they love too
much and obliterate the boundary between themselves and their
children. If a mother isn't sure where her skin ends and the child's
begins, the child's pain is worse for her. The child's pain is her
pain. This may sound poetic, but a child burdened with being his
parents' consolation is cheated out of just one thing: a life of his
own.

Children have feelings, a rich variety of feelings in response to
the rich variety of life's experiences, and those feelings are as

innocent and unwilled as the color of their hair or eyes, but equally a part of who they are. When parents are aggravated by a child's excesses—of mood, of activity, of appetite, of energy, of fearfulness—they often respond with intolerance. Imagine saying to a child: "Oh, I don't like blond; that's an unpleasant color. As long as you are blond I won't pay attention to you, or the attention I do pay you won't like." Silly, right? But is it? There are hundreds of ways parents tell children not to feel what they feel, but they all boil down to: "Don't cry; it's all right." It's *not* all right!

"It's all right" is one of the biggest lies parents tell. Everything is "all right" if hurt isn't real, if the child's feelings don't count, if it doesn't matter that you shamed her or that Melissa said she was stupid. The misstatements of consolation are lies that seal away hurt as effectively as sweeping dirt under the carpet. If a parent, in his or her pride, does not allow a child to suffer, then a little pocket of suffering will be sealed away in memory, unexamined, unresponded to, unhealed.

Parents who cannot tolerate their children's anxiety give the children a power they don't need: the power to blackmail them with unhappiness. If a parent calmly acknowledges the child's upset, mild anxiety gives way to calmness. But some parents cannot make an imaginative leap into the child's life, cannot tolerate the child's upset, cannot keep it straight that parent and child are two different minds and sensibilities, rather than one wise adult and one little unformed mind needing control. Such parents often respond with trite, patronizing, comments: "It's okay." "Don't worry." "It doesn't matter." Children need something real, something authentic; not condescending kindness, but rather a sincere understanding of what they're feeling and a demonstration of tolerance of their right to those feelings.

The cranked-up sentimentality some parents pass off as appreciation may not be something you or I would do. But we might fall into the habit of trying to make our children happy and good by bribing them with praise. Ironically, lavish praise can have an unanticipated side effect. The seeds of perfectionism are sown whenever love, acceptance, and pride in self become contingent on performance. Children praised and admired primarily for their achievements may grow up to be highly successful, yet inside they may feel empty and alienated, loved for their accomplishments rather than for themselves.

The most important way for parents to build self-esteem in their children is not by praising them or by being permissive. It is by accepting and acknowledging the children's feelings, opinions, and wishes. Not giving them license to act however they wish, but validating their right to think and feel whatever they wish. Let children know you understand what they want, how they feel, and what they think, *and* that it's okay.

This principle is easy to understand—and easy to forget. For example, a family is coming out of a movie, everyone seems to have had a good time, and ten-year-old Suzi pipes up, "I didn't like it; it was boring." She's not unhappy, just stating her opinion. But that's not the way Dad hears it. He picked out the movie and is attached to his choice. So he snaps, "You never like anything! You're such a grouch!" Suzi feels ashamed and shuts up. Next time she'll know better than to say what she thinks.

If she were more grown-up than most of us ever are, Suzi might simply get angry at her father for being intolerant. But when little kids (from about two to fifty or so) get yelled at, they feel bad about themselves. Children *internalize* their parents' reactions, take them inside and make them their own. What was her crime? Having an opinion? Not liking something? Daring to be different from her father?

The best way to help build children's self-respect is not to teach them that they are terrific (strong, pretty, smart), but that they are okay. Okay is better than terrific. It's real.

HOW TO RECOGNIZE WHEN A CHILD IS ASHAMED

Children are famous for their honesty, and they're not shy about announcing what they want either: "Cookie!" "I wanna go home!" But often, when it comes to their most important and conflicted emotions, children cannot or do not put their feelings directly into words. Instead, they show us signals, often nonverbal. Shame is too complex and frightening to talk about in the usual way. Children can't usually *tell* their parents that they're ashamed; they can only *show* it by their actions.

The signs of shame are nonverbal: lowering the eyes, hanging the head, blushing, running out of the room. Embarrassment, the mildest version of shame, is not too difficult to spot, partly because it usually arises in an obvious social context. When little ones are embarrassed about showing off or meeting strangers, they may hide behind Mommy or Daddy, or if they're home, they may run out of the room. Since embarrassment is less painful than acute shame, older children may tell you that you're embarrassing them. When parents shame their children inadvertently—by finding fault or praising them in front of their friends—the children usually respond with a jokey protest: *"Mom . . . c'mon, Mom!"* It's not the criticism or the praise; it's the audience. With shame, the audience is all important.

More troublesome and harder to spot is the acute shame that a parent inflicts on a child. It's hard to see and sympathize with the child's shame when we're caught up in an emotional interchange. This usually occurs in one of two ways. The first is the cold, cutting comment delivered by a parent who cannot or does not control the child more directly: "Never mind, *I* took out the garbage; God knows when *you'd* ever get around to it." "You make me sick." "You're such a baby!"

Young children usually react to this kind of humiliation by crying and protesting. And that's when worse trouble can start. A shamed child is in real pain. He's not just mad or sad, he's scalded. Put yourself in the child's place. Think of yourself as a ten-year-old. You forgot to clean your room and your father screams at you. You're little and he's a giant. His face is immense and twisted with rage. You can feel his heat. The Daddy-who's-supposed-to-love-you screams terrible things at you. How would you feel?

Parents locked in battle with their children may not understand or accept what the child is feeling. We lump their agitation into familiar categories—"mad," "upset," "temper tantrum"—and be-

cause shame is not one of those familiar categories, the shamed
child is cheated out of understanding.

*Twelve-year-old Doreen was the official patient in the DeSilva
family, but as far as I was concerned the major problem was
that Mrs. DeSilva took out her frustration over an unhappy
marriage on her daughter. Mr. DeSilva worked long hours and
brought work home with him. His computer was a distraction
that shielded him from daily emotional involvement with his
children. He was "concerned" but distant, abandoning his children to the wife whose anger he could not deal with. Most of
the first few sessions were taken up by Mrs. DeSilva's complaints about Doreen: She never cleaned her room. She
dumped wet laundry in the hamper. She borrowed her mother's things without asking. Et cetera, et cetera. All the heat in
the family was in this pair, locked in a cycle of control and
rebellion. My strategy was to pull them apart, get Mr. DeSilva
more involved with discipline, and maybe then wake up the
sleeping conflict that kept husband and wife apart.*

*Mrs. DeSilva readily agreed to step back and let her hus-
band step in. She was tired of all the fighting and tired of playing the bad guy. Let him do it. Where she was shrill, he was
reasonable. (Why not? He didn't care as much.) He explained
things carefully to Doreen and tried not to criticize her too
much. Things went better until one evening when Doreen had
a temper tantrum and Mr. DeSilva blew up. He told her to finish her milk, and she became hysterical and ran up to her
room. Why did she do that? I wondered. He didn't know. So I
set up what family therapists call an enactment, a dialogue in
the session designed to reveal the family's dynamics: who talks
to whom, in what way, and who does or doesn't interrupt.*

*"This is puzzling. Would you talk with her now to see if you
can help her put her feelings into words? Help her explain
why she got so upset. Here, let me turn your chairs to face
each other."*

"Why didn't you want to drink your milk?"
"I didn't feel good."

He then proceeded to give her a long, oh-so-reasonable ex-
planation of why she should have finished the milk. He'd al-
ready poured the milk, she needs to drink more because the
pediatrician said that would help her get fewer sore throats,
she doesn't drink enough milk, milk is an essential ingredient
for building strong bones, and so on and so on. Mr. DeSilva
was very reasonable. Meanwhile, his twelve-year-old daugh-
ter's head was sinking slowly into her chest. So I intervened.

I went over to Mr. DeSilva and shook his hand. "Congratula-
tions."
"What for?"
"You were great."
"What do you mean?"
"You won, she lost."
"But that's silly, that's not the point."
"Oh?"

Because he was caught up in his own point of view, Mr. DeSilva
couldn't see Doreen's. Couldn't see that by lecturing her about
how stupid she was, he was humiliating her. She couldn't tell him
what she was feeling because she didn't understand; she just felt
bad. She'd tell him later, just like she told her mother—by not
cleaning her room, by picking on her little brother, and by mis-
placing things.

Probably the hardest time to recognize a child's shame is when
it's most important, when a shamed child becomes enraged. When
a child feels humiliated, he may become foot-stompingly outraged;
he is I-am-wronged! Let him rage if he needs to, or run out of the
room if he must. That's where kids run into trouble. When they are
acutely ashamed and the exit is blocked. This often happens when
parents cannot distinguish between a temper tantrum and a furious shame reaction.

One of the easiest ways to spot a temper tantrum is to notice
when it occurs. If it happens right after the child has been told,
"No, you can't have that," the message is fairly simple. By scream-

ing and crying, the frustrated child is trying to force the parents to bend to his wishes. (Children reared in homes where discipline is relatively clear-cut know that a tantrum will not work.) If the emotional display is a dramatized attempt to get what the child wants, remove the audience; leave the room.

Parents are susceptible to temper tantrums because they can't stand to let their children cry and carry on. The same anxious intolerance makes them interfere with a shamed child who just wants to be left alone.

When your child bursts into tears and runs out of the room, it's natural to want to go after him. It's natural to want to soothe the child or talk him out of his "temper tantrum." But children who run out of the room aren't asking to be soothed. No kid is dumb enough to throw a temper tantrum away from the audience. A child who runs into his room crying is upset, possibly ashamed, and wants to be left alone.

Give children room to hide when they need to. It's an exercise in realizing the limits of parental control. We can't control their feelings; we can't prevent them from getting hurt, and we can't make hurt go away. We can comfort them when they're upset and want to be comforted. But often when they run crying into their rooms it's because someone made them feel ashamed, and shame is so painful that they've momentarily lost control of their feelings. They need time alone to regain their composure. Let them have it.

Unfortunately, adults who don't recognize a shame reaction, or can't tolerate a child's upset, get into a pattern that makes things worse. They demand to know what's wrong, as if a child convulsed with emotion could say.

The shamed child already has a sense of rage and dismissal, as though his experience is a fact that is being ignored, trampled on, and belittled. As long as the parent keeps badgering the child, the fantastic wrongness of shame is aggravated by anger and helplessness. If the parent persists and blocks the child's exit, the child's outrage swells into a moral hysteria. Every atom in the child's being screams: *"Leave me alone!"* *"Let me out of here!"*

*   *   *

Children don't label their experience as shame. Imagine a little boy storming out of the room in tears after his mother told him that she took the garbage cans out to the curb because the garbage man came early. Why would a child get so upset? Only being ashamed of himself for being irresponsible can explain the intensity of the boy's reaction. But if you asked him what was wrong, he'd probably say, "Mommy yelled at me!," or perhaps, "Nothing, leave me alone!" What can you say? Nothing. Leave him alone.

What to do while the child is out of the room: Think about what might have shamed him. How might you have offended his dignity? How might you have treated him like a baby? Did you imply that his opinion is wrong or doesn't count? That his feelings aren't legitimate? The way to decode an "excessive" or "inappropriate" emotional response is to figure out the personal significance that would explain it. Injuries to self-respect can be as bruising as muggings.

What to do when he comes back: After the shamed child has calmed down a little, you can approach him and begin to restore the bond of understanding. Don't expect an angry, ashamed child to get over the rage right away. Rather than ask, "Why were you so upset?" let the child know that you already have some understanding by saying something like, "Boy, you're really mad." The instant the child feels understood, there will be an immediate release of feeling. Acknowledge his feelings, but don't expect to be immediately rewarded. Expect an angry response and accept it.

The same sensitive children who become enraged with shame often pester their parents with excessive bragging.

When a child demands "too much" attention or seeks "too much" praise, some parents feel they should curb the child's craving, lest the child become spoiled or addicted to attention. This is an exaggerated fear. The child who demands attention is demanding what she needs. If your child boasts, give her a little taste of what she wants: a hero's happiness. Every child dreams of consequentiality.

It may be hard to respond enthusiastically to a child who is bragging. At least be understanding, be tolerant. Recognize that children need to have their healthy exhibitionism responded to; be responsive.

TEACHING COMPETENCE: AUTONOMY VS. SHAME AND DOUBT

So far my message to parents has been simple, emphasizing one thing above all else: tolerance. Self-respect is a product of acceptance and appreciation. Show your children respect by accepting and acknowledging their opinions, their feelings, and their individuality. But this message only pertains to half a parent's job: nurturance. Now I want to discuss the other half: teaching and disciplining children so that they will grow up competent and respectful of the rights of others.

According to Erik Erikson, the second year of life, when the toddler is developing muscular control, is a critical period during which the child gains a lasting sense of autonomy, or when shaming and loss of self-esteem lead to a pervasive sense of doubt and shame.[2] Like Freud, Erikson exaggerated the extent to which development occurs in critical stages; the alternatives he describes are major but ongoing determinants of the child's self-image. A sense of mastery makes a child feel proud and contributes to self-respect, whereas a sense of incompetence leads to self-doubt and insecurity.

Small children are thrilled when they can do things for themselves. They love the independence and autonomy of self-care, but they easily become frustrated by failure. Too much failure leads to shame and insecurity. It isn't, of course, just the child's abilities that count, but how parents respond to the child's efforts.

Unfortunately, parents are often more focused on what they can teach their children than responsive to the child's own initiatives. Most parents are obsessed with teaching and preaching. Letting children be who they are and become all that they can be means not hurrying them to grow up, not trying to teach them before they're ready. The parent who ridicules, laughs at, or gets angry at the child's failures makes the child ashamed and insecure. That's obvious. Just as important, if less obvious, parents who push children to attempt too much too soon are also fostering insecurity.

Wise parents take a healthy middle ground between doing everything for their children and doing nothing for them. Every time I make a suggestion like this—especially one so brilliant as "take a healthy middle ground"—I'm aware that as parents we tend to be blind to our own biases. The parent who's inclined to do too much for her children thinks that approach is natural, while the parent who doesn't help enough thinks that he is doing the right thing. The fact that parents sometimes come in pairs, with different ideas about how to raise children, leads to a certain amount of tension, but it also makes it possible to correct biases—*if both parents express their ideas and work out compromises.* The other important thing to keep in mind is that children's responses to their parents should be considered feedback, information about what works and what doesn't.

Recognize and encourage success, but *do not* make the mistake of magnifying the stakes by lavishly praising accomplishments. Take a light attitude toward successes and failures, especially when the kids are little.

Children between the ages of three and six need to discover that they can master a variety of skills in spite of their frustrations. They need encouragement to sustain their efforts—encouragement, not a lot of pushing. Remember, the most important thing for parents to teach their children is not how to do any particular thing but to feel a sense of mastery and to feel good about themselves.

How should a parent respond to a child's inevitable slip-ups in the process of acquiring bodily mastery? With tolerance. That means accepting that children make mistakes *and* accepting that they feel bad about those mistakes. This challenge begins acutely with toilet training. Some children are extremely ashamed of "mistakes." Let them know it's okay: "That's okay, honey, you don't have to be grown up all at once." And if they do get upset, let them know you understand that, too: "You feel bad, don't you?"

Yes, but we all screw up sometimes; we all lose our tempers and yell at the kids or show disgust. What can you do when that happens? Don't expect yourself to be perfect. Remember, a parent's minor empathic failures contribute to a child's formation of a stronger self by teaching them to rely on themselves for understanding and forgiveness. What should you do if you inadvertently shame your child? Speak to the child after you both calm down. Apologize. Will an apology after the fact undo the hurt from a traumatic humiliation? No, but it will help the child learn that humiliating interchanges may be someone else's fault. This helps inoculate the child against future humiliation.

THE CHILD'S RIGHTS AND YOURS

The two biggest mistakes we parents make are: (1) not establishing sufficient control over our children's behavior, and (2) interfering too much in their lives. Both problems stem from a failure to distinguish between the child's rights and our own.

Parents with self-respect love their children and do a lot for them, but they still maintain and protect a boundary around their own lives. Moreover, they respect the children's rights to think and feel and choose what they want—maybe not always to *do* what they want but certainly to want.

Parents who confuse love with permissiveness fall into a pattern of not setting and enforcing rules. Such parents spend a lot of time nagging. Ineffectual nagging comes about when parents try to control too much of their children's behavior. It starts early, when parents translate love into lenience.

There is a false dichotomy between being strict and being kind—actually, they tend to go together. To remain sympathetic to children, it is necessary to teach them to obey. A parent locked in a struggle for control with a child is too exasperated to show consistent understanding of the child's feelings.

Effective parents establish firm control early in their children's lives, and use it sparingly. They make clear and consistent rules *and* back them up. Children learn from consequences. If the consequence of every third or fourth thing they do is that their parents nag them, they will learn that their parents are nags and that they themselves are not worthwhile.

The most common alternative to effective discipline is yelling. Yelling at kids, like nagging, wounds their pride, and does more to add to the quota of shame than to establish discipline. A child who gets yelled at—to you it may feel like explaining, to them it's yelling—feels he is being bossed around, feels hated, feels that nothing he ever does is any good.

A Healthy Family Has Clear Boundaries

A clear boundary between generations puts the parents in charge, allows them to claim their own rights and privacy, and helps them respect the children's freedom and autonomy within their own orbit.

One reason children misbehave is that parents don't form a united front. Children aren't strong enough to resist a parent's authority unless they are standing on someone else's shoulders. Children identify with their parents. When one parent deprecates the other (such a spineless way to fight back!), the child may take pleasure in being treated as a confidant. Parent and child are partners in crime: "We think Mommy's outbursts are hysterical." "Don't pay any attention to your father; you know how he is." Unfortunately, the child is mocking part of himself.

Another place where it's important to honor the boundary between generations is in handling sibling rivalry. Sibling rivalry is not just a matter of competitiveness and the selfishness of spoiled children. It's rooted in an absorbing and relentless desire to be loved and valued. The daily and usually excruciating struggles between siblings come about because a child cannot allow himself to be second best or devalued, much less left out. ("You gave him more!") The shakier the child's feeling of worth, the more minutely he has to compare himself to those around him to make sure he doesn't come off second-best.

Don't interfere. Let brothers and sisters work out their own differences. They may fight and be mean to each other—some of that is inevitable—but if parents interfere, the fights will never get settled, only interrupted, and the kids won't learn how to handle conflict with peers. Sibling rivalry comes from a blind drive to be special. Show each child that he or she is special, but stay out of their fights.

Poor discipline and intrusiveness make parents intolerant of their children, and so does failing to lead full satisfying lives of their own. One of the most important tasks for parents is to preserve their own lives—separately, by keeping themselves vital and happy; and together, by making time for their intimate relationship. Parents whose own narcissistic needs (satisfaction, attention, and appreciation) aren't met, often use their children for narcissistic gratification.

It is in the family that American men and women try to make up for the anxieties and deprivations suffered in the outer world. If our jobs make us feel inadequate and we fail to establish our personal autonomy in the outside world, then we attempt all the more to exercise control in the family. This leads many parents to blur the boundary between themselves and their children. One of the saddest things parents do is use children to live out their own dreams and live up to their expectations. Our love and their littleness makes us think we own them, tempts us to run their lives. Don't. Let them be themselves.

When our children make the mistake of daring not to be invented by us, when they reveal, perversely, minds and wills of their own, we are greatly troubled. It starts with the "terrible twos," that period in the careers of novice parents when they first reveal their frustration and intolerance of the fact that their small fry want to become little persons in their own right. Imagine getting worked into a temper just because a tiny child is practicing autonomy. Many times I've reminded patients and friends who complain about their children's willfulness and defiance that they will someday be proud of their children's spunk and strength of character. Children *should be* full of energy and hard to tame—other people's children, anyway.

As children grow, parents should allow them more volitional control and show increasing respect for their ideas and opinions. "Because I said so" is the best answer to a small child who wants to know why he has to do something. Older children deserve an explanation. This shift conveys respect for the child and helps build self-respect as well as responsibility.

Parents who respect the child's rights, and their own, are best able to handle fights—I mean "disagreements." Explain the "no": "No, I won't drive you to the concert on Sunday night, because I don't want to drive that far, and I don't want you out on a school night." But don't argue. Don't debate. And don't escalate: "If you dare take the bus, I'll ground you for a month."

One more point: These confrontations may be humiliating for your children. They're getting older and beginning to think of themselves as mature. They see your "no" as a put-down. If they need to storm out, don't block the exit. Let them cool off.

LISTENING

The single insistent theme of this chapter is: Parents build children's self-respect by accepting them. Once you learn to distinguish between your rights and theirs, the most important thing to remember is to honor your children's worth as individuals by accepting and appreciating them. Translating this into practice means learning to listen.

Perhaps you've noticed that a lot of adults don't listen very well. Some people are obvious about it, like the men and women who always seem to talk about themselves: their days are busier, their problems larger, their aches and pains worse, and their successes more significant than yours. Some people ask you about yourself, but you get the feeling they don't understand and don't care. It's cold, and it hurts. Most of us learn to take turns, but the best turn is our turn. From the boors who talk constantly about themselves, to the reticent ones who avoid hurt feelings by keeping their feelings in check, we all hunger to express what's in our minds and hearts, and to be listened to and understood. The need, expressed or suppressed, is greatest in grown-up children who weren't understood and appreciated when they were young.

Little children leave no doubt about their need for their parents' time and attention. They clamor for it like hungry little animals.

To listen well, a parent must hold his or her needs in check. This is easier if your needs are being met. But, easy or hard, listening is part of your job as a parent.

Suppose you come home from one of those terrible, mind-numbing days at the office, and your child starts to tell you she's bored: "There's nothing to do." You say: "Don't be so negative, there's plenty to do. Why don't you call Kim and see if she can play?" Wrong answer. The most important thing to do is simply acknowledge what the child is feeling: "Nothing to do? That's too bad, honey. Have you been bored all afternoon?" It's easier to listen if you don't rush to solve the child's problems for her, or defend yourself against the need to by denying them. Another trick that makes it easier to listen is to remember that children's requests and complaints have an *expressive* and an *instrumental* component. First, acknowledge the expressive component; worry about the instrumental part second: "Why do we have to go there!" "You hate it, don't you?"

When parents are put on the defensive, they often respond in ways that shame their children. Take, for example, the constant questions of a four-year-old: "Why is the sky blue?" "Why does the sun shine?" Your aim in answering should be to respect and encourage curiosity and initiative, not discourage it. Give simple answers. If you're stumped, ask the child: "I don't know, what do you think?" Most children already have or think they have an answer to the question they're asking.

"Why are hills high?"

"That's a good question, why do you think?"

"Because the Indians piled up the dirt."
Accept the child's answer, don't criticize.
"Oh, that's interesting, who told you that?"
"The kids at the park said the hills were Indian mounds."

It's foolish to play the child's game of protesting the rules with an endless series of rhetorical questions: "But *why* do we have to go?" Most questions, however, are sincere and deserve an answer. Don't ignore or dismiss children's questions. They are the child's way of showing initiative. Questions can also open doors to the imagination. Indulge your children's imaginative flights. Listen and follow, even lead a little.

I remember one time my son and I were walking across the Brooklyn Bridge. I'd seen so many romantic pictures of the bridge and always dreamed about seeing it for myself. As we walked back from the Brooklyn side, I was drinking in the fabulous Manhattan skyline and ignoring my son. When he interrupted my reverie by asking, "How much would it take to buy Manhattan?" I was annoyed. What a question! I'll bet even Donald Trump couldn't answer that one. But I tried to respond: "I don't know, Paul, probably many, many billions of dollars."

"If I owned a time machine, I would go back in time and buy New York City. Then I would rent it out, but only to people who agreed to keep it clean." And he went on from there, building a wonderfully imaginative plan for making New York a fantastic place to live, filled with special delights for both of us. Listening to his fantasy turned out to be the best part of the whole weekend.

Little children can be hard to listen to because they talk so much; older children can be hard to understand because there's so much they don't want to talk about. A classic example is when a parent asks, "What did you do in school today?" and the child answers, "Nothing." It hurts to be shut out.

Listening to your children means listening to what they're saying—even if it's "Leave me alone"—not making them say what you want to hear. Teenagers may not want to discuss anything having to do with their sexuality. It's private. The same may apply to less obviously personal subjects, like what their friends are doing or what happened in school. Children avoid talking about subjects that are too personal or make them feel vulnerable. There are moments, like at the end of a long and tedious day at school, when almost anything feels too personal to discuss. After a day of being the subject and object of close attention at school, children often just want to be left alone. Their "nothing" isn't coy or lazy or withholding, it's self-protective. They're telling you that the subject makes them feel more vulnerable than they want to feel. Respect the child's boundary around the personal. Show interest, but don't press. If the child doesn't want to talk, back off.

What children don't want to talk about has to do with timing as well as topic. Busy parents are eager to make the most of the precious time they have with their children. When they're together, they want to hear all about what's going on in the children's lives. But the kids may not feel like talking at that moment. You can't program "meaningful" conversation. Kids tend to talk seriously only when it's their idea. This usually occurs spontaneously, in the midst of everyday routine. That's why "quality time" is no substitute for being there.

Whether and when children feel free to open up to their parents depends upon the reception they expect. If you demonstrate to your children that they can talk things over with you, without fear or judgment, they will. If you don't, they won't. If you accept your children's right to protect themselves with silence when they feel the need, and demonstrate understanding when they do express themselves, they will open up to you, in their own good time.

LETTING YOUR CHILDREN GROW UP

One reason being a parent remains an amateur sport is that as soon as you get the hang of dealing with your children, they get a little older and throw you a whole new set of problems. Successful parents must learn to shift their style of parenting to accommodate their children's development.

Although children are constantly growing and maturing, the process is usually slow enough to allow parents to keep up. There are, however, at least two times when events quicken and it's a real challenge to accommodate: one is adolescence, the other is starting school.

When they leave home to venture off into twelve or twenty years in the educational system, children go armed with more or less self-respect, depending upon the security of self-worth and ideals built up in the early years of childhood. Children leave home to go to school, but they do not, of course, leave their families. (Despite what some "independent" people think, we never leave our families.) The nature of the school experience depends very much on the parents' response. If the boundary between family and school is clear, parents will give children enough room to explore, while still providing emotional refueling in the form of reassurance and support. If this boundary is diffuse, parents will interfere too much. If it is rigid, parents won't know what's going on, and won't be there to help when necessary.

Handling the beginning of school illustrates how positive parents respect their children's right and need to grow up during a period when the parents are still clearly in charge. Now let's turn to adolescence, a transitional period—for teenagers learning to become adults *and* for parents learning to become parents of adult children—when control gradually shifts from parent to child. One self-image has to give way and be replaced by another, and one style of parenting has to be modified to adjust to the adolescent's growing autonomy. The more room parents give, the less need teenagers have to rebel.

The first commandment for parents of adolescents should probably be: Thou shalt not become a force against which to rebel. The three most common ways to break this commandment are trying to overcontrol teenage children, overreacting to their challenge to parental ideas and values, and interfering with their allegiance to the peer culture.

Some parents are willing to grant freedom, but cannot tolerate rudeness. Like everything else in family life, adolescent rudeness is a function of interaction. It's not just something *they* do; it's something they do in reaction to their parents. Teenagers demand to be treated like people with a right to their own opinions. Often without realizing it, parents insist on talking to teenagers from the same one-up position they used when the children were small. The "rude" response is a protest against what feels like a shameful put-down. For example, most eight-year-olds will accept their parents' right to end a discussion with "Because I said so . . ." Most fifteen-year-olds won't. Don't provoke rudeness by talking down to your teenagers. And—this is important—you can avoid escalating arguments into power struggles by tolerating your children's right to *say* what they think, even if it means calling you names or using language you don't like.

Another reason for rudeness is that adolescents become intolerant of their parents. The same children who once looked up to Mommy and Daddy as giants who can do no wrong, now look down on them as old fogies who can't do anything right. This disdainful attitude is a natural stage in the evolution of the family system and the evolution of the self. If parents are threatened and fight back, they fuel an escalating series of conflicts, which in many cases are never settled, only broken off when the children leave home.

Adolescent fault-finding should not be mistaken for disrespect. Even when they begin to speak in those hateful condescending tones, adolescents still respect and identify with their parents. Insolence and identification occur at different levels of consciousness. Ironically, while they oscillate between asceticism and indulgence, adolescents continue to have excessive internal standards. In an effort to contain their impetuous and unruly desires, they exaggerate standards of conscience to minimize conflict. They tend to judge their parents by these same standards.

Teenagers try to make up for the painful loss of dependence on their parents with relationships outside the family. They now look away from the family for models of identification, which become more compelling as the need for shoring up self-respect becomes greater. In early adolescence, children, especially girls, are sustained by passionate friendships. Later, these give way to crushes, which in turn lead to dating—or what passes for dating these days.

Wise parents respect their teenagers' right, and need, to spend time with and be loyal to their friends. This doesn't mean that "So-and-so does it" is an adequate justification for their staying out later than you want them to on a school night or letting them go to unsupervised parties, but it does mean that you should be as tolerant as possible of your children's need to accommodate to the culture of their peers. Empower your children to make decisions on their own. Remind them that they have choices, and that they don't have to do things they don't want to do just to go along with the crowd. But at the same time, be sensitive to their awkwardness and anxiety about social pressures.

Some of the self-confidence associated with adulthood comes not from increasing maturity but from the fact that by controlling the choice of companions and social settings, adults can construct their world in a manner that enables them to display talents and avoid betraying faults. Adolescents are insecure because every day they are exposed and tested and denied the opportunity adults have to avoid situations that reinforce self-doubt. Understand the oppression of being watched and respect their need for privacy.

The dynamics of adolescent rebellion may be simple, but parenting never is. Adolescents still need access to their parents. For all their proud self-assertion, they are children, and they still need support and understanding. The boundary between parent and child should be clear enough to give adolescent children room to grow and explore but not rigid enough to deny them the nurture they still need. Give them roots, and then give them wings.

Respect and tolerance are the mature, self-confident parents' responses to their children's growth and development. While these important responses are relatively silent, especially when heartfelt and genuine, they are nevertheless pervasive. They are an expression of parents' relative self-respect as individuals and relative cohesiveness as a couple. Parents who respect themselves and each other will welcome and respect their children's growth toward self-reliance.

Positive parenting is a balancing act. Children need nurturance and control, but, as I've explained, this must be balanced with respect and tolerance for their growing autonomy. Of course it's easier to accept and respect your kids if you accept and respect yourself. In the chapters that follow, I will describe how to expand the limits of the self—not by denying problems, but by facing shame and choosing self-respect.

III

·······

BREAKING THROUGH
TO SELF-RESPECT

13
· · · · · · ·

Facing Shame and Breaking Through to Self-respect

THE PROBLEM OF CHANGE

Once there was a hopeless neurotic, an obsessive-compulsive who could not stop tearing paper. The experts tried everything—analysis, drugs, even shock treatment—all to no avail. The patient was so preoccupied with tearing paper into little strips that he couldn't work, couldn't eat, couldn't sleep. In desperation, they called in the greatest expert of them all, Mel Brooks. Imagine Brooks as a psychiatrist: that pugnacious fireplug draped in a dirty white coat, stethoscope hanging around his neck, the wild hair, and that gravelly, insinuating voice. After a careful interview, Brooks the brilliant hit upon the solution; he commanded the patient: "Stop tearing paper!"

This case study taught me that although the truth is sometimes simple, many people can't seem to do the one thing they most need to. If the paper-tearing patient were around today, he could probably find books exploring the Paper-Tearing Syndrome and experts eager to blame the whole thing on his parents. He might be comforted to have a label for his problem, reassured to know he's not alone, and perhaps feel vindicated by the status of victimhood. But would he stop tearing paper and start facing what he's afraid of? Not likely. Real personal change is rare and difficult.

Many people seek psychotherapy for their griefs and longings, hoping to change their luck by changing themselves. Psychotherapy *can* help, but entering psychotherapy doesn't bring about change, only confronting personal limits and conquering fears does that—inside or outside of therapy.

Before we can reach self-respect we must face shame. The alternative—ignoring shame or pretending it doesn't exist—results in, at best, a facade of confidence. Real self-respect takes more than positive thinking; it takes active change. We must break through avoidance and denial, face the truth about why we rely on these mechanisms of defense, and we must go beyond understanding to forge honest relationships based on sharing the self we really are and not on performing a self we think others will like.

Real and lasting change comes from looking in and reaching out. Cutting through repression and ignorance of one's own mind reveals hidden wants and fears. This increased understanding is a start not a finish, a means to expand the range of experience, to feel more, to think more, and to do more. Understanding initiates change, but exercising understanding takes courage, takes action.

Instead of working harder to deny shame, we can work harder to understand it, and we can act to begin overcoming its grip on our lives. Genuine self-respect is founded on acceptance and understanding. Reversing the development process by which we learned to be ashamed begins with uncovering and facing that shame.

FACING SHAME

Facing shame means three things. First, we must recognize the role it plays in our lives: Beneath our insecurity and avoidance lies shame, making us hold back and leaving us so sensitive that we overreact to criticism and rejection. Second, we must begin to understand all the ways we hide from shame: our defensive mechanisms, habits of avoidance, and techniques of distraction. Finally, we must discover what it is about ourselves that we are ashamed of.

We discovered in the first part of this book that we don't usually appreciate the role shame plays in our lives because its effects work below the surface of awareness. Shame is so painful that we hide from it. We learn not to face the painful discrepancy between the self we wish we were and the self we think we are. We cope. We don't take risks and we don't reveal certain wants and needs; instead, we develop habits of avoidance that enable us to live and act with a certain security. If we don't have much fun or make friends easily, don't take chances, and worry about what people might think if we said what we thought and did what we wanted, we tell ourselves that's what it means to be a grown-up. The result is a lingering feeling that something is missing and a nagging fear of unworthiness.

So although we don't often see it, shame organizes our lives and shapes the face we turn to the world. Beginning to understand shame and avoidance is the beginning of being able to do something about it.

As you'll recall from Chapter 7, shame originates in anxiety over self-expression and the need for acceptance. When we express ourselves and are appreciated, we feel proud. But when we express ourselves to someone who turns away or criticizes, we feel scorned. The closer to the heart the expression, the more humiliating the rejection. We feel flawed: dirty, weak, defective—ashamed—all of which raises the specter of unlovability. It hurts and we want to hide.

Facing shame involves recognizing it, understanding how it works, and confronting what we are ashamed of, but in life, unlike books, this is all part of one process, as the following example illustrates.

When Darcie went back to graduate school at age forty-one, she felt insecure and out of place. She was certainly as smart as the other people in her program, but they all seemed so sure of themselves. They didn't hesitate to speak up in class, whether or not they had anything worthwhile to say. Her own reticence, she felt, was not only isolating her, but also making her resent her self-assured classmates for dominating the airspace. So when she attended a visiting professor's lecture, she

*resolved to force herself to ask a question. The talk was pomp-
ous and abstract, but Darcie understood it well enough to
raise a question about one of the professor's points. As soon as
she sat down, one of the radical instructors in her department
stood up to say that Darcie had missed the point entirely, and
then went on to say what he always said, that the whole thing
was a matter of the* haves *exploiting the* have-nots. *Darcie was
mortified. She knew her position was valid, but she couldn't
stand being put-down like that, and so she withdrew even further into silence.*

*There are two points I'd like to make about this story. The
first is that avoidance feeds on itself. The less we risk, the less
we venture, the riskier venturing becomes. By speaking up so
rarely, Darcie made herself extremely vulnerable when she
did say something. (If Mel Brooks were around, he'd tell her to
speak up more.)*

*The second point is even more important. What was Darcie
ashamed of? She thought the problem was "speaking up"—she
was "shy," "reticent," "afraid of getting criticized." All that is
certainly true as far as it goes, but it doesn't go far enough.
When people rise to ask a question at a public lecture, they
may simply be seeking clarification, but often the latent
agenda is either showing off or being aggressive. (The more
apprehensive one is about saying something, the more likely
one of these hidden motives is operating.)*

*It turned out that Darcie was ashamed of both showing off
and being aggressive. Neither continued silence nor more
speaking up alone would have resolved her isolation. What
did help was understanding that she was ashamed of showing
off and getting angry, and discovering how she got that way.
(Remember, it's hard to think about how you* learned *to be
ashamed and* feel *ashamed at the same time.)*

*Darcie grew up in a large family where calling attention to
yourself was discouraged. "Good children" looked after themselves and didn't make waves. These things weren't exactly
said, but they were powerfully enforced by concealed coer-*

*cions. Conflicts were never openly expressed and anger was
something you swallowed. Darcie's parents tiptoed around
their differences and taught Darcie that being loved meant being "nice."*

*Darcie's uncovering her anger illustrates the discovery pro-
cess of facing shame. Later we'll see how she moved toward
self-respect by learning to express her anger.*

The place to look for shame is behind avoidance. What if Darcie
were to speak up more in class, what would that mean to her?
What if you were to do what you're shy about doing, what would
that mean? Take note of when you hold back and when you are on
the defensive. How do you feel? How do you behave? What do you
say and do? And what do you *not* say or do? If you are willing to
put in a little time and effort, and stir up a little anxiety, you can
make a list with two columns: situations you avoid or that put you
on the defensive, and the style of your defensive maneuvers. You
probably already know a great deal about your own avoidance and
defensiveness, but if you are willing to learn a little more, ask
someone you trust to go over your list and discuss it with you.

The most obvious candidates for what we are ashamed of are
faults and failings. There is some truth to this. We're ashamed of
how we look, we don't think we are smart enough, and we've
done some things we aren't proud of. But if we look into the
shame beneath avoidance, we'll usually find certain strivings
about which we are in conflict. We're ashamed of being unattractive because secretly we wish we were so good-looking that
others would be drawn to us. We think we aren't smart enough
because we're dedicated to the proposition that intelligence can
conquer the world. Remember, shame is the painful discrepancy
between the self we *wish* we were and the self we think we are.
We may not admit them, even to ourselves, but our wishes are
enormous.

Need makes us weak or, to put it more accurately, discovering
our neediness makes us feel weak. If only our need weren't so
strong!

LOOKING IN AND REACHING OUT

The shamed self is a weakened self. Therefore, undoing the effects of shame means strengthening the self. But what does that mean?

Most people who are insecure and ashamed of themselves are aware of their vulnerability to the reactions of others. They know how badly they crave attention and how devastated they are by criticism and rejection. Unfortunately, many people conclude that the solution must be found within themselves. If only they were stronger, they think, then they wouldn't be so dependent on the opinions of other people, wouldn't be so insecure, wouldn't need people so much. It's a defensive wish.

Men and women who become bodybuilders imagine that if they spend enough hours in the gym they can make themselves strong and beautiful, attractive and invulnerable. It's a compelling fantasy. Some people wish they could build self-esteem the same way. You can't. The sense of self is formed in interaction; it's re-formed the same way.

We've seen how shame begins in childhood, when the child exposes vulnerable aspects of the self and runs head-on into attack or rejection. Such collisions are so terribly painful that we learn to anticipate and avoid them. As a result, the affect of shame replaces the fear of external punishment by humiliation, scorn, and contempt. Ever after the shamed child is wary—careful not to show too much, not to be too open, lest the tender wounded parts of the self once again meet with rejection and more shame. Reversing the process means reversing the process. Not hiding, but exposing the genuine unvarnished self: expressing honest feeling, asking for what we want, saying what we think, having fun, and getting angry. This must be done gradually and with people who are likely to be receptive, and it must be done with full awareness of what can happen: Sometimes, taking risks, trying new things, or telling the truth about our feelings will be met with acceptance, sometimes with a cold shoulder or a hot rebuke.

Personal change always involves some pain, that's why we get stuck and stagnant. Breaking out of fixed and narrow habits is liberating but risky. The risk is making mistakes, saying something or acting in a way that someone may not like, occasionally even making fools of ourselves—or to put it more accurately, reexperiencing shame. The difference between learning to be ashamed in the first place and occasionally encountering shame in the process of deliberately expanding the limits of our lives is that if we understand the process, that moving forward and living more openly will now and then expose us to shame, we can avoid moving back. If we understand how shame works, our actual encounters with it will be less devastating. Even when we're hurt and feel like withdrawing or punishing our tormentors, we'll know why. Knowing why enables us to pause between hurt and reaction. We can retreat if we choose, but we don't have to do so blindly.

This is a critical point: Change takes action as well as insight. Understanding what holds us back—and why—helps us know what needs to be done. But doing it takes courage.

As Darcie discovered her anger, she began to express it, at first tentatively. One Saturday afternoon her friend Rochelle stopped by on her way to doing some shopping and asked if Darcie would mind watching her kids. It was a thing Rochelle did often, and usually, although she was annoyed, Darcie didn't complain. This time, however, she said, "It's okay today, but next time call, okay?" Rochelle, who wasn't used to directness from Darcie, acted hurt and said, "Well if it's too much trouble, never mind," and left with her kids.

Darcie felt awful. Maybe she shouldn't have said anything. Maybe she should call Rochelle and apologize. After thinking it over, she decided that she had the right to complain. She also realized how uncomfortable she was with the idea of doing anything that might be selfish or demanding. That's why Rochelle's reaction made her feel so bad.

Darcie decided to do nothing. She didn't call Rochelle and she didn't work herself up into self-righteous anger either. She just waited, and endured worrying about what Rochelle would think. Two weeks later, Rochelle called and asked Darcie over for supper. When Rochelle didn't mention what had happened, Darcie realized that it had only been a minor annoyance to her friend. She was the one who was afraid to speak up; she was the one who was afraid of getting angry; and she was the one who was ashamed of being demanding. Her friends had gotten used to her being Old Faithful; they'd get used to her being more honest.

The capacity to tolerate painful affects is essential to seizing life and making it work: It is our inability to experience limitations and deficiencies that keeps us alienated from our authentic selves and keeps us from venturing fully into the world. The unwillingness to take risks and endure some pain keeps us from getting past where we're stuck. If instead of learning from life's failures, we take them as confirmation that we are shameful and unworthy or that "nobody understands," then we are condemned to hang back, turn inward, and continue to live with painful self-consciousness.

The antidote to self-consciousness is action. The more we reach out—acting on the world—the less likely we are to worry about ourselves.

It's only when our involvement is interrupted that we become self-conscious. Boredom makes us withdraw, and so does hurt. The subject breaks away from the object, and "I" becomes "me." Self-consciousness is magnified the more one has something dangerous or unlovable to be ashamed of. An extreme example is schizophrenia. The self of the schizophrenic splits into voices he hears in his head, first urging and then accusing. For the rest of us, shame, the lingering residue of old hurts, heightens self-consciousness and traps us in self-doubt. Our "voices" are full of doubt: I'd better not ask. What if they don't like me? What if I can't think of anything to say? These thoughts are torture. Doubt is torture.

The antithesis of anxious self-awareness isn't proud self-awareness; it's acting on the world. Self-consciousness dissolves with energetic participation in life. The self that's busy living has less time for brooding self-watching.

Living honestly means pushing through self-doubt and being real. It's all very well, of course, for *me* to urge *you* to begin living more honestly; it's not my neck you'll be sticking out. The call to live honestly, naturally, isn't new, of course. Much has been written about the natural, unrestrained freedom of human nature, much of it appealing, much of it simplistic.

From social philosophers to encounter group leaders to radicals of the 1960s, there have always been voices urging us simply to live fully by living freely. Rousseau urged a return to nature; Herbert Marcuse urged us to shed "surplus repression"; Jerry Rubin urged us to "let it all hang out"; even Ringo Starr sang, "All you gotta do is act naturally." One of the most moving and fully realized pleas for the unrepressed life is contained in Norman O. Brown's *Life Against Death.* Brown calls for a resurrection of the body as the seat of primary pleasure, and for the abolition of guilt and shame. The message is appealing.

Dedicated revolutionaries, prophets, and simplifiers envision a utopia with perfect freedom from the inner restraints of the superego and the outer authority of culture. Unfortunately, we cannot undo shame by willing it, or do away with vulnerability by denying it. Reading about acting unashamed is wonderfully liberating. Living it is a different story.

We *are* vulnerable. Simply dropping defenses exposes us once again to the pain that was the reason for erecting the defenses in the first place. We can begin to relax the grip of shame by reaching out—trying new things, taking risks, opening ourselves up to other people—but it's important to realize that we will get hurt along the way.

Shame-anxiety is not only the result of infantile fantasy but also of self-conscious adult reality. The woman who has trouble saying no may very well disappoint family and friends if she does. The man who hesitates to make demands (out loud) can count on some of the resentment he fears if he begins to say what he wants. Both of them will be tempted to retreat from these unwelcome reactions and withdraw even further into old habits of avoidance. Here's a brief example.

For the past couple of months I've been running at lunchtime with a new running partner. Although Susan doesn't run as far or as fast as I'm used to, she's fun to talk to and I enjoy her company. From the start, however, she worried out loud that she doesn't run fast enough and is holding me back. I tried to reassure her that it's okay. Recently, however, she came back from a two-week sailing vacation, happy, tanned, and out of shape. After a couple of days of her running so sluggishly that I could hardly run slow enough to keep back with her, I decided to be direct:

"Susan, we've got to get you in just a little better shape, so you can keep up."

"I can't believe you said that!" she said. "I thought I was doing pretty good to come back after not running at all and do this well."

Her response upset me quite a bit. Was she just kidding around, or did I really hurt her feelings? I'm the kind of guy who worries a lot about these things. (I like to think that I don't want to hurt other people's feelings; the truth is I can't bear anybody getting mad at me.)

What to do? The obvious thing to do—talk it over—is the second thing to do. The first thing is for me to come to terms with how I feel and what I plan to do about it. My impulse was to apologize, and although it's possible to apologize for hurting someone's feelings, I felt as if I'd be apologizing for myself—"I'm sorry I was selfish, demanding." She'd probably say it was okay, and I'd redouble my resolve not to tell the truth about my feelings.

Change is a three-step process: You try something new; other people react to the change; and, usually, you change back. The alternative is, of course, to persist, to resist the pressure to change back. When shame-sensitive people risk overcoming habits of avoidance, the risk is that someone will respond critically. They might.

Dealing with criticism for trying something new is, like all change, a three-step process: You try something new; you get criticized; and you feel more or less mortified. This feeling triggers automatic defensive reactions, usually an impulse either to withdraw or to counterattack. Pause. Stop and search this reflex response. There's no special formula for this process; just catch yourself in the act of emotional reactivity, and think about what's going on. This delay, this consideration, gives you the chance to respond more thoughtfully: to apologize, not for being yourself, but for hurting the other person's feelings, if you choose, or simply to let the other person be annoyed.

In dealing with my worry about Susan's response to my asking her to run a little faster, I decided that it was important to my self-respect not to apologize. Instead, I gave some thought to why I'm ashamed to make demands (it was discouraged, to put it mildly, in my family) and what would be so terrible if she got mad at me? (By the way, some of you may be surprised that this incident upset me. That's the way it is with shame. What shames or embarrasses one person often seems trivial to others. Moreover, in my place, many people would be able to apologize with no loss of self-respect. That varies, too. It's easier to apologize for hurting someone's feelings when you don't feel ashamed of your actions.)

The self gains strength from becoming part of a web of relationships, not by accumulating power and not by becoming self-sufficient. "Self-sufficient" is an oxymoron. It's important to reach out to others, but this doesn't mean calculating how to please or how to avoid rebuke. Reaching out means being ourselves, means being vulnerable. Our defenses protect us, but they also keep us from touching and being touched. Only by opening ourselves up to people, being real, can we be accepted and confirmed.

DOING AND BEING

Self-respect begins at home, with reassuring acceptance of who we are. But since who we are is manifest in what we do, it's primarily our actions, rather than our being, that stimulates our parents' response. Anxious parents may, for example, show more love and appreciation for the child who stays close to home and doesn't take chances. Or, to choose a different example, a father, unsatisfied with his own accomplishments, might praise his daughter lavishly for good grades but ignore or discourage her interest in sports. To the extent that appreciation is only conditional, we develop an act; we perform the self we think people will love.

Shame is being afraid to be and show who we are, what we genuinely think and feel, what we spontaneously enjoy.

Most adults live their act. I don't mean that most people are false and phony, they aren't. I mean that most adults are so used to doing what they think will lead to approval, and not doing what they think will lead to rejection, that the act becomes habit, and it's hard to tell where the false self ends and the real self begins.

There are people whose false fronts are plain to see. We can see through our father's obsequious ways; his "courtesies" are really designed to get people to pay attention to him. And our mother-in-law never gives a straight answer when we ask her what she wants to do ("I don't know, we'll have to see what Dad wants") so that she can manipulate events without seeming to. (It's easy to spot falseness in our parents and in-laws; we're so much better than they are.) But for the most part our persona, the face we project to the world, is well practiced. Besides, we're not trying to fool anybody; we're only doing what comes naturally. We just want to be loved.

I've always considered myself a generous person. I give a lot of presents and do a lot of favors. It may be both obvious and understandable, but to me it has been wincingly painful to discover that I often do these things so that people will like me. ("Gosh, that Mike, he's a great guy.") Years ago when I gave my wife an expensive camera for her birthday, she got mad at me. "We can't afford that!" I was so hurt, full of self-pity: *Gee, she doesn't have to get mad at me; all I did was try to give her something nice.* All I did was spend a lot of money so that she'd be grateful. She didn't want that camera, and we *didn't* have the money. It was a hard lesson. Now that I'm more aware of this dynamic, I occasionally realize that the present I think of sending to someone is motivated more by a wish to be appreciated than by unselfish generosity. Sometimes I send the gift anyway, sometimes not. And best of all, sometimes I know that the flowers I send to congratulate a friend or the baseball cards I buy for my son are just for them.

Most of us overwork certain areas of our lives. We are demon workers, wonderful mothers, loyal children—strivers, achievers, doers, self-sacrificers. Why? Most of us are doers because we like what we do, but we overdo because we're searching for self-respect. Stop looking for self-respect in success, motherhood, achievement, or self-sacrifice. You won't find it there—unless the achievement and self-sacrifice is a creative expression of a secure self, rather than a substitute for being loved and appreciated. The irony is that we can never really be appreciated by trying to be appreciated, only by being ourselves.

I once knew a kid in junior high who was very shy. He thought that if he became a star basketball player people would like him, so he shot baskets ever day after school alone until dark. That shy, lonely boy developed a wonderful jump shot and became a shy lonely basketball player.

All the effort we put forth to score points doesn't score love. If you find joy in your work, then work. If you truly love doing things for your kids and don't need to bend them to suit your wishes, then go ahead and devote your life to them. But don't look for self-respect from doing. Doing, when it isn't a natural product of being, is living a false self.

The term "false self" brings to mind blatantly neurotic or deceitful facades, like Charles Dickens's Uriah Heep, the oily, unctuous clerk whose fawning protestations of " 'umbleness" hid his cold, calculating schemes. But the false self isn't always obvious.

One of the most likable people I've ever met was a young psychotherapist whom I'll call Felix. Everybody liked Felix. What made him so popular was that he always noticed and commented on what people did and said. If you wore a new shirt to work, he'd notice: "Hey, new shirt, nice!" And he had a wonderful knack of picking up the emotional essence of what you were trying to say: "You really worry about that stuff, don't you?" "That's great, you sure did a nice job with that." What a pleasure it was to be with such a warm guy! What a relief after all those people who can't stop talking about themselves!

And yet, Felix was lonely. He had plenty of company but no intimacy. Behind his attractive expression of interest, he was locked inside himself. He did with his friends what he did with his patients, reflected their feelings. The fact that he was so good at it that no one noticed, doesn't alter the truth: He was ingratiating. (We usually don't spot the effort behind a person's charm until we see them turn it on to someone else.) Felix wasn't a selfish or calculating person. He truly liked people and wanted to be liked himself. Only he wasn't himself; he was what he thought people wanted him to be, a good listener.

Be kind, but be yourself.

We begin to overcome shame when we risk dropping our act, the false self, in favor of feeling and thinking and saying and doing what we really feel.

Once in a while it's helpful to remind yourself that, although others may react to what you do, your intrinsic worth doesn't depend on any particular actions. If someone loves you, they love *you,* not your acts. Real love means accepting, cherishing the whole person. So it is with self-respect. Separate yourself from the outcomes of your actions. Differentiate between your core self and other, peripheral, attributes or activities. Other people may react to the clothes you wear, the favors you do, or the work you produce; and their reactions, appreciative or critical, certainly have an impact on how you feel. But your clothes and your favors and your accomplishments aren't you. They might represent what you like or what you did, but they are not *you,* not your central being.

It's a little embarrassing to say so in this context, but I've always been very concerned with appearances—not with being staid or proper, but with dressing well. When I was a skinny teenager, I avoided short-sleeve shirts that exposed my puny arms. As an adult, I'm picky about the clothes I buy (I might go to five stores to buy one necktie) and careful about what I wear to work. (My alibi is that it's important to my patients that I convey a look of authority and respectability.) As you might guess, I appreciate other people who dress well, men and women, and I'm somewhat disdainful of people who don't have good (i.e., my) taste in clothes. However, despite all this calculation about clothing, I've often admired people who don't seem to worry about what they wear. I remember, for example, Harvey Jackins, the founder of Re-Evaluation Counseling, who radiated self-confidence— U.S. Marine haircut, outrageously blue Hawaiian shirt, and all. People with self-respect dress the way they want to, the hell with what other people are wearing. These people can break the rules, ignore or even defy convention, because *they don't care*. They don't worry. Their self-esteem doesn't depend on appearances; it just is.

Real self-respect means making peace with who you are, including weaknesses as well as strengths, talents and limits, likes and dislikes. Harboring a denied defective self-image requires constant defensive vigilance. It also precludes learning from life's failures.

Facing what you consider your shortcomings is one way to discover the sources of shame within yourself. Remember, making shame more understandable makes it more manageable. At best, you can work on accepting yourself, your whole self; at least, you can recognize the weak spots in your self-esteem.

There's a wonderful scene in the movie *The Boys in the Band*, when Harold, the guest of honor at a birthday party, shows up late. The host, who has been made to wait and worry, meets Harold at the door and shames him, or tries to, for being late. I wish I could quote the exact exchange, but it goes something like this:

Michael: "You're late! You were supposed to arrive at this location between eight-thirty and nine o'clock!"

Harold: "What I *am*, Michael, is a thirty-two-year-old, ugly, pock-marked neurotic—and if it takes me a while to pull myself together and find something to wear that isn't totally ridiculous before I can get up the nerve to show this face to the world, that's the way it is."

Here was a person with a full quota of insecurity, but nevertheless reconciled to himself.

Once you become reconciled to yourself, then you can dance as though no one were watching. Let go. Be.

BEING AND DOING

It's all very well to emphasize being over doing, to say that self-respect is intrinsic to who we are, not dependent on what we do, but the relationship is circular. How we feel about ourselves affects what we feel free to do—and our tolerance for making mistakes and enduring failure and criticism. But it's also true that what we do and how we deal with the consequences feeds back to how we feel about ourselves. The more we respect our own being, the freer we will be to act openly in the world, *and* the more we learn to act openly, the more we come to respect our own being.

The antithesis of inhibition—naturalness—is doing what you want and saying what you think, concentrating on acting on the world rather than worrying about the possible criticism of the self doing the acting. When you are self-conscious, try shifting your focus outward; concentrate on the sights and sounds of the world instead of on your self. Instead of worrying about what others might be thinking about you, think about them. Don't be interesting, be interested.

Each time you reverse the shame-inhibition process, each time you go ahead and approach a stranger or try something new, you gain increasing freedom to act—and be. Self-consciousness begins to lose some of its paralyzing hold on you.

Overcoming inhibitions—doing instead of worrying about it—is a little easier when you realize that time is passing and life is now. As long as we are double-minded about what we do, doing and watching ourselves do, we lead half lives. Living more fully has two stages. We initiate fuller life by wishing, and then enact it through deciding. Don't wish for a "fuller life"; get in touch with your emptiness and boredom and anxiety and depression, and wish for what's missing—friends, play, full engagement with your work, closer ties to your family. Make it specific, and then make it happen.

When we speak profoundly about discovering the true self and optimistically about reaching out to others, we must at the same time deal with everyday hurts and slights, lest they wound the spirit and erode self-respect.

It's criticism that wounds us, wounds us because even though it may be criticism of what we've done, it feels like rejection of who we are. Suppose a wife finally decides to tell her husband that she's tired of always being the one to make social arrangements, and he lashes out at her, "You're always complaining! Why must you be so selfish?" She's stung; she feels rejected. Maybe she was right all the time. Maybe the only way to be accepted is to be helpful, motherly. Maybe honesty is the worst policy.

What gives anyone else the right to stand in judgment of us? *We* do, if we deal in judgment. We judge others because we judge ourselves. This form of contempt isn't an automatic reaction to shame, the way rage is. It's learned from parents and playmates. Putting others down is a defensive way to inflate the self—not inflate, really, but ward off self-doubt. Criticism, blaming, and fault-finding are self-doubt projected outward. You can practice acceptance by learning to accept others; give up expecting people to be different than they are. Accepting others is the first step toward accepting the self.

In trying to explain how to break through from shame to self-respect, I've emphasized looking in and reaching out, coming to terms with yourself and opening up to others, each effort reinforcing the other. Your relationship with yourself has everything to do with your relationships with other people. Progress in these two domains, personal and interpersonal, is circular: Self-acceptance improves relationships, improved relationships enhance self-acceptance. Now that I've explained the outlines of change in this chapter, I will elaborate in those that follow, beginning with making friends with the self.

14

·······

Making Friends with Yourself

With friends we are easy. There's little need to perform or prove anything, because we know they like us. We don't have to get dressed up or be all smiley or have successes to report when we call on friends; we just have to show up. That's the wonderful thing about friendship: acceptance. We accept our friends, they accept us.

Our good friends value our positive qualities, recognize our shortcomings, and love us anyway. Wouldn't it be nice to turn that compassionate acceptance inward, to make friends with yourself?

A RETURN TO THE SELF

Most of us rush through youth with our eyes fixed on the future. When we're eight we want to be twelve, when we're twelve we want to be eighteen. At twenty, our energy is focused outward, on making our way in the world, having fun, falling in love, and getting ahead. In our thirties, we consolidate those preliminary choices and readjust those that don't work out. These years are hectic and hurried. We may have a lot of self-doubt, but we don't have a lot of time for self-reflection; in fact, for most of us, the self is a taken-for-granted background of experience.

As long as we're preoccupied with problems at work and frustrations at home, we can safely maintain that our dilemmas are out there. Our conflicts are with supervisors and colleagues and deadlines, with husbands and wives and children; all we need is more time and energy. If only we had less to do, and more cooperation, think of all the fun we'd have.

The real struggle isn't in our families or our careers, it's in ourselves. That last sentence is what I wrote in my first draft. I liked it. It had the ring of clarity that comes from reducing the complexities of life to simple pronouncements. Unfortunately, it isn't quite true. Our challenges are outside *and* in. There's work to be done in the world, and work to be done on the self.

When I was thirty-five I sought out one of the gurus of self-fulfillment. Things weren't going well. I was working all day and coming home at night to a tired wife and two small children clamoring for attention. It wasn't much fun. After listening to my complaints, the guru told me that I should get busy and earn some more money, so that I could catch up with my bills and buy some leisure. It wasn't what I expected to hear, but it was good advice.

But one day, when we've climbed high enough to reach a plateau, we look around and see where we've gotten to, and what we paid to get there. We've given everything we've got at home and at work, and we wonder, where is the satisfaction and meaning we thought would follow? We've accumulated families, careers, and possessions, all of which may leave us with a residue of disappointment. Promising happiness, they do not provide it; yet they remain as enduring reminders of the unkept promise.

When we round up the usual suspects for cheating us out of contentment, they turn out to be circumstantial (not enough time, not enough money, too much work, other people), over and done with (mistakes and missed opportunities), and otherwise outside our control. Yes, there are things to regret, but regret only distracts us from unused life that's available. Regrets are sad but safe. Safer than discovering disowned parts of the self, and facing the shame we must uncover in the process.

GETTING TO KNOW YOURSELF

Getting to know yourself is easy, like driving at high speed in heavy traffic and studying what goes on under the hood at the same time. After a while, we find out what the motor can and can't do. We also discover a few clunks and knocks, some of which can be fixed, some of which can't. We may even learn a little about what causes problems—driving too hard, too fast, or starting out too late—but most of the real problems, as you know, are caused by other drivers.

Ordinarily, getting to know ourselves is something that happens unself-consciously. It's not something we *do;* it just happens. Successes and failures teach us about our talents and shortcomings; friendship and love teach us about longing and vulnerability. Most of our attention, though, is focused out, not in—like drivers in heavy traffic. When accidents happen, it's generally because of what someone else did, though sometimes we wonder.

Sydny was an arrestingly attractive woman, a tall redhead wearing a black dress and a wide gold necklace, who began with a familiar opening. "I'm not sure whether or not I need therapy; maybe you can tell me if I'm crazy or not." She was joking, of course, trying to cover her embarrassment about asking for help; at the same time, she was expressing real doubt about whether she needed it.

She went on. "I've had a bad two years. The problem is my family—not my marriage; I'm lucky, we have a wonderful marriage. It's the boys."

Both the seventeen-year-old and the fifteen-year-old had given her a lot of trouble. The older boy fell in with a bad crowd and started drinking heavily. He was defiant at home and noncompliant at school. The fifteen-year-old was just the opposite. "He's like me," Sydny said, "a hard worker, eager to please—an overachiever. Last week he got a ninety-nine on one of his Regents exams, and now he wants to pay fifty dollars to take it over. He thinks he should have gotten a hundred."

Problems? Yes. Pathological? No. Sydny and her husband had done all the right things on their test, the boys. They'd been firm about the drinking, insisted on the boy's entering an alcohol rehabilitation program, and even went to Tough Love to reinforce their sense that serious problems call for serious discipline. They'd been good with the younger boy, too, trying to reassure him about his ability and their love, but also accepting his need to prove himself.

In the process of trying to cope with these two difficult adolescent passages, Sydny read a lot of self-help books. The books were interesting but disquieting. One in particular, Robin Norwood's Women Who Love Too Much, *made her wonder if her idea of herself as well-adjusted wasn't somewhat self-deceptive. "I didn't used to think it mattered, but I had a very unstable childhood." Her parents divorced when she was five, her father died when she was ten, and her stepfather had a terrible temper; but she doesn't remember these disruptions having an effect on her, only on other members of the family. When her father left, she felt sorry for him—having to live on his own—but she didn't blame her mother. Her stepfather had a cruel streak, but he mostly took it out on her sister. "He liked me; everybody's always liked me." But now she wondered, "Maybe I've just been covering up."*

Here was a well-adjusted woman who'd been through a hard time. Like all hard times, Sydny's had tested her coping mechanisms and made her aware of some underlying insecurity. Her joke—"maybe you can tell me if I'm crazy or not"— wasn't a joke after all. She really wondered if she'd been hiding basic, unresolved problems all these years. (What an opening for a therapist!)

Here's what I told her: "You've had a lot to cope with; it's worn you down, made you question yourself. You wonder if maybe all the disruptions you had growing up did leave you with some deep problems and you've just been denying it all these years. I think you really did come here wanting to find out whether your personality is basically healthy or unhealthy.

"I don't think it's either one. There's a third possibility: I

*think you are well-adjusted, the way you've always believed,
though there's some unfinished business you haven't dealt
with. Some unexplored anxieties and old griefs. But that
doesn't mean you're basically unsound. I think that you have
some unresolved insecurity and that probably underneath that
is a basically solid personality. As for therapy, do you have to
explore these underlying insecurities? I don't think so. It might
be useful, but it isn't necessary."*

*When more than the usual number of problems tested Syd-
ny's coping skills, she discovered her strength and weakness.
Because she'd always taken the former for granted, she paid
more attention to the latter. She's not alone.*

A lot of us make similar discoveries. The facade cracks and we
get a glimpse of the underside of our personalities. When we see
flaws, we wonder if the basic structure is faulty. The parents we
used to think were okay turn out to have a lot of annoying qualities, and we begin to see how much we're like them. After so many
years in a marriage or a job, we start to realize that what's been
holding us back isn't entirely *them;* it's our own limitations. Maybe
we aren't as well adjusted as we thought we were. Maybe we'd
better not look too closely. Maybe.

Because the emotions we push down and away from awareness
are uneasy ones, these are the first layers of the suppressed personality we stumble upon. When troubling memories and doubts
become conscious, we often suspect that the real self is defective:
Underneath the reasonably secure self we've managed to construct lurks a flawed and fragile one.

It's true that for the majority of sensitive people, the real self
remains hidden. But the real self is as likely to contain as many
strengths as weaknesses. It's not a question of either/or, strong or
weak. We're both.

It isn't just weaknesses we are afraid of. We're also afraid of our
powers and possibilities. Strengths can be every bit as threatening
as weaknesses, potentiating as they do buried dreams and exposing us to the risk of conflict with others, conflict we've learned to
avoid.

Because it means confronting unsuspected weaknesses and un-used strengths, getting to know the real self can be painful. In-creasing your self-awareness may initially make you more self-conscious, more sensitized to your limits, and more aware of the discrepancy between the real you and your ideal self-image.

One of my patients once complained that, although we uncover a lot in our sessions, after she leaves she forgets what we talked about. When I asked her what she did after she left my office, she said that she walks to the parking lot—thinking over what we discussed—and then she gets in the car and turns on the radio. My brilliant prescription? Leave the radio off. It made a big difference.

So it is with most of us. When we uncover something embar-rassing or uncomfortable about ourselves, we don't hold the thought for long; we turn away. Important discoveries about the self are often painful, at least at first, and the human mind doesn't readily dwell on conflict, so we drift off, or turn the radio on. I mention this because in order to get to know yourself it may be necessary to break away from everyday routines and distractions. That's why people go on retreats. Reflection is best done in soli-tude.

Some of the experiments I'm going to suggest can be done just sitting there, but going for a long walk and thinking over what you discover is a good idea. Getting away for a weekend of contem-plation is an even better idea. You need time and space to search for meaning in your life. Don't distract yourself. If, in the process of trying to get to know yourself, you find yourself drifting off or running away, just notice; don't be too self-critical. Notice, and bring your attention back to the task at hand.

Looking in the Mirror

The first exercise requires a notebook, a mirror, and honesty. The notebook is for writing down your observations, the mirror is for looking at yourself, the honesty is for looking hard.

Spend fifteen minutes examining yourself. Start with the physical you. What is your best feature? How would you describe yourself to a stranger? Imagine meeting yourself for the first time. What would be your first impression? How could you make a more positive impression? What is your worst physical attribute? How have you tried to cover it up? Now imagine a friend looking at that part of you. What would the friend say?

What parts of your body could use some improvement? Are you willing to do anything about it, or can you accept that part of you the way it is? (The only alternative to changing or accepting is continuing to think, "Ain't it awful." You can do that if you like, but I don't recommend it.)

Now, describe your personality. What are your strengths? Weaknesses? What have you always wished were different? What have you tried to change? Hide? What have you tried to hide or change that is really part of you? Imagine describing those attributes to a friend. What would the friend say? Think of someone with a trait you admire and wish you had. Would you trade? Would you take all of that person and give up all of yourself?

These are large questions. Take your time.

The Story of Your Life

Imagine writing a screenplay of your life. Where does the story begin? Who are the major characters? Who is directing the movie? What were the big wins and losses? What were the payoffs and costs?

Who is responsible for the conflicts? Which of the conflicts could be eased or prevented if the characters knew more? What is the turning point? What might have seemed unfortunate but turned out to be valuable? How did the negative past, your sadness and tragedy, shape you and deepen you, make you more sensitive and sympathetic, and stronger?

After you bring the story up to date, project it into the future. What will happen five and ten years from now if the characters just go on as they have? How could things change for the worse? How could the characters change for the better? (Was your first thought about how other characters could change, or how you could change?)

When you examine the past and imagine the future, you will see some things you like, some you don't. You can wallow in regret or figure out why. For example, why were you so insecure at a certain time? Where are you with that now? What can you do about it? Where are you heading? Will you take steps to create satisfaction with friends? Family? Work? Play? It's up to you.

Strengths and Weaknesses

Make a list of ten words or phrases that describe you best. Then rank these characteristics from 1 (your most important characteristic) to 10 (least important).

Rank

I am _____ _____
I am _____ _____

How many of these items are positive, negative, and neutral? Add up the ranks of these three categories.

_____ positive (hard-working, successful)
_____ negative (out of shape, afraid of anger)
_____ neutral (woman, thirty-five)

Which items would a friend rank as most important? If you don't know, ask.

As you do these exercises (or for those of you who don't like to play games, as you think about them), you will become more aware of what parts of yourself you feel okay about, and what you are ashamed of.

Some of our shame is tied to specific memories. Shame gnaws at our insides. Whenever something triggers one of those awful memories, shame sharpens its teeth on us. That's why we push the memories away. We shove them back down into the unconscious where they chew away at us, uninhibited by logic or understanding.

Memories of Humiliation

Shame is so hard to bear, it's a little easier to begin by thinking about a painful time when somebody else unfairly humiliated you. What happened? Why were you so humiliated? How is that experience still affecting you?

Memories of Shame

Humiliation happens. It hurts, but not as deeply as those things you've done that you are truly ashamed of. Don't turn away.

Make a list of five things you've done that you are most ashamed of. You've probably confessed some of these things. Can you bear to tell someone else?

Now think about the worst. Write a short story about it. Make the story dramatic. I recommend using the third person. ("There was a person who . . .") If you don't like to write, go for a long walk or, better, find someplace quiet to sit and think it over. But keep your mind on the task. Close your eyes and remember the incident.

A few years ago, psychotherapist Irv Yalom and two colleagues studied encounter group leaders, trying to figure out what makes the best ones effective. What they discovered was that the most effective leaders first evoked strong feelings, and then helped participants understand and reexamine their experiences.[1] That's what I'm going to suggest here. Close your eyes. Remember. Focus. Make it real. See what everything looked like. Feel the feelings.

After you focus on what happened as vividly and for as long as possible, think about the impact, the cost, the unfairness of having to feel as you did. Then rethink what happened, using the third person. Explain why the person felt so bad. Explain the person's motives. Explain how the person might have reinterpreted what happened. Explain how much of a burden the memory is. Remember, understanding shame is essential to freeing ourselves from its grip.

Repeat this exercise on two or three subsequent occasions. Each time, try to make yourself feel as upset as possible. Purging shame works partly by catharsis—feeling your feelings as intensely as possible, expressing them as vividly as possible, *without* any repeat of the original consequences. The more upset you can make yourself feel, the better. Go through several memories using the same procedure.

Aspirations

Remember, it isn't just our real qualities that get shot down; it's also our inflated aspirations.

Make a short list of your grandest dreams. These can be pipe dreams, like being a movie star or a professional athlete, or ambitions you now think were extravagant. Then go back and write down some ideas about what feelings of weakness or inadequacy these fantasies might be compensating for. (Dreaming of great wealth, for example, might be a way of compensating for feeling powerless, or unloved, or deprived of fun.) Next, note some of the experiences that disabused you of these grand illusions and what the consequences have been. Finally, for each inflated aspiration, make a realistic appraisal of your abilities and consider what you might have done, or still might do, with such abilities.

Before going on, let's see how our images of ourselves become so fixed.

SELF-SCHEMAS

Psychologists call enduring beliefs that people have about themselves *self-schemas*.[2] These define our sense of self and determine how we approach certain situations, which affects how we behave, which in turn cements those self-schemas. Consider, for example, a man who thinks of himself as shy. If he goes to a party, he doesn't talk much—he's shy—and he has a bad time. On the way home he thinks, *Yes, I'm shy, and I hate parties*. It's feedback, but it's rigged.

Shame-sensitive people have negative self-schemas. They sense themselves as weak and inadequate, though they may not be consciously aware of these feelings because they cover them up. Negative self-schemas hold us back by priming anticipatory anxiety and inhibiting enthusiasm. The woman who thinks of herself as "overly emotional" assumes that she'll cry if she speaks at a graduation or a wedding party or a memorial service. Moreover, she assumes that crying is bad, "overly emotional." So she swallows her feelings, a slave to her negative self-image.

We control the present and limit the future with negative self-schemas. We select and organize information, then edit it and store it in memory in ways that are often self-critical and self-limiting, consistent with our secret shame about ourselves. In other words, we worry too much.

But *why* do we worry, especially about things that might be embarrassing or shameful? Because traumatic shame, unanticipated shame, catches us off-guard and hurts worse. We know this is true *because it's happened before*. We incorporate loathing and degradation from our parents' most angry and rejecting comments. It doesn't matter that they showed us love most of the time. Ugly incidents stand out.

Worrying about what might happen (or might happen again) contributes to a spiraling increase of anxious inhibition—like what happened to the shy man at the party. Worry is mainly anticipatory; it refers to possible future events. When we worry about past events, it's because we anticipate future consequences of those events. "I shouldn't have done that" may mean "He's going to kill me when he finds out!"

It's not so easy to just stop worrying, but by noticing and verbalizing negative thoughts you can lessen their grip on your mind and actions. Monitor your worry and learn to identify its initiation as early in the worry sequence as possible. Don't try to stop worrying; instead, shift the focus of your attention from yourself—how you'll do, what they'll think—to the situation itself. The same thing works with self-schemas that are really put-downs, with which we beat others to the punch of criticizing us. Notice yourself doing this. Notice your expectations before important encounters. Notice your negative self-evaluations. Notice how they influence what you think of the situation, and how they hold you back.

Self-schemas are not necessarily negative—*I'm shy, I'm no good at sports*—but they do tend to be self-protective. When something bad happens, many people persist in believing that it wasn't their fault. How often have you heard someone describe an argument and admit they were at fault? Most arguments are the other person's fault. We can't bear to admit that we were wrong or that we made a mistake, because we're ashamed.

The self-protective schemas that won't allow us to admit we're wrong cause a lot of problems and a lot of conflict. Afraid of the possibility of being "wrong," we often try to prove ourselves "right"—often at someone else's expense. Notice how many painful arguments are between two people each trying to make the other "wrong" and themselves "right." Much of the contentiousness dissolves as soon as one acknowledges that the other is right. (Actually, the other person is always "right," in the sense of having a legitimate point of view.)

Another self-protective schema applies to people who live by the code "the best defense is a good offense." Better to criticize others than risk any chance of being criticized themselves. Anything to avoid the dread possibility of being wrong.

The idea that self-respect means to think well of yourself—to be proud, optimistic, and self-confident—leads, paradoxically, to problems. To accept ourselves deeply we must know ourselves deeply. For that it is necessary to recognize and accept our own weaknesses. Healthy self-respect is not so much feeling perpetually good and worthwhile, but rather the ability to manage feelings like inadequacy, weakness, or incompetence.

Self-based experience has a peculiar characteristic: Attempts to exclude or reject part of experience leads to a more global loss of awareness. So in order to be in contact with one's own feelings, it's necessary to tolerate negative self-feelings.

TELLING THE TRUTH

When we're honest with ourselves, one of the things we notice is that we aren't always honest. We lie to the world and to ourselves about what we feel, what we think, and what we want. Some of this is deliberate. We're "tactful" when we don't mention that we didn't really like the gift somebody went to so much trouble to pick out. We're "kind" when we reassure our friends ("That was great, you really did a nice job"), not because we mean it but just to boost their egos. We're "polite" when we make polite conversation pretending to be interested, when we're bored and wish we were someplace else. Okay, so we lie a little; we only do it because we're considerate, and deceitful.

We lie to ourselves, too, of course; but we can't afford to know this. Lying has to do with not respecting ourselves. When we don't tell the truth about what we feel, it's because we don't respect ourselves and our right to feel what we feel, think what we think, and want what we want. We fool ourselves about this dishonesty, telling ourselves it's because others are overly sensitive or insufficiently understanding. If only we could find the right person, we could tell the truth. The truth is, we lie a little everywhere, even when you'd think we wouldn't have to.

Lorraine first consulted me when, in her mid-thirties, she was considering leaving her husband for the man she loved. She did leave her husband, but became acutely depressed for having committed the sin of selfishness. Because Lorraine was so depressed, my treatment was more supportive than analytic, meaning that I intervened more often, asked leading questions, and occasionally gave advice (for example, about getting a lawyer to protect her rights in the divorce). It seemed to work, and after a few months Lorraine was doing well enough to do without therapy. I saw her again a couple of years later when her lover left her (for an older woman). Again she was depressed, again my treatment was active and supportive, and again it seemed to help. The third time Lor-

raine consulted me things were different. She was about to finish graduate school and begin a new career. This time she was not depressed; rather, she consulted me because she wanted to discuss her new career and because she was considering getting into long-term exploratory psychotherapy, which she thought should perhaps be with a new therapist. (Silently, I agreed, because I felt that it would be hard to switch from the active, supportive role I had adopted to a more neutral and analytic posture.)

In the fourth session Lorraine was discussing an impending job interview about which she was quite nervous. At one point she said, "What if the interviewer asks me a question about my specialty and I freeze up?" When I suggested that she just remember the basics, she blew up. What followed was a long, vehement speech about how I never seemed to give her credit for being very smart—"What makes you think I need you to tell me something as obvious as that?"—and that I had always treated her as helpless and incompetent. It hurt to hear this, but she was right. She went on to say that the same thing always happens with men, and that it must have something to do with how she presents herself. "I must act helpless when I idealize a man and then when I get over the idealization he's still treating me as though I were nothing." In this, too, she was right, and wrong, at least with me. Relationships are always a two-way street. Perhaps Lorraine had been a little helpless with me (after all, she was depressed), but I could see that when I abandoned my usual restrained, analytic stance, I had been too "helpful"—in other words, intrusive and patronizing.

The reason it took so long for Lorraine to tell me that she hated my condescending manner was that she was afraid of her anger, and afraid of my retaliation. But an even more powerful motive for secrecy was that she was ashamed of herself for being "the kind of person who acts helpless." When Lorraine found the courage to risk being punished for her anger, and to admit that which she was ashamed of, she not only *cleared the air between us but also helped us both to understand ourselves better.*

Lorraine's anger was a catalyst to understanding her shame. Anger is often a clue to shame.

Lying is protective, but it keeps us from breaking through to self-respect. Practice telling the truth. Try simply saying what you think and feel—no more, no less. Notice how often you deny certain feelings, hide your opinions, and pretend to think and feel what you do not. It may be painful to notice all the little lies and half-truths you tell, but noticing bad habits is a step in the direction of changing them.

You may discover something else if you begin to be more honest. We don't always know what we think or feel. You'd be surprised at how many people don't even know what makes them mad or what they really like. They're too worried about doing the right thing to figure out what's right for them.

When I grew up, politics was an important subject of conversation in my house, and I thought I knew a fair amount about what went on in the government. Unfortunately, I didn't really learn to think about the issues, only to categorize politicians as good guys or bad guys. The good guys were the people my parents liked, liberal Democrats, and the bad guys were conservatives and Republicans (which used to be redundant). So while I could play the game of discussing politics, I never learned to look behind the labels or to think about the issues. Oh, I knew what I thought about certain issues, but only after I read James Reston and Tom Wicker.

Discovering in myself the habit of picking up and passing on received opinions was very painful. (Knowing that others do it doesn't make me less ashamed.) A lot of people are like this. We're devoted to brands of food and clothing that we couldn't identify without the labels, and we automatically take on opinions from respected sources.

Here's an experiment that takes a little effort but can be very enlightening. Make a list of everything you strongly believe in. For instance, Democrats are better than Republicans; classical music is harder to enjoy but more "important" than pop music; exercise makes you healthy and feels good (when it's over); Blue Nun is better than New York State wine; Yale or no Yale, George Bush is a lightweight. For each entry, note where and how you formed that opinion. You may be surprised at the results.

It turns out that telling the truth about what you think often means saying, "I don't know," or "I haven't thought that through yet." While saying "I don't know" may be a step in the direction of honesty for opinionated people, those in the habit of not figuring out (or admitting) what they want may need to move in the direction of saying, "This is what I want." Those who hesitate to admit uncertainty may be afraid of being stupid, while those who hesitate to say what they want may be afraid they'll be rejected if they make demands. If you can't allow yourself to make mistakes, you can't take chances and can't risk spontaneity. If you can't allow the possibility of wanting something others might not, then it's hard to say what you want. Start by saying what you want, *then* listen to what others want and work it out.

Telling the truth about your feelings is not, of course, the same as saying whatever you feel like. It's the difference between the backseat driver who says, "You're driving too fast, slow down!" and the passenger who says, "I'm scared, would you please slow down?" It's the difference between saying, "That was a stupid movie" and "I didn't like it." It's a big difference.

There's jargon for this, jargon that seems a little cutesy, but it does clarify: Make "I" statements. "*I* would like to see such and such movie." "*I* prefer the window open." "*I* think Dan Quayle is cute." The "What would *you* like?" and "What do *you* think?" can be either implied or spelled out.

Telling the truth is a form of self-assertion and therefore may remind you of what you've heard about "being assertive." It conjures up a brash and bellicose image, which is unfortunate for two reasons. If our image of assertiveness is associated with rude and aggressive people, this only serves to reinforce our natural tendency to avoid conflict by repressing our own legitimate wants and the aggressiveness sometimes necessary to promote them. If being assertive means demeaning others the way George Steinbrenner does, or grating on the nerves like Howard Cosell, or being a crybaby like John McEnroe, or flaunting one's possessions like Donald Trump, we don't want any part of it. Are these people obnoxious? Yes, of course they are. But why do we love to hate them? Why don't we simply ignore them? Because by dissociating ourselves from their distasteful brand of aggression, we can repudiate aggression in ourselves. As long as we're ashamed of our own assertiveness and can project it onto public figures who epitomize the worst aspects of arrogant egotism, we can safely continue to deny the claims of our own narcissism. But you don't have to be pushy or loud to be assertive. Being assertive means standing up for yourself, not stepping on other people.

The second, and more troublesome, problem with our image of being assertive is that thinking of assertiveness as uncompromising honesty is appealing but self-defeating. Unassertive people often imagine that to be assertive means to be totally forthright, and that's impossibly hard to live up to.

Real self-assertion is about getting what you want, not saying what you want. Assertiveness has to do with forwarding the aims of the self, saying what you mean wherever possible, but, perhaps more important, doing more of what you want and less of what you don't want.

Again, the underlying problem is that unassertive people not only don't say what they need to say, they also bottle up their aggression. So when they imagine that being assertive means making bold statements, it's not just a misunderstanding, it's a self-protective misunderstanding.

One of the reasons we hold back is to avoid conflict. If you say simply what you want (or think or feel) and avoid discharging repressed hostility ("You always . . . !" "You never . . . !") there will be less conflict—less, not none. Tell the truth, simply, and be prepared to withstand—listen to and acknowledge—negative responses. Some people are stuck wanting to tell someone something but are afraid of a negative reaction. I hear this all the time. "I'd love to tell my parents that I wish they'd call and ask if visiting at a certain time would be convenient, instead of just telling us they're coming on such and such a date, but I'm afraid that if I say that they'll just get mad and not visit at all." Tell all of that. "I've wanted to tell you something, but I've been afraid you might get mad. . . ."

Conditioned by shame to suppress much of what makes us human, we become our own oppressors. We dissimulate for fear of being rebuffed, disapproved of, contradicted, criticized, or made to feel foolish. We lie to avoid conflict. When lying becomes habit, we choke off realms of inner experience and avoid avenues of real-life action out of fear and shame. When we tell the truth about what we think and feel, we become more authentically ourselves.

When we say "yes" to what we really want and "no" to what we don't want, we chip away at numbing routine. New interests and activities emerge, some of which have been dormant over the years. The more honest we are about what we want to do, the more time we have (make) for hobbies, athletic activities, classes, reading, and music. Extricating ourselves from pretense and habit is liberating, like that wonderful last-day-of-school feeling in June. Freedom is exhilarating, and disquieting. Unfortunately, when we do make time for ourselves, we may discover that we've forgotten how to play.

REDISCOVERING PLAY

When children play, they do so with abandon. What they abandon is self-consciousness. Grown-ups have a hard time doing that. We're more tightly wrapped, and for that reason most of us have to do something to release the playful child within us. We can't just *be* unrestrained, we have to overcome restraint.

Some of us feel comfortable playing tennis or running or dancing. We know how to play these games: We know the rules, we have the right clothes, we know what's going to happen, we've done it before. Grown-ups can play, but playing isn't grown-up. "Grown-up play" is an oxymoron. To play, we must let go, like children. Pure play is pure release.

A lot of us are too caught up in the serious business of life to make time for play. We're too busy, we're too tired, we're too stressed out—we're too uptight. The longer and harder we work, the more caught up we become with Achievement and Responsibility, and the more out of touch with the world of the senses. Starting a long time ago, we learned to subdue the urge to run and jump and play—first, to do well in school; later, to advance our careers. A lot of us overdid it.

It's disheartening to discover that over the years we've lost some of our capacity for enjoyment. We find ourselves at places of fun, like parties and picnics, thinking about getting home when we don't have to, or just not enjoying ourselves the way we used to. Or we try too hard, in that self-conscious smiley way that older people take on when they've been allowed into a children's party. It makes us feel sad and stale, as though losing a certain unreplenishable moisture.

By now you know one big reason why adults have such a hard time dropping their guard, letting go, and loosing the spontaneous playful self. That's right, shame. Because play is a creature of the unrestrained self, it's dangerous to the extent we regard the self as suspect and vulnerable to judgment. It's hard to fool around if you're afraid of looking foolish.

A successful woman in her late thirties told me the following story. At the last minute she decided to go to a conference because she was feeling stale. Maybe she needed some new ideas. It was good to get away, but the conference was disappointing; most of the presentations bored her. Then, quite unexpectedly, she made a discovery.

She was having breakfast with a colleague in a garden restaurant at the Ritz Carlton. The tables were arranged around a sunlit courtyard with a tulip garden and a large pond at the center. In the pond was a little house on stilts with a platform sloping down into the water. Before she could figure out what it was, half a dozen ducklings poked their heads out, waddled down the platform, and plopped into the water. They were so sweet! Old enough to venture out fearlessly, young enough to still be fuzzy.

The conversation didn't quite hold her attention. Her mind was with the ducklings, and she watched them out of the corner of her eye. Such carefree little swimmers! They splashed around and chased each other—it was pure play, or so it seemed. If the water was cold or the ducklings were hungry, she didn't notice. The eyes of her mind saw only their freedom and play, and her own sense of being a prisoner of responsibility and habit.

After breakfast she decided to skip the morning's presentations and go for a walk. She walked for over an hour, turning things over in her mind. What made the image of those ducklings so compelling? They were free, that was it. She, on the other hand, felt used and tired. Her career and the marriage and the children had tightened their grip on her life, leaving her boxed in and worn out. She didn't need to get away, and she didn't need new ideas; she needed to have some fun. And she would, too. When she got home, she'd make some time for herself, go for walks at lunchtime, get together with friends, maybe sign up for swimming at the Y. She was lying to herself.

When she got home, time passed and life resumed its course. Play? Someday.

What held this woman back? What holds most of us back? It isn't just that as obligations rise, spirits flag, although that's part of it. We've forgotten how to play; it isn't "important," so we don't make room for it. And when we do feel like playing, we aren't sure how to go about it.

The idea of willed pleasure seems paradoxical; we expect to release pleasure. When we were kids, we never had to *try* to have fun. Now that we're adults, we have trouble releasing ourselves from constraints. Negative thoughts distract us and compete for our attention. We have a lot to get done, and we worry about deadlines and the kids. It's possible to stop yourself from thinking negative thoughts and, instead, concentrate on fun: It takes letting go.

One of the ironies about play is that you can't *try* to let go. What you can do is create a context for letting go. Finding your context is important, a place where you can let go and be free. Some people can play where others can't. If you take an activity too seriously, it's not play.

Real play is gloriously pointless. Playing to score points is contradictory. When ten-year-old boys go out to "play" basketball wearing elaborate uniforms in front of parents exhorting them to win, it isn't play. This structure, this conditioning, spoils play for a lot of us. When I was a kid, I loved to play tennis. I played a lot and got good at it. (The more time passes, and the fewer witnesses, the better I was.) When I started working summers, I quit playing. I cared too much about the game to just fool around occasionally at it. Then, in my sophomore year of college, I decided to try out for the college team. Although I was the fourth-ranking player on the varsity team, I wasn't nearly as good as I had been. My mind remembered how to play, but my body didn't cooperate. It was terribly frustrating. Every night after practice I'd come back to the dorm muttering and slamming doors. One of the older students (twenty-four), Brechar Hemaphlard, from Thailand, said to me, "Why do you do it? You don't seem to be having any fun." *Foreigners*, I thought, *they don't understand anything*. What's fun got to do with it? Wouldn't anyone who could play a sport at the varsity level do it? Besides, it used to be fun, maybe it will be again. It wasn't, and so I eventually did quit.

There are two morals to this story. The first is that it's hard to have fun if you are too caught up in winning or doing well. The second lesson is that it's hard to have fun if you feel like a klutz. The experience of incompetence takes the joy out of it. In the case of my tennis, it wasn't just that I wasn't good at it, it was that I wasn't as good as I felt I should be. Incidentally, I tried tennis again when I was about thirty and found that I was just as good and just as bad, but I no longer cared. It had become just a game.

One of the contexts for having fun is being with friends. It's hard to play by yourself. One of my patients recently reminded me of this. She was talking about working too hard and not having enough fun, and so I asked her what she does to play. She plays board games. *Board games?* Yes, but she plays with friends and they use the game as a vehicle to fool around. They kid and joke around, and make up new rules to suit their mood. They don't care about winning or losing and it isn't a test of their intellects. They just play.

Playfulness, like other moods, is infectious. This emotional contagion is one reason people go to sports events. You certainly can't see as well in the stadium as you can watching TV at home. People pay all that money and go to all that effort not just to see the game but to get into the mood of the crowd. To let go, scream, and cheer. It's fun, but we need permission, and need a context. People go to rock concerts for the same reason.

It's hard to play by yourself, but here is another paradox: Shame-sensitive people have a hard time playing in front of other people, finding it nearly impossible to escape the confines of self-consciousness. They're too concerned about being watched to concentrate on doing.

Play is a way to break out of our shame-conditioned shells, but that doesn't mean we can just will ourselves to drop self-consciousness, to simply decide to stop worrying about being clumsy or looking foolish. Our restraint is defensive, but we are defensive for a reason. We're vulnerable. Relaxing defenses is the key to successful play; ignoring them leaves us exposed to the possibility of traumatic shame. Still, the world is full of people who confidently say to others, "Don't worry, be happy."

Relaxing is easier said than done. Here's one suggestion: Learn to dance—or just start to dance. But make it easy on yourself. If you can't dance in front of people, do it alone. Find some music that moves you and turn it on. Turn it up. Move. Once you become a little more comfortable with yourself, venture out and play in the company of people you like, friends whose good opinion isn't at issue. Run, jump, throw, catch. If you can play a sport and really get into it and let go, fine. Give it a try. Otherwise, find an outlet where you *can* let go.

Play needn't be confined to games. Work can be play. Some people are lucky enough to work at something they love, something that allows them to be creative. You can make your own luck by introducing a spirit of play into your work.

Nearly everyone recognizes the crucial role of play in the arts. A jazz musician, for example, creates novel rhythms and melodies by improvising, fooling around. You can emulate this creative involvement by suspending the rules, pushing the limits, breaking new ground, and getting fully involved. Play is the freedom to go out on a limb with the knowledge that you might fall flat on your face, but also with the knowledge that *it doesn't matter.* To play at work, it may be necessary to make it not matter, to experiment with flexibility by disconnecting yourself from self-scrutiny and outcome.

Take writing. Many people approach the blank white page with all the enthusiasm of a high diver who's not sure he can swim: *What if I don't have anything to say? What if it's clumsy and awkward?* Successful writers are not people who don't have such worries, they are people who trick themselves past them. A technique many writers use is "prewriting." They set that intimidating first page aside and make tentative, freewheeling notes. They jot down ideas they feel strongly about, they make lists, they free-associate. They don't worry about what they write or how they write it: It doesn't count; it's just fooling around. Later, when they come back to these visions, some need revision, some may be thrown out, and some may be just fine. The same process of releasing your vision can be applied to almost any kind of work by suspending your concern with outcome. Just brainstorm.

Another way to play at work is to have a group of congenial colleagues with whom you can loosen up and toss around ideas. This *does* require a little luck. Still, we can work with what we've got.

To release creative group effort it's necessary to unlock the usual routines and roles. It helps if you respect each other enough to be honest and take chances, and it helps to introduce some kind of novelty to break down everyday inhibitions (occasionally meeting outside the office, for example).

*   *   *

Two groups of people who have trouble playing are men and women. Men may be more likely to take the fun out of their games by being hung up on scoring points, and women may be more inhibited about unleashing their aggression, but men and women alike have a hard time releasing themselves from fear of embarrassment. As we've seen, a lot stands in the way of play, but one thing I haven't mentioned is the simple art of making time for yourself. And here, I think, women have a harder time than men. Some men are too caught up with their work to take time for play, but most men have an easier time than women at being good to themselves.

BEING GOOD TO YOURSELF

Many of us have a surprising and deep-rooted resistance to anything that smacks of simply having a good time. We have a hard-wired association between pleasure and guilt, at violating others' rights to our time and energy, and shame, over giving in to the weakness of self-indulgence. We're ashamed of our appetites and anxiously driven to achieve or serve in order to prove to the world that we are what we worry we aren't: worthwhile, worth loving.

Many of the men I know are too busy working in order to get Stuff and Be Important to take time for themselves. They don't take time for breakfast, or sit still long enough to read the paper, or make time to be with their friends. They aren't unselfish, just busy. Women are busy, too, but they're more likely than men to be ashamed of anything that feels selfish, whether it's play or career advancement. They're too busy looking after other people. On good days, selfish women think: *They need me.* On bad days: *They're so damned selfish! Nobody does anything around here but me.* They'd love to take a day off, spend some money on themselves, let other people pick up some of the slack, but they can't. That logic serves their purposes. It protects them from conflict with those who depend on them and from the shame of feeling selfish.

Instead of belaboring the reasons we aren't good to ourselves, let's see what can be done about it.

You might start by taking a look at how you're spending your time—what you're doing and why, and what's missing. Of the things you have to do each week, which are important and satisfying, and which do you do merely because you have to? It might help to actually make a list. Now examine the reasons you "have to." You may discover a couple of themes in your motivation. Some people tie themselves down with obligation so that others will appreciate them, some so that nobody will get mad at them. Try to be honest with yourself about this.

Being more honest with yourself about your motivation may help you realize how many things you do because you lack the self-respect and confidence to say no. Would someone whose self-respect was absolutely secure worry as much as you do?

You may discover that some of your obligations and imperatives are optional. You don't *have* to do the laundry for teenagers who don't cooperate. You don't *have* to come home at a certain time every night. You don't *have* to accept extra work whenever you're asked. (Remember, one way to say no is to say, "I'd love to, but I can't.") You may, however, decide to continue doing most of these things. Don't berate yourself for doing things to avoid rocking the boat or in hopes others will appreciate you. Being a friend to yourself means taking a look at what you're doing, modifying some things and accepting others.

While we're on the subject of how you spend your time, it might be interesting to consider how you choose your vocation. Does your choice of a career reflect capitalizing on your strengths or compensating for your weaknesses? Did you join the ministry trying to be "selfless," ignoring your own unruly needs and giving too much of yourself to others? Did you become a therapist to help other people resolve problems that plague you? Did you become a police officer to deny fear? A teacher to avoid confronting grownups? Did you decide to work for the government or other large institution, rather than go into the private sector, for security? Has not making waves, ignoring problems, and keeping out of trouble become more important than creative challenge? How much of what you do is an expression, and an enhancement, of your self-respect? How much of what you do is designed to elicit approval from other people?

You don't always need someone else to feed your self-esteem. You can sit down and do good work, or exercise vigorously, or clean up your room for your own satisfaction. No one knows about it, but you feel better. Cultivate this capacity to confirm yourself.

How about all the fun things you don't do anymore? Make a list of some of the things that used to give your life zest and meaning. It might be playing tennis, painting, reading, fishing, listening to music, hiking, going to museums, having people over for dinner. Now write down the reasons you've gotten out of the habit of doing these things, without blaming other people. If you don't have people over for dinner anymore because your spouse complains or doesn't like your friends or won't help, put that down as "*I* don't have people over because *I* haven't been willing to insist." If you don't take time to get together with your friends because you have to get home to cook dinner, put that down as "*I* haven't been willing to drop the ball, just not cook dinner and let them fend for themselves." Got all your excuses in place? Good. Now you don't have to change a thing.

Of course it's not just habit that holds us back. Here's a little experiment (it's only a "little" one, you can do it) to test the elasticity of your restraint. Make a list of your favorite activities. Estimate how often you used to do these things, and how often you do them now. Increase the number of times you do these things for one month. (I'd suggest keeping a record.) In the process, you may discover more flexibility than you thought, and you may start to be more aware of what holds you back and why.

HEALTHY PLEASURES

When I talked about guilty pleasures in Chapter 6, I explained how we get hooked in cycles of control and release, and I described how these cycles, in which shame is the stimulus and the response, lead to "immoderate appetites," "passive escapism," "shameful pleasures," and "secret vices." Now I'm saying be good to yourself. Is this a case of damned if you do and damned if you don't?

The difference between guilty pleasures and healthy pleasures is that guilty pleasures make us feel ashamed afterward; healthy pleasures make us feel good and they enhance our self-respect. The problem is, of course, that some people are so uptight, filled with shame and guilt, that they don't allow themselves any fun, while others fool themselves into thinking that they're so overworked, overwhelmed and put upon, that they've earned the right to indulge in binge eating, heavy drinking, or pornography. Unfortunately, there is no formula for distinguishing healthy from guilty pleasures.

We know that certain things we do aren't good for us. Whether it's something as innocuous as watching tired comedies on TV every night or as self-destructive as binge eating, we just can't seem to quit. *Trying* to stop may, in fact, be part of the problem.

Trying to stop ourselves from bad habits is often part of the control and release cycle. Take overeating. Most diets are yo-yo diets. Self-deprivation builds up cravings—physical as well as psychological. So we bounce back and forth between overcontrol and overindulgence. Condemning ourselves (*This is really awful, I've got to quit doing this*) may give us a temporary incentive to "reform," but rarely works. It's hard to change something you don't understand.

If they bother to think at all about what's behind regressive indulgences, people generally think of them as ways to gratify themselves when stress is high and other sources of gratification low. In lives hemmed in by obligation and restraint, the most readily available pleasures are those someone can sell us: material things, passive entertainment, sugary foods, and mood-altering drugs like alcohol, caffeine, and nicotine. These guilty pleasures are gratifying, but they are also self-soothing—and there is an important difference.

People trapped in guilty pleasures are often critical and unable to empathize with themselves, unable to soothe themselves in other ways, and unable to trust others to provide empathy. Most of the people who indulge in guilty pleasures are otherwise deprived—deprived of creative stimulation, sympathy, and the healthy pleasure of moderate doses of a wide variety of satisfactions.

We rely on regressive forms of self-indulgence to soothe painful feelings, and in the absence of other reliable forms of soothing, we come to overrely on them. When this happens, guilty pleasures may seem maladaptive and may induce shame, but it is important to realize that they are effective methods for soothing a damaged self in a frightening world.

Notice *when* the urge for self-indulgence strikes. Pay attention to where you are, what you're doing, and what you're thinking about at the moment you begin to plan your next indulgent binge. It's likely to be when you've worked hard to accomplish something and feel you deserve a special reward, or when you've been hurt, disappointed, or frustrated. These are times when the self needs responding. People with more self-respect have the capacity to give themselves some of this sympathy and approval. People with less self-respect have a greater need for external infusions.

Instead of condemning yourself for guilty pleasure, try to understand your need, and try to build a broader network of satisfactions. The next time the urge for guilty pleasure strikes, consider substituting a healthy pleasure. (It's much harder to *stop* doing something than it is to *start* doing something else.) Go for a walk, or to a movie, play ball, cuddle, read a book. Open yourself to novelty. Get out and look at the stars, go for a swim. Do something different. You may find more satisfaction and less shame.

15

....

Kinship and Friendship

What would it mean to have solid self-respect? Many people think that if they had self-respect, they'd be secure and their relationships would be successful. They'd be complete; finished products. It doesn't work that way. The self-sufficiency we long for is partly an ideal, partly an illusion. The truth is, we never outgrow our need for other people.

Self-respect does not unfold in a vacuum, free from the influence of family and friends, and it does not endure in a vacuum. By the time we're grown, our characters have been molded by years of relationships. Those whose parents yelled at them ("You never do anything right!") or who paid hardly any attention to them, grew up ashamed and insecure; while those fortunate enough to have parents who always seemed to understand and appreciate them, grew up more or less self-respecting. But no matter how lucky or unlucky we were growing up, we still need other people. Even if we're sure of ourselves, we need a network of relationships to express and fulfill our social nature and to sustain the self's need for understanding and appreciation. *And,* even if we're unsure of ourselves, we can transform the quality of our lives and become more self-respecting by developing relationships with people who accept us.

The quality of our connections and the quality of our self-respect are circular, each feeds the other. And like all things circular, change in either one leads to change in the other. Anything that bolsters our self-respect will improve our relationships, and anything that improves our relationships will bolster self-respect.

THE SOURCE OF SELF-RESPECT

The source of self-respect is the family, more particularly our relationship with our parents. Their respect for us, their acceptance of our feelings and opinions, is what builds *self*-respect and shapes the face we turn to the world. Our relationship with our parents is the source of all subsequent relationships.

Most of us leave home on the brink of adulthood. Right in the middle of transforming our relationships with our parents from an adolescent to a mature level, we interrupt the process to set out on our own. Notice that I said "interrupt," not resolve. Most people reduce contact with their parents and siblings to avoid the anxiety and conflict of dealing with them. Once out of range, people forget or deny the discord. Still, they carry around old difficulties in the form of unresolved sensitivities that flare up in intense relationships wherever they go. Having learned to ignore their own role in family conflicts, they are unable to prevent recurrences in new relationships. For most of us, the incomplete transformation of our relationship to our parents is the most important unfinished business of our lives.

Distancing

We leave home with a well-defined set of expectations about relationships and with a particular pattern of coping with conflict. Most of these coping patterns rely on some form of *distancing* to manage anxiety in relationships. The instinctive response to threat is fight or flight. Distancing is a universal mechanism for avoiding the threat of emotional distress.

It's so common for mobile, middle-class Americans to move away from home to pursue educations and careers that it isn't always obvious that part of the need to leave home is to put distance between ourselves and our families. Some people don't move out of town; instead, they withdraw emotionally: They keep conversations superficial, reveal little about themselves, and use third parties as buffers. Some of us are aware of our distancing. We avoid visits because they're so difficult. Or we visit but make a point of not talking about anything personal. Some of us aren't aware of our distancing because it takes the form of long-practiced and seldom-questioned routine. We don't have intimate conversations with either parent, because we're never alone with either parent. Mom-and-Dad come as an indivisible pair, a single, hyphenated being. If our parents are divorced, we may be close to one at the expense of distance from the other, or we may distance ourselves from both to avoid being caught up in their conflict. Perhaps we don't know how obliged we are to avoid certain subjects, because it never occurs to us to broach them. But regardless of how aware or unaware we are of our distance from our parents, we tend to think it has to do with them. What we seldom realize is that distancing is about us.

The more we manage emotional intensity by distancing ourselves from members of the family, the more we bring that unresolved sensitivity into other relationships, especially intimate ones.

Shame and Emotional Fusion

What has all this got to do with shame and self-respect? Shame is a major source of our emotional sensitivity and tendency to overreact. Each of us becomes reactive in the face of sufficient anxiety. When anxiety reaches a certain point, we react by falling back on a set pattern of responses. These vary from person to person, but most of us have a characteristic style of navigating relationships under stress: pursuing, distancing, overfunctioning (taking over and doing things for others), or underfunctioning (becoming dependent). These patterned responses, automatic anxiety-driven responses, are the product of *emotional fusion.*

Fusion does not mean closeness in the sense of intimacy; it

means a breakdown of objectivity and autonomy. Emotional fusion weakens the boundary between thoughts and feelings: When our intellects are flooded with feeling, we are incapable of objective thinking. Emotional fusion also blurs the boundary between one-self and others—like the woman who takes responsibility for her husband's moods, or the man who assumes his wife is angry at him whenever she isn't smiling. Because we're less able to think clearly and less able to remember that we're different people, we react emotionally as though there is no boundary between us. We're thin-skinned.

The two boundaries blurred by emotional fusion, between emotion and intellect and between ourselves and others, are strengthened by self-respect and weakened by shame.

Self-respect makes us level-headed and stable, able to pause between action and reaction and therefore less vulnerable to over-reaction. Shame makes us hypersensitive, quick to become our anxious, emotionally reactive, worst selves rather than our calm, best selves. Fusion makes us unstable. Unable to resist the gravitational pull of anxious reaction to others within our orbit, we're less able to stay on course. We can't tolerate differences of opinion; we have to make other people wrong to make ourselves right; we feel we have to change them to be the way we want them to be.

Self-respect enables us to be close without fusion. Our boundaries don't melt in the heat of emotion. We have integrity. Self-respect lets us tolerate differences, and therefore makes us capable of true intimacy.

Respect for Differences

We're drawn to people like ourselves. When you meet someone who shares your interest in music or movies or hiking or who reads the same kinds of books, you feel a kinship and an attraction. Discovering and sharing similarities of taste and habit and opinion feels wonderful, and wonderfully reassuring. The more similar you are, the safer it is to open up. As long as the two of you are on the same wavelength, there's less static and little danger of misunderstanding.

In any relationship, differences inevitably emerge, and they seem to bother us more the closer the relationship—and the closer the differences touch on what's important to us. It's disappointing to discover that a friend thinks the movie you loved stinks. But it's really upsetting when a spouse or lover differs with you on something as important as sexual practices or dislikes your best friend. Such differences are painful. But it's really emotional reactivity to differences, not the differences themselves, that causes us so much distress.

I've seen couples in my office fighting like wounded animals over such trivial things. Once, for example, a woman said she didn't see any reason why their son shouldn't watch professional wrestling on TV if he wanted to. Her husband was furious. She *knew* he didn't approve of that trash! She was *ruining* the boy's mind. Such a fuss. It wasn't just Hulk Hogan and Andre the Giant that bothered him, it was his wife's dissent. He grew up in a family where differences weren't tolerated. His parents masked disagreements and conflicts with a facade of togetherness, because they had an unnatural dread of separateness. They never argued openly about anything, but then they didn't talk much either—too many unsafe subjects.

If we can't tolerate differences, we have just three choices: combat, surrender, or distance. When there are too many differences, there isn't much of a basis for a relationship. But with no tolerance for differences, there's no room for separate identities, no room for divergence of opinion or interest, and no room for real intimacy— to be able to be who you are in a relationship and allow the other person the same privilege.

Shame is the enemy of intimacy. It makes us hide our thoughts and feelings from others because our defenses are brittle. We haven't learned to control our quixotic tempers or sulky retreats. Given that our reactions to hurt feelings are relatively fixed, what are our alternatives? One is to continue to rely on distance, physical or emotional, to minimize anxiety in intimate relationships: We can make ourselves tough and mean, impenetrable to hurt. Or we can reduce emotional reactivity at the source.

Nowhere are we more vulnerable to shame than with our parents. After all these years, we still crave their approval—and they still give it about as much as they ever did. When we avoid our parents or keep relationships with them on a superficial level, we aren't being cold or unkind. We're avoiding shame and anger—shame for being so vulnerable, anger at not being appreciated. In the search for self-respect, getting closer to our families is the final exam. Improving family ties accomplishes two things: It extends the network of sustaining relationships, and it overcomes unresolved emotional reactivity. By going back to the source of our feelings about ourselves, we can make peace with the past and come to terms not only with our families, but also with ourselves.

MAKING PEACE WITH YOUR PARENTS

As long as our parents are still alive, each of us has two relationships with them. One is based on the past and consists of memories we have of growing up, feelings about those memories, and judgments we make about the memories and feelings. The second relationship is the actual ongoing relationship (for better or worse) with the flesh-and-blood parents who exist in the present. Unfortunately, the first relationship, the one in our minds, is more alive for many people than the second one, the real, contemporary relationship. The first can poison the second, like sewage seeping into a flowing stream.

The past is gone, but we can't let go of it. We brood over old injustices and long for missing appreciation. We do things to make our parents admire us, which is not necessary, and we try to change them, which is not possible. We love them and resent them.

Some of us can't stop wishing our parents were different. We'd rewrite the past. Maybe we still can. Others, anxious and bitter, avoid their parents altogether, thereby keeping the past frozen in memory.

We can't change what our parents did—or how we responded. And we can't change who they are. What we can change is our relationship to them.

In *The Power of the Family,* I wrote: "And what about the past?

Your mother's harsh treatment, your father's neglect, all the ways they let you down? Does all this go away, or cease to matter? No, but it's over. As for the parents you remember, forgive them. Perhaps you can understand why they did what they did. Perhaps not. But believe this: They did the best they could. We all do."[1]

I wrote that from the heart. But I was wrong, naive. My sentiment overlooked bitterness and denied anger. I now believe that healthy relationships with our parents go through stages. Honesty and self-respect demand that we face up to our indignation. Ignoring our resentment, pretending not to care about the annoying things they did, and do, is another form of emotional distancing.

The Stages of Reconciliation

Little children idolize their parents. Even if our parents aren't perfect, self-respect demands that we see them in the best possible light. We're theirs, and they are what we will be. The fewer faults we see, the better.

Adolescent rebellion serves self-respect by loosening family ties and freeing children to become themselves. Teenagers struggle to redefine the rules, and demand to be treated with respect. They don't want to be like Mommy and Daddy anymore, they want to be themselves. (They may even be ashamed to be seen with their parents.) Once parents were perfect, now they're the reverse. Later, after we've left home and been on our own for a while, we start to realize that they aren't so terrible after all. This familiar scenario overlooks just one thing: Our parents really do have annoying habits; they really did hurt us.

The third stage in the evolution of parent-child relationships, distancing, is also necessary. New families need room to function, and new adults need room to consolidate their independence. The ideal might be independence *and* healthy contact with parents, but the reality is that we need some distance to allow us to concentrate on our new lives.

Before they can reconcile with their parents, some people must go through a period of angry self-assertion. This is not the most mature stage of relationships—maturity is being emotionally connected without being emotionally reactive—but it may be a necessary stage to go through. Ignoring the past, their mistreatment and our anger, alienates us from ourselves as well as from our parents. Pretending to get along with someone we're still angry at leaves a wall of silent bitterness between us. Let me tell you about the person who taught me this.

When she came to see me at age twenty-six, Judy was a robust, attractive, single career woman, bright and full of energy. But try to tell her that! As far as she was concerned, she was a clumsy, overweight, undereducated neurotic. You name a fault, she claimed it.

Judy's severe and obsessive self-doubt took the form of incredible procrastination. Afraid she might do something wrong, she put off doing things at all. Bills piled up. Deadlines came and went. She had to check and recheck everything she did for fear of making a mistake. Before she left the house, she had to reexamine all the electrical appliances and countertops to make sure she didn't leave anything undone. She even had little rituals for parking her car to make sure she didn't leave the lights on or her keys in the ignition. Her life was a mess.

When I asked, "Whose voice do you hear saying you screwed up?" Judy burst into tears. No words, just sobbing that went on for several minutes. She had a hard childhood. Her mother was always putting her down, and her alcoholic father beat her. Nothing she did was good enough.

Looking back, I think I prolonged Judy's shame by trying too hard to be reassuring. She'd tell me some "awful" failing of hers, and I'd say, "That's not so terrible. Lots of people do that." She liked being reassured but didn't always believe it. "You don't know how bad it is." And then she'd tell me more embarrassing symptoms of self-doubt, more compulsions, more rituals.

After wearing out the subject of how awful she was, Judy began to talk more about her mother's cruelty. She was unpredictable. Sometimes she was kind and loving; other times she was brutal with humiliating comments. "There's no telling what mood she'll be in. She just flies off the handle; it doesn't seem to have any relation to anything I do." Judy would look in her mother's eyes for a weather report, and if she didn't see storm clouds, she felt safe. Drawn to the warmth, Judy would often run right into a thunderclap of humiliation. At first, when she talked about her mother's mistreatment, Judy cried a lot, but it wasn't long before she got angry. She began to show me what she called her "spunky side." In fact, she wasn't spunky in the sense of being strong willed and spirited, she was sarcastic and biting. Judy's "spunky side" felt better to her than cowering in shame, but it was just another form of emotional reactivity.

As Judy began to come to terms with her past, she started getting more involved with life in the present. Partly she was ready; partly I pushed. She got a better job, looked up old friends, and started dating. Her first move in the family was to withdraw. Instead of always going to family gatherings, where she always felt picked on, she started staying away. For the first time in her life, she felt in control. She didn't have to submit to humiliation; she didn't have to go. The hell with them.

Eventually, Judy felt sufficiently strong to plan a reentry into her family. This time she would visit and attend family parties a stronger, more self-assured person. I was delighted.

Every couple of weeks she'd come in to tell me proudly how she was standing up for herself with the family. I was not delighted. What she meant by standing up for herself were aggressive counterattacks. For example, when Judy went to a family party at her "snotty, stuck-up sister-in-law's" and her mother said, "I'm glad you could join us," Judy let her have it. Told her off. Telling me this, Judy was so pleased. I had to bite my tongue. I wanted to say: Fine, but wouldn't it be better just to remain calm and not rise to the bait? *But I realized that I was wrong and she was right.*

Judy's anger was something she had to get through. It was an intermediary stage between silent humiliation and the calm composure that self-respect makes possible.

When we revise our past, getting angry at our parents may be a necessary stage if we are to switch from thinking of ourselves as (shamefully) inadequate to thinking of ourselves as (shamelessly) mistreated. We're okay, they're not okay.

So what if we have to exaggerate their faults and mock them to our friends? Maybe we need to give ourselves those booster shots of scorn. Anger has its place in face-to-face encounters, too. If your mother acts wounded when you want to visit a friend over the holidays, or your father changes the subject in the middle of your telling him about one of your successes—and you are defenseless—you just feel bad: disloyal; boring. They're right, you're wrong. Getting mad is better than feeling bad. Shame on your mother for being so possessive. Shame on your father for being so insensitive. (It's better than shame in you.)

Some people complicate their lives and relationships by thinking that when they discover anger, self-respect demands they show it. They take the advice to "get in touch with anger" as permission to condemn and berate their parents. In fact, with anger, the important thing is to feel it, not necessarily to show it.

Your anger may be upsetting, but think of it as transitional, a rite of passage separating you from negative attitudes, demands, and expectations. Anger is part of the separation phase, separating your response—shame—from their stimulus. Later, when you really are separate, you can differentiate your response from their stimulus without having to resort to distance or indignation. After you've felt your anger and the power anger bestows, strive for acceptance. Accepting them is also accepting yourself. Once you can let your parents be themselves, without feeling the need to change them, you can relax and be yourself.

Defining a Self in Relationship to Parents

Making peace with your parents finally boils down to being in emotional contact with them, being yourself, and letting them be themselves. It's almost as simple as staying in touch and avoiding emotional reactivity. The reason I've taken such pains to explain distancing, emotional fusion, reactivity, the possible need for an angry phase, and respect for differences, is that ignorance of these mechanisms can defeat even the most well-intentioned efforts at reconciliation. Emotional reactivity is so powerful and toxic that it's essential to think through and plan your efforts to improve relationships.

Planning should start with an assessment of the current status of your relationship. (Incidentally, it's best to work on one relationship at a time. When I speak of "parents" plural, it's only for convenience.) First consider the level of intimacy you have with one parent, and plan to move one step closer. If you're never alone with your father, for example, arrange for the two of you to spend a little time together. Go for a walk. Take him out to lunch. Or if your conversations with your mother are generally about third parties (your father, your obnoxious sister), plan to steer the conversation around to what's going on in her life and yours.

The second step is to figure out the basic pattern of the relationship. It should be easy to come up with what your parent does that annoys you. Start with that, but also notice how you respond. That may be a little harder—harder but imperative. Becoming more aware of the waltz the two of you do and anticipating the other person's steps distances you slightly and enables you to see what's happening without becoming totally caught up in the emotion of the moment. Anticipation mutes emotionality. Recognizing your own steps makes you even more objective and helps keep your toes from getting stepped on.

Stuck relationships with parents usually come in one of two forms: hot or cold—intense and conflicted or peaceful but distant.

Irene and her father were locked in an intense emotional relationship. They loved each other but fought all the time. When I asked Irene to describe what her father did that upset her, she said, "He's impossible! He argues about everything. He's always trying to tell me how to run my life, and if I ever try to talk to him about something I'm doing, he interrupts to tell me what his second cousin once removed did or what the man on the bus said."

The capacity to hurt grows out of closeness and need.

Irene's father was well positioned to hurt her. They were intensely involved with each other, each one vying for appreciation in a form the other didn't show. What made Irene's father so hard to talk to was that, unlike most of us, he didn't know how to hold his claws in during an argument. It didn't take much to get him going, and his passionate tongue-lashings were becoming unbearable.

Irene was able to get closer to her father and calm down the relationship by working on it in stages. The first thing she had to figure out was what she was doing that contributed to the blow-ups. That was the hard part.

What Irene did when her father was being difficult was try to endure her annoyance without saying anything. If she was on the phone and her father started lecturing her, she'd hold the mouthpiece away and roll her eyes at her husband, saying, "See? He's off again." After a while, though, she'd get mad and blow up. By then it was too late to be reasonable. She'd yell at him, he'd yell back, and then one of them would slam the phone down or storm out of the room.

Irene's first change was simple. She started speaking up about her annoyance before she got mad. If her father changed the subject when she was talking or didn't get what she was saying, she spoke up. And—this is critical—it worked to the extent that she talked about her feelings, rather than criticizing him. "Hey, Dad, I wanted to finish telling you about. . ." works. "You're always changing the subject" doesn't. The one thing that defeats most efforts to open up to parents is that people confuse talking about their feelings with telling their parents off.

The next thing that Irene tried to tackle was her father's overbearing control. When he told her what to do, she felt humiliated, treated like a child. Irene's usual response was to argue, which only made him more insistent or resulted in his criticizing her (!) for being a know-it-all.

I suggested a couple of alternative responses, tricks that often work with advice givers. She could joke with him about being so helpful, or she could stop resisting and start asking for so much advice he'd get sick of it. Irene didn't like either suggestion. She didn't want to be sarcastic and phony, she wanted to be real.

Irene figured out that the main thing was to try something different with her father. What she came up with was to not say anything when he started giving advice. Just not respond at all, to wait until he talked himself out. It worked. Irene's lack of reaction conveyed her lack of interest in advice, without the usual argument.

By this point, things were going so well that Irene decided to try to make her conversations with her father more personal. First she'd try to get him to talk about himself, then maybe he'd be receptive to a more personal exchange. It sounded good.

Unfortunately, neither Irene nor I anticipated her father's response. When she invited him to talk about what was on his mind, he launched into bitter recriminations about how everyone, including Irene and her brothers, disappointed him. This was hard to listen to, and at first Irene couldn't. She'd get upset and cut off the conversation. After we'd had a chance to talk about it, she decided that it was hard to listen passively while her father put everybody in the family down, so she decided to try listening actively.

The next time her father started in on what ungrateful sons he had, Irene reflected how sad he sounded. By acknowledging her father's feelings instead of reacting to his attacks, Irene was able to listen to his denunciations without getting upset. Her nonreactive response had a powerful effect on her father and the relationship. He began to talk more about himself and less about other people, and he became much more receptive to Irene's talking about herself. He'd still occasionally launch into one of his patented attacks, but since they no longer had the power to set Irene off, they rarely lasted long.

When you consider the combustibility of emotions between fathers and daughters, it's hardly surprising that Irene and her father had a stormy relationship. In most families, when there's that much tension, people have an emotional cutoff. In Irene's family, however, a powerful ethic of togetherness kept them from avoiding each other.

This was not the case with Mel. He and his mother were distant, and he didn't like it.

Mel left home at eighteen to join the air force and see the world. Then, at twenty-four, he went to college, married, and settled down—if you can call it that. As a rising executive in a large company, moving up meant moving his family every three or four years. Maybe it was all the traveling that made Mel long to reconnect with his roots and get closer to his mother. But she was so resolutely unresponsive that Mel began to worry that she had something against him. She rarely answered his letters, seemed annoyed or uncomfortable when he called, and usually made excuses when he asked her to visit. Her rebuffs singed his pride.

Mel couldn't figure it out. Maybe his mother didn't like his wife. Maybe she was bitter about his joining the air force. Maybe she didn't approve of his choice of career. These unanswered questions worked on his nerves, leaving him frustrated and making him bitter.

When Mel consulted me for help in getting close to his mother, the first thing that struck me was that they were locked in a pattern of pursuit and distance. It was ironic that Mel couldn't see it; he was such a distancer himself. The problem was that, now in his thirties, he was lonely for lost connections, and, unfortunately, the person he most wanted to get closer to was the expert who taught him how to distance.

Like a lot of people who try to improve frustrating relationships, Mel thought he had tried everything. He had called, written, and visited. He even tried staying away for long periods of time. Finally, in desperation, he'd written his mother a long letter asking her what was wrong. Even that did no good. She answered obliquely, saying nothing was wrong; don't be silly. Clearly, the "everything" that Mel tried was all one thing: pursuing a distancer.

After we talked about it, Mel realized that his strategy was counterproductive. Once he recognized his part in the pursuer-distancer dynamic and understood that there are gradations of intimacy, Mel was able to stop pushing his mother for more intimacy than she was comfortable with. But like all strategies to change behavior, this one might not have worked without some understanding of what was motivating Mel's behavior in the first place.

When he was eighteen, Mel wanted to get as far away from home as possible. He didn't have many friends in the small town he grew up in, and his family felt confining. When he got far enough away from home and firmly enough on his own two feet, Mel realized that he was lonely. He'd hoped for a revival of the special bond he once had with his mother. They were so alike. She was smart and sensible, always a welcome relief from his father's effusive sentimentality. What Mel hadn't realized was that their closeness was based on just being together in the everyday course of life. They never talked much about personal things, because neither one of them was much of a talker. Now Mel was trying to become a more open, expressive person, but his mother wasn't. The thing that bothered him about his mother—her emotional reticence—was exactly what bothered him about himself.

Finally, Mel also realized that he was putting so much energy into his relationship with his mother because he was neglecting other relationships in his life. Focusing on one relationship at the expense of other aspects of one's life overloads that relationship. The intimacy Mel was hoping to achieve with his mother would have distracted him from, but not truly compensated for, the fact that he still didn't have many friends and that his relationship with his wife was emotionally distant. He hadn't originally talked about his distance, because he hadn't thought about it, except in terms of the one person most like him. So while he was able to improve his relationship with his mother by keeping conversation relatively light when he was with her, he began to make more significant

*progress on becoming intimate by talking more with his wife
and spending more time with friends.*

Mel had hoped for a restoration of lost intimacy with his mother.
He settled for ordinariness. Most of us bring needless tension to
relationships with our parents until we let go of unrealistic expectations. We go on wanting something from them: a father to hug us
without being asked; a mother to tell us how proud she is of us; for
them to say "I really, really, love you"—demonstrations of love
and affection, declarations of respect. We long for them to change,
to apologize, to make up for what we think we missed. The one
thing we can't let go of wanting may be the one thing they don't
know how to give—or show. We never really grow up and grow
into self-respect until we stop needing our parents to make things
right.

Our parents are not who we need them to be; they're just who
they are. What's more, they may not be the people they used to be.
They're getting older. They may not want to be the parents who
take care of us anymore. There comes a time when they need to be
taken care of, when we must become our parents' parents. We
become the ones who are a little more understanding, sympathetic, and supportive.

Such a shifting of roles takes place gradually, but one thing isn't
gradual. As soon as adult children cease to demand what their
parents are not equipped to give, the relationship improves dramatically. The minute that happens, we can make peace with them,
and with ourselves.

THE REST OF THE FAMILY

It isn't just our parents who drive us crazy. They may be the most
important, but they aren't the only difficult relatives in the family.
There are the brothers and sisters who resolutely resist our efforts
to get close to them, and there are the ones we wish would leave
us alone. There are the helpless uncles who can't seem to manage

their own lives, and the helpful aunts who can't stop trying to manage ours. And, of course, there are the in-laws who never really understand that you aren't one of their children who they can control and regulate.

Most of our relatives don't have any tricks up their sleeves. Their actions only surprise us because we keep looking for them to do what we wish they would do, or what *we* would do. They do what they do. (If chronically late Uncle Louie spoils Thanksgiving dinner, it's not simply that he's late, it's that you wait for him.) Once you learn this, you can stop being so surprised and upset. You can let them be who they are. (You might as well; they will be anyway.)

Self-respect empowers us in relationships, even with difficult relatives, by making us clear about who we are and what our rights are, and by making us tolerant of other people's rights and ways. If we aren't easily threatened, we don't have to be defensive. In putting this principle into practice, there are two guidelines worth keeping in mind: taking a firm stand, and staying out of triangles.

Taking a Stand

More than once I've encouraged someone to take a stand who then translates that into telling someone off. Taking a stand does *not* mean telling someone off. It means clarifying how *you* feel. Sometimes this means setting limits on what you feel you can tolerate, other times it means saying you wish you were closer.

Coping with difficult people means coping with your reaction to them. Some people are too difficult—too boring, too critical, too competitive, too selfish. With them, you may have to resort to distancing—avoid them or placate them. If, for example, your father-in-law is totally impossible (for you), perhaps you'll need to insulate yourself with emotional distance to keep the peace, and your sanity. Keep things superficial. Don't reveal anything about yourself. Be pleasant; avoid closeness; "yes" him. No, that's not the ideal, but life is tough enough without having to make a project of improving every difficult relationship. Sometimes it just isn't worth the effort.

No one would deliberately walk into a mine field, but the more people we invest with the power to make us explode, the less freedom of movement we have. We avoid certain people to avoid tension, the tension that comes from activating parts of ourselves of which we are ashamed, and exposing ourselves to the possibility of humiliation or rejection. We don't avoid Uncle Louie simply because he's argumentative and critical, but because we're too ashamed of our own anger, or powerlessness, to fight back. So we avoid the Uncle Louies of the world and we mock them, shrinking our life-space and ourselves.

The secret of dealing with difficult people is to avoid becoming reactive and defensive. Respect yourself and the boundary between you. Let them have their point of view. Acknowledge it. Figure out your point of view and state it, directly, calmly. Sometimes we feel embattled, but we don't have to fight back to be ourselves. We are ourselves.

Shirley had a blow-up with her mother-in-law that ended with Shirley saying she would not show up for a family portrait. Even though she felt a little guilty about it, Shirley thought she needed to draw the line with this woman who was always intruding, always making demands. Later that same day, Shirley's sister called and wanted to know what happened. Shirley got upset and hung up. According to her, the problem is her sister, "She's nosy, critical, impossible. What could I say?"

The vast majority of the time when somebody asks, "What could I say?," there is an obvious answer: a direct response. "What could I say?" means "I didn't dare be direct because so-and-so would have given me a hard time."

Shirley's avoidance is defensive, but not stubborn and not stupid. It's based on a correct assessment of her own vulnerability. If she tells her sister what happened, and her sister does what she does, Shirley *would* feel guilty; she *would* get angry. In order to protect herself from rejection and attack, she shuns intimacy— with her sister, definitely, but to a lesser extent with anyone else who triggers feelings she isn't comfortable with. The place to break this cycle of avoidance is in the reflex, defensive response to upsetting feelings. "What could I say?" *You could have told your sister what happened.* "But then she would have argued with me, told me

I did the wrong thing." *So?* "So, I would have gotten all upset!" *Maybe. Especially if you felt that you would either have to agree with her—let her be right and you wrong—or change her mind— make her wrong so you could be right. You could let her have her opinion, and acknowledge it without necessarily agreeing with it.*

Letting other people have their point of view and sticking to yours helps head off upset. A little more difficult, and a little more important, is handling the upset when it occurs. The most important thing is to own it as your upset, your feelings. Don't make the other person responsible. Don't attack; say how you feel. Respect yourself enough to acknowledge: *That hurts; that made me mad; I'm sorry;* and, so hard for some people, *I don't know.*

Self-respect strengthens the boundary between ourselves and others. We're us; they're them. They are entitled to their feelings and opinions, and we are entitled to ours. The more ashamed and defensive we are, the more easily we allow this boundary to be violated. We can't tolerate criticism or anger because it hurts so much. The mortification comes from a reexposure to the injuries of childhood, and the hurt goes to the heart of the self.

Sometimes taking a personal stand can help overcome an emotional cutoff. One of the saddest things that happen in families are the feuds that erupt in conflict and end in no contact. These cutoffs have been called "emotional divorces," but the emotional pain persists. Often the underground intensity from a cutoff does not surface until a family occasion brings it up.

Hugh and his brother, Brodie, were only two years apart. Growing up, they fought a lot, as brothers do, but they were constant companions. Now all that was changed. It changed when Brodie's wife had a blow-up with his mother. Hugh wasn't sure what had happened between his sister-in-law and his mother, but he was sure what happened afterward. Total and complete cutoff. Both women were hurt and bitter. Both felt wronged, and neither was willing to break the silence. Brodie, caught in a loyalty conflict, chose not to rock the boat at

*home, and so he, too, stopped calling and visiting his family.
That meant Hugh didn't get to see his brother. He wasn't sure
why. It just seemed that Brodie and his wife were avoiding the
whole family.*

*Although he didn't like it, Hugh got used to the idea of being
cut off from his brother. He had tried a few times to mediate
between his mother and Brodie's wife, but with no luck. Neither one would agree that maybe the other one had a point,
or maybe it didn't matter and they should apologize. Then
Hugh tried to reach out to his brother, writing to say he missed
him and suggesting that the two of them get together. No response.*

*Married with children, Hugh's life was reasonably full, and
he didn't think much about the broken bond. But then when
his second child's christening was scheduled, he realized how
much he missed his brother and how badly he wanted him to
come. At the first baby's christening, his wife's large family had
all been present, but since the only family Hugh had was his
parents and his brother, his brother's absence really made him
feel cut off.*

*Hugh missed his brother, and he decided that it was impor-
tant for him to let Brodie know. When he asked me about getting in touch with his brother, I suggested he think about
writing to Brodie in such a way as to share his feelings and his
point of view—without blaming the brother or his wife or trying to fix the family feud. (Getting in touch with a cutoff relative, as Hugh was trying to do with Brodie, works best if the
person trying to get in touch concentrates on sharing his feelings and desire to get together without trying to change the
other person.) The point of Hugh's letter, then, was to let his
brother know how he felt; not to make his brother come to the
christening, but just to let him know that he was wanted.*

Here is a part of the letter Hugh wrote:

Dear Brodie,
    I have a problem. Megan's christening is coming up and I know I'll
really miss you if you don't come. I don't want to impose or make

demands on you—I'm sure you have enough problems of your own to worry about. So I've decided to write and tell you how I feel, but leave what you decide to do completely up to you.

Hugh went on to tell his brother he loved him and missed him. He said he understood, or at least could guess, how difficult the family feud must be for Brodie. And he said that it was sad that the brothers and their children were getting older without knowing each other. Then he closed by repeating that he really hoped Brodie would come to the christening, but that he would certainly understand if he felt he couldn't.

What happened? What happened was that Hugh felt better after mailing the letter. He tried hard to concentrate on the good feeling of saying how he felt without thinking that now his brother had to come or the whole effort was wasted. In fact, Brodie did not come to the christening. He wrote to explain that it was just too awkward to come because it was a family affair, but he suggested instead that the brothers meet halfway between their two cities for dinner. These dinners became a regular occasion, every month or so, and the two brothers slowly started rebuilding their relationship.

Staying Out of Triangles

Although we think of relationships as occurring between two people, the smallest stable unit of relationship is three. Dyads are unstable; cycles of closeness and distance produce instability, and one or both people move toward a third party to stabilize the relationship. The outsider is inclined to be jealous and resentful. Instead of considering what the source of the problem might be, the neglected one is likely to feel bitter: "You're always working." "How about making me number one once in a while?"

When shame and insecurity make it hard for us to express our anger or desire directly to the person concerned, we divert it to someone safer. Whenever you find yourself tangled up in an unproductive relationship, it's a good idea to consider that the relationship may, in fact, be part of a triangle. If it is, you can begin to resolve the problem by recognizing where the real conflict lies.

One of the most common situations where relationships become bogged down in triangles is divorce and remarriage. It isn't just the complicated connections, it's all that anxiety. Consider, for example, the case of Hal and Robin.

Hal and his wife Robin sought my help in dealing with problems with his children and his ex-wife. They described Adrienne, the ex-wife, as totally unreasonable—"a bitch on wheels." She had custody of the two girls, and although she and Hal had a clear agreement about visitation (the girls spent every second weekend with him), she frequently changed plans and either made the girls late or kept them from visiting at all. She was nasty to Robin and refused to let her in the house to pick up the girls. The younger daughter, Elizabeth, age twelve, seemed to accept the new marriage and was always happy to visit. Ashley, fourteen, was a different story. She was very snotty toward Robin and several times refused to come for the weekend.

Hal and Robin agreed that Adrienne was moody and mean, but disagreed about how to handle her. Hal was for peace at any price. Robin felt they should be firm with her. What did I think?

I helped Hal and Robin see that a difficult situation was made more difficult by a series of overlapping triangles. Then I suggested that the three of us work out a plan for breaking every one of these important relationships into a direct, one-to-one relationship, keeping each one between the two people involved. The first and most important triangle to untangle was the one involving Hal and Robin and Adrienne. Robin's nagging Hal to get tough with his ex-wife only displaced conflict from where it belonged (between Hal and Adrienne) to between the two of them. Robin could see that. Once she agreed to let Hal handle his ex-wife however he chose, he decided that all he wanted to do was calm her down so that she would stop interfering with his daughters' visits.

I suggested that Hal write Adrienne a letter expressing sym-

pathy for all she'd been through, which was hard for him, because he was so aware of all that she had put him through. But he was willing to do it if it would pacify her and keep her from causing trouble. Robin could see that it was a reasonable strategy but worried that if Hal was nice to Adrienne, she might come back into his life and displace her. Considering how completely cold Hal had grown toward Adrienne, this was a remarkable fear. Yet it certainly helped explain what made Robin so insistent that Hal stand up to Adrienne and tell her off. Hal reassured Robin that he didn't care at all about his ex-wife and that there was no way he wanted even to be friends with her.

Hal's letter had an immediate and significant calming effect. Adrienne stopped interfering with the girls' visits and Hal was able to work on his relationship with his older daughter. With the situation greatly improved, Hal and Robin thanked me and said good-bye.

Two months later Hal called saying, "Everything is awful. Can we see you?" When they came in, Robin spoke first. The older daughter, Ashley, had come for the weekend and, although she was now very sweet and loving with her father, she was deliberately cold toward Robin—"as though I was just in the way." At one point, Ashley came out of her room and showed her father some photographs of a school trip. "Both of them completely ignored me." Robin was crushed. She spent the rest of the weekend in her room crying. "He's happy, he doesn't care. I wish the kids would just disappear."

When I asked Hal if he could understand how his wife felt, he responded defensively. "Nobody seems to realize that I have a relationship with my children. I have a responsibility to them. Why must you overreact so? What am I supposed to do?"

Untangling this triangle took figuring out what made each of them feel so vulnerable. I started with Robin. Why did it hurt so much to be ignored by a fourteen-year-old girl? It turns out that Robin had been a very lonely teenager, shy, unpopular, and extremely insecure. Ashley's coldness toward her made her feel humiliated because it stirred up all that old hurt. That, Hal could understand and empathize with. He, on the other hand, was so insecure about his daughter's affection that he was afraid to show support for Robin when there was any tension between her and the girls.

Hal and Robin had already understood how triangles complicated their relationship with each other and with the girls. Now that they better understood each other's insecurities, they were able to be a little more understanding and a little less emotionally reactive.

Moving toward connectedness with the larger family is one of the best ways to bring more self-respect to other relationships. It gives us the security of being anchored in many relationships and the flexibility of being able to relate successfully to a diverse group of people. The more flexible and rounded our relationships, the more flexible and rounded ourselves.

FRIENDSHIP

No one questions the value of friendship, but a lot of us don't have many friends. Oh, we have friends all right, but we don't spend as much time as we'd like with them. Too bad, because friendship has the same double benefit as improved family ties—strengthening the self and enjoying the pleasures of company—without all the tension.

Unlike family, we choose our friends. The relationship is voluntary and optional; we can leave if we want to, and therefore it's safer to be honest and take risks. We can talk over painful and embarrassing subjects, reveal self-doubts, try out different sides of ourselves, and learn to be who we are.

The most intense friendships are formed when we're young, when we're less tied to competing obligations and more willing to open our hearts. I remember that wonderful feeling of talking for hours with my friend Ed at college, impelled by the momentum of some deep and inexplicable sympathy. We admitted our faults, admired each other's virtues, and trotted out our prejudices for comparison. Most of them fit. There was the pleasure of saying anything I wanted, and the pleasure of hearing Ed say everything I'd always thought but never expressed. I can see clearly the student union where we talked, sitting at those heavy wooden tables scarred with initials. There we were, the two of us, with all our fears and flaws, and the hopes we still dared to believe in, and our failures; there we were, eighteen and twenty. That was a long time ago.

After college, Ed and I kept up our friendship with letters and calls and visits as long as we could. But the slow accretion of competing interests gradually eroded the connection. We never stopped caring about each other, we just started caring about other things more. Whether or not you'd say we're still close depends on your definition. We love each other and it never takes long to open up again, but a thousand miles is a thousand miles. A lot of people cherish someone far away but don't have many active intimate relationships with people closer to home.

Whether your friends are shared or yours alone, friendships do not just happen; they have to be made. Making friends means meeting people and opening up to them. Unfortunately, many of us come to friendship wounded. Shame breeds fears that make us wary of entering into relationships. It's not just that we hang back, but that we don't know when to let our guard down—and how far.

Turning an attraction into a relationship takes self-disclosure, first of attitudes and opinions, and later of deeper and more personal feelings. Friendship grows with mutual disclosure, but disclosure should be paced to test for receptivity and reciprocity.

Some people wait too long for reassurance that others like them, and therefore hesitate to make overtures that might move the friendship along. Others rush into friendships without waiting for signs that the other person is interested, and often end up getting hurt. They're so hungry for appreciation that they fail to realize that not all friendliness should be taken personally. The job candidate who invites the friendly interviewer out for a drink is such a person. The person who mistakes friendly work relationships for friendship is another.

Not everyone wants friends, and not everyone who is friendly to you wants to become your friend. Nor is every isolated person unhappy about it. People who have experienced rejection in the past, and who blame themselves for it, are likely to avoid friendship out of fear of further humiliation. They are socially unadventurous, reserved, and cautious; they are hesitant to open up and quick to react to slights.

When you find yourself hurt and tempted to withdraw because of something a friend did, you might want to think about why you're so sensitive. Perhaps, for example, you grew up jealous of your siblings and insecure about your parents' respect. Now you may overreact to finding out that the friend who was too busy to do something with you is off doing something with another friend. If you are shame-sensitive to rejection, you think, *Ah-ha, I knew it. He (or she) really likes that other person better than me.* If you are secure, you don't give in to jealousy; you know that friendship is not a competitive sport. Figuring out what in your makeup makes something hurt so much doesn't make that hurt go away, but it may put the hurt in perspective and enable you to react more calmly.

What should you do when friends disappoint you? Many people try to manage distress in a relationship by suppressing it. They get along fine until emotional conflict triggers one of the as-yet-unresolved patterns of emotional reactivity they brought with them from home.

Brian and Roger were close friends for five years, until Roger's repeated refusals to visit except at his house or on his terms restimulated Brian's feelings about his mother's distance and drove him into bitterness and retreat. Why didn't Brian speak up? Because he was angry and didn't know how to deal with anger except by withdrawal. When something happens that makes us feel like a rejected child, we instinctively assume that the only options we have are those we had as children. The alternative—respecting ourselves and each other enough to say simply what we feel—doesn't occur to us. Old hurts leave us scarred. Part of the self nurses old injuries and fears, takes pride in autonomy, and harbors the illusion of self-sufficiency. If people can hurt and disappoint us, then the safest thing is not to need them.

You can respond to inequity by adjusting your attitude about it, or actually doing something about it. Are the payoffs worth the cost? Is the neglect really a statement about you, or the other person, or circumstances? As for doing something about it, you can give up, sulk, or speak up.

Incidentally, although we more often worry about getting less than our share in relationships, a sense of inequity can also arise when one person feels that the other does too much. The self-respecting person doesn't calculate whose turn it is to come up with a kindness or a favor, but balance in a relationship requires an exchange, not one person doing all the giving.

All of us go through difficulties in our friendships. Most of us lose friends we would have liked to keep, and all of us see relationships going sour and becoming unsatisfying from time to time. Conflict can actually strengthen a relationship if it's handled right. Resolution of the conflict reaffirms the partners' faith in each other, as well as reminding them that they have chosen to work through problems because they don't want to part. Resolution of conflict means talking about it, expressing your side—talking about your feelings, not blaming or accusing—and listening to your friend's side.

Some people are only willing to express positive feelings, and often overdo it. They don't respect themselves or the other person enough to talk about anger or hurt or feeling rejected. They control these feelings at a cost—to themselves and to the relationship. Giving more than your share in relationships doesn't really make other people like you. It may tie them to you in gratitude and guilt, but this isn't the stuff of friendship. We give too much when we don't respect ourselves enough. It doesn't work.

True friendship is mutual, balanced, sharing. No earthly experience or human emotion, from joy to anger, or shame to sadness, is unprecedented or incapable of being shared. When our lives are thoroughly witnessed, we are not alone; we are worthwhile.

16

· · · · · · ·

Overcoming Shame
in Love and Sex

The clearest way to organize this chapter about love and sex would be to discuss first one and then the other. This arrangement would be both logical and faithful to our parents' teaching: First comes love, then comes marriage, then sex. But as you well know, the relationship between love and sex is far from logical, and love doesn't necessarily come first. The relationship is circular not linear. So is this chapter.

Shame protects intimacy, but ends by undermining it. By facing and overcoming shame we make ourselves more capable of intimacy, and our relationships more fulfilling. But the circularity I referred to means that in order to overcome shame you have to work on relationships.

SHAME AND SEXUALITY

It shouldn't be too surprising that we're ashamed of sex. Shame, as you'll recall, clusters around weakness, dirtiness, and defectiveness, and sexual shame touches on all three.

Of all the lessons of childhood, none is taught with such force as self-control. We are vulnerable to shame about almost anything that ties us to nature, anything that makes us susceptible to forces

that are impervious to our own will to control—eating, elimination, and, of course, sex. These expressions of our untamed nature
keep us from transcending our animal underside and make us
vulnerable to judgment. We're ashamed to be weak, and sex is a
weakness.

The association of sex and dirtiness begins with lessons about
hygiene. Children learn early that urination and defecation are
messy—dirty—and must be controlled: held in and then put in a
special container, kept in a private room, that disappears them. If
human waste is dirty, then so must be the organs that expel it.
These "private parts" must be cleaned and covered up. Human
babies aren't born with this knowledge; it has to be taught.

Once, when my son was a baby and I bent over to change his
diaper, he peed in my face. He didn't exactly do it on purpose, but
he certainly didn't seem upset about it. He smiled. I mention this
now not to revenge myself by embarrassing him (oh, no!), but to
illustrate that children don't start out ashamed of natural body
functions. We teach them. Imagine a five-year-old peeing in his
father's face. It's almost inconceivable, isn't it?

Parents don't intend to teach shame, only modesty. (If it were
modesty people learned instead of shame, why would so many of
us cringe in embarrassment when a lover moves his or her mouth
down on us?) Likewise, with the control of sexuality, the goal is
not to condemn sex but to tame it. The direct association between
sex and shame often begins with masturbation. Parents who feel
uncomfortable when their children touch themselves may show
their discomfort with anger, stern warnings, or disgust: "That's
bad." Don't ever touch yourself *there.*" Some children stop. Most
don't. The urge is strong, and so, instead of stopping, they hide.
Excitement and shame grow up together.

This brings us to the whole matter of why sexuality is such a
universal problem. Sex may be a part of our animal nature, but it
is not just a human animal who is driven by sexual desire, it is a
human *person*—a self who feels and acts and *judges* those feelings
and actions. Sex is of the body, and the body, in its nakedness and
need, is close to the vulnerable heart of the self. Sex is inseparably
bound up with self-respect, and both are tied to love relationships

with intimate others. Sex is a vehicle for the expression of love, and love is a vehicle for the expression of sex.

LOVE AND SELF-RESPECT

In love, the self changes shape. We're not merely sympathetic *toward* our lovers, we're *connected* to them in the bond of love. Love widens the scope of self-respect, forming a new, joint, wonderfully enlarged identity. One plus one equals one: two *I*'s become one *we*. Later, one plus one equals three: two *I*'s that form a *couple* also, eventually, reclaim their separate identities.

In growing up and separating ourselves from our parents, we gradually strengthen the boundary around ourselves. We remain a Smith or a Jones, but we become progressively more a Mary or a Johnny—sons and daughters still, but also separate selves, more and more autonomous, more and more independent. We form our own opinions, make our own plans, and extend our privacy. When we're intimate with someone, physically and emotionally, we open up the boundary around our private selves to let the other in close. Being "in love," infatuated, is to want no boundary between you and your lover but to have a strong boundary protecting the two of you from outside intrusion. You're always thinking of the other person, wanting to touch and be together, excited in the other's presence, and you want to be alone together.

Infatuation is transformed into romantic love, or else it fades away. The boundary around the self shifts to include the other, whose well-being now affects your well-being, and the boundary around the couple shifts as well.[1] The notion of boundaries draws attention to the dynamics of exclusion and inclusion. A couple must redefine boundaries with family and friends, teaching them, for example, that to include one is to include both, and limiting intrusion into their privacy. ("No, Dad, you can't come on the honeymoon.")

But boundaries are also very much a function of what's inside the boundary. The more fulfilling their love, the more likely a couple is to maintain a firm boundary around their relationship. Likewise, the boundary between the couple reflects both their relationship with each other and their relationship with themselves.

In love, we drop the walls we build around ourselves. How soon and how high we raise them again depends not only on the progress of love but also on how secure we are. However, as I shall explain, we aren't stuck with how secure we are. We can choose how to respond to hurt feelings. Insecure people have a strong impulse to react defensively in the face of hurt—withdraw, stay angry—but *they can choose not to,* especially if they understand that it is *they* who are being sensitive and they who can choose how to respond.

Now that we've seen how shame is tied to sex, and both love and sex are linked to identity and self-respect, let's examine the uneasy accomplishment of mature love and sexual fulfillment.

GROPING OUR WAY TOWARD INTIMACY

No need to explain the powerful conflicts surrounding sexual desire to anyone familiar with Freud (or anyone who was ever a teenager).

When it comes to sex, teenagers are in an impossible position. Physically, they're charged and ready to go; emotionally, they're uncertain; and socially, we demand that they wait. No wonder their first experiments with sex are conducted in secrecy. In Chapter 11, we saw how adolescents begin to experiment with sex, first alone in their rooms and later pairing off in private. Shame plays a useful role, guarding their privacy and protecting their tender researches, but shame often overplays its role, making them worry that sex is dirty.

From the first, our relationship to the erotic impulse is ambivalent. We're attracted to sex like dogs to a sizzling steak: The delicious smell drives us crazy, but we're afraid to sink our teeth in and get burned. Anything that hot sets up a powerful approach-avoidance conflict. Unfortunately, no one can tell us when to yield and when to resist; that we have to figure out for ourselves.

When they fall prey to erotic imaginings and become caught up in a fever of their senses, adolescents often think of themselves as depraved. Why? Because giving in to temptation means not only doing what is forbidden, but also that you have an uncontrollable inner demon. Sexual fantasies frighten as well as fascinate.

Excessive shame turns teenagers away from healthy sexual experimentation. Some of these anxious adolescents repress their sexuality and find release in sublimating activities, while others retreat further into sexual fantasy. No wonder teenagers dedicate themselves so all-consumingly to erotic reverie; fantasy is a victory over limitations and frustrations that represents a protest against shame while at the same time reinforcing it.

Their dreams are endless. Girls dream of dark and handsome princes who will be drawn to them just because they're themselves. They won't have to do anything; they'll be swept away. Shy and lonely teenage boys excite themselves with images of big-breasted women, all lewd and knowing, willing to make the first move. They dream so many dreams, and then worry about the selves doing the dreaming.

Many people worry that their fantasies are perverse and that this reveals an ugly truth about them: *They* are perverse. Perhaps this is the place to make an important point about sexual preferences. There is only one sex drive—a biological urge that becomes attached to anything associated with its satisfaction. A person who gets sexual satisfaction while looking at photographs of women wearing stag-magazine lingerie will be turned on by these things. It's sad that men become conditioned to respond to pornographic images instead of the real women who are available to them, but it isn't perverse. Likewise, a person who has sexual pleasure with persons of either sex will be attracted to members of that sex. Remember this when you're tempted to condemn yourself, or your partner, for particular sexual inclinations.

Grown-up sexual intimacy requires that we know how to give and receive sexual pleasure. If we cannot, we feel "impotent" or "frigid," or at the very least inept. Unfortunately, most people emerge from adolescence with secret doubts about their sexual adequacy. When our sex lives turn sour, we often accuse (if only silently) our partners of wanting too much or giving too little, but it is really ourselves about whom we worry most deeply. Maybe something is wrong with us.

Although we express intimacy in relationship with another person, our capacity for intimacy is our own. What anxious adolescents and frustrated married people have in common is a tendency to project blame for their frustration, instead of facing their own insecurity and shame.

> *I recently treated a couple in their late twenties for a sexual problem. Rodney was suffering a disorder of desire. He just wasn't interested in sex. "She's always pestering me; it gets on my nerves." Brenda was frustrated and hurt. "He never wants sex anymore. He thinks we have to be getting along great to have sex. If we had sex once in a while, we'd get along better." Like any couple, they had some problems of communication, but I felt they could profit from a direct, behavioral approach; so I explained how negative thoughts inhibit desire and how anxiety inhibits excitement. Then I taught them how to stop thinking negative thoughts and concentrate instead on feelings of physical pleasure; and I explained how they could decondition anxiety by relaxing first and then going slow. The couple made rapid progress with their homework assignments until one evening when they decided to go to bed even though they were quite tense.*
>
> *Brenda was angry and discouraged, and it showed. Rodney felt accused and wanted to have it out.*
>
> *"You act like everything is my fault. This problem involves both of us. I'm tired of being blamed all the time."*
>
> *"It's not my fault you never want sex!"*
>
> *Here, two grown-up people of goodwill regressed into a couple of kids trading recriminations. Each one blamed the other. There's nothing new in that, but why?*
>
> *It's one thing to realize (and have it reinforced by a thera-*

pist) that problems in a relationship aren't either person's fault; they're problems of the relationship, of chemistry and history. It's another thing for a woman to feel undesirable and for a man to feel inadequate.

What works to relieve upset in an intimate relationship is a complementary response. Had Rodney responded to Brenda's look of hurt and anger by saying, "What's wrong?" and then listening, she would have felt better. Then maybe she would have been receptive to hearing his side, though perhaps at another time. Or, if she had responded to his defensive protest by absolving him of blame, he might have calmed down. Instead, they responded symmetrically, which escalates conflict into a battle. But no wonder, each of them was feeling ashamed about core issues of their gender: for her, not being attractive; for him, not being potent.

At this point, I shifted the focus of therapy, interrupting direct practice on relaxing into desire for an exploration of the shame and self-doubt that made each of them so vulnerable to signs of rejection. This was not, however, a lengthy trip down memory lane. All that was necessary was a brief excursion into history, long enough to identify some of the sources of their insecurity. Brenda couldn't forget that no one asked her out in high school; Rodney still worried about not being able to have an erection the first time he went to bed with her. These revelations were enough to help them see why they were defensive and realize that they could choose not to overreact. After three sessions of exploration, we returned to the direct approach, and two months later we terminated. Things were going better for Rodney and Brenda but, more important, they left with an understanding of the possibility of choosing not to respond defensively to each other's upset.

The seeds of sexual conflict may be sown in childhood, but the growing season is adolescence. Earlier I mentioned the adolescent dilemma of being physically ready and eager for something still forbidden. The opposite danger also exists: giving in to sex too quickly.

THE PROTECTIVE VALUE OF SHAME

Bad timing can spoil a good relationship. Two lovers who rush to couple when either one isn't comfortable open the door to anxiety. Anxiety is greedy; it may begin with penetration but can spread out to consume the rest of the sexual response.

Shame, in the form of modest reticence, creates a space that allows lovers time—time to get to know one another, and time to slowly open themselves to each other. To intrude brusquely is to violate the other's intimate self. Shame resists sex that is exploitive, that is not accompanied by a loving attitude. To violate this restraint is to risk killing sexual passion and turning desire to disgust.

Shame inhibits the sexual response until the person feels responded to—as a person—and cared for. Perhaps this is more true for women than men. A woman may need reassurance that a man wants her and not just her body. She is painfully aware that her own distinctive personality can be dispensed with in the sexual act. The alternative to a sense of shame is not free and unfettered sex. People do, of course, couple without caring. Men are notorious for their ability to divorce sex from caring, or as an elegant but honest woman once told me, "Most men would fuck a chicken." Women, too, are capable of divorcing sex from love, enjoying what Erica Jong called the "zipless fuck." But such unfeeling intercourse is not liberated, it's corrupt.

Shame withholds surrender until the lover shows evidence of caring. Love itself may not be essential, but it safeguards something that is: trust. Love is the protector of sexual pleasure because it makes us feel safe to collapse into physical pleasure without fear or shame, to become, for a time, two animals enjoying each other.

An adolescent girl who succumbs to desire (or gives in because she's afraid to say no) may feel "dirty" and "weak," rather than "decent," "self-respecting," and "strong." Her anxious parents nag her not to wear her fig leaf too short. It isn't ladylike to be overly inviting. Maybe she should follow the example of Sleeping Beauty who awaits the passing prince in a state of suspended animation. Meanwhile, she sees her uninhibited sisters, who are using sex to bait popularity, branded "loose," "cheap," and "shameless"; some even become pregnant.

Boys have their own problems. They want sex but equate potency with power. They're afraid to be soft, afraid to be tender, afraid to be weak. Many are ashamed of touching. Boys get to a certain age and their daddies no longer hug them, and they're embarrassed to hug anyone. When they get to be young men, they overcome their inhibition to hug and be close only when they're driven by desire. Unfortunately, by then the affection isn't necessarily affectionate.

Problems or not, adolescents eventually grope their way toward each other. They come to sexual maturity full of longing and misgiving. Searching for some means to satisfy the longing and overcome the misgiving, many stumble into what seems to be the solution: romantic love.

THE ROMANTIC SOLUTION

Romantic love is the nearest adult equivalent of the early bond between infant and mother. The two people who fall in love may be grown-ups and much of their relationship may take place on a grown-up level, but their intimacy stirs primal needs and longings—and exquisite emotional sensitivity to acceptance or rejection, pride or shame.

Ironically, although the lovers cherish one another, they re-create each other as something more and less than who they really are. When our needs are intense, we relate to others as *selfobjects,* Heinz Kohut's term for a person we respond to not as a separate being but as someone-there-for-us.[2] Lovers love each other and use each other as selfobjects for maintaining, restoring, or consolidating the inner experience of the self. The lover's affirmation, admiration, and responsiveness feeds our self-respect. No wonder we idealize the people we love.

Think of the lover as someone permitted well inside the social boundary around the self, and you'll realize why that person becomes part of the self. There is a blurring between what we want and what we see in the other person—and between how that person responds to us and how we react. The intensity of acceptance and rejection is a function of two things: the significance of the person responding, and the significance of what is being responded to. It may not matter much if a stranger criticizes something that isn't close to the heart of your concerns, your messy car, for example. It does matter when someone close enough to regulate your self-esteem criticizes something that feels like part of you, especially something tender and private that only emerges in the intimacy of intimacy.

Romantic love follows a predictable course: from attraction, to testing for receptivity, to closeness, and, sadly, to the tension that inevitably enters every intimate relationship.

Attraction

The lure that catches a trophy-sized northern pike can be little more than a colored strip of metal. The bait flashes by and the fish sees what it wants to see: a succulent minnow. First the flash, then the strike, then the hook. Dumb fish.

Human beings are, of course, quite a bit more sophisticated. The lure that catches a lover's eye may be long red fingernails, a flash of thigh, her smile, his tall good looks, her quick wit, or his playfulness. (It's not only glamour that we're attracted to; sometimes we're attracted to vulnerability, which seems to offer the safety of a bargain with someone who cannot easily afford to hurt us.) Lovers aren't fish, so easily hooked; they'll want to get to know each other. But as women know better than men, there's no getting to know somebody without that initial attraction.

Today's woman may feel free to make the first move, but her

success depends, at least partly, on her ability to be seductive and fascinating. This puts her in a bind. She's caught between the need to attract and repel, to draw toward her the special men she finds worthwhile, while keeping others away.

In October 1989, Larry King interviewed a woman who was abducted and raped. One of the points stressed by the defense at the rapist's trial was that the woman's dress indicated loose morals. About half of the viewers, men and women, who called in to express their opinion agreed that she shouldn't have been dressed so provocatively. None of the callers actually spoke the words, but many implied that "she was asking for it." And so, if the New Woman makes herself attractive, she may invite attack, not only in the form of male aggression but also in the cruel logic of the double standard.

Regardless of how little or how much conflict she feels about sexuality, a woman must learn to walk a tightrope in public, inviting appreciation but not unwanted attention. She may feel torn between submitting to aggressive exploitation or denying her sexuality—her attractiveness as well as her own desire. The same woman who feels shamefully anxious about her sexual interests can also feel shamefully unimportant to a man, a mere object over which men excite themselves in order to gratify base needs. It's so confusing.

Men have it easier. They're a little more likely to be appreciated for their accomplishments rather than their looks, and they're a lot less vulnerable to unwanted attention. (In the 1960s, Harvey Jackins advised male counselors who were propositioned by women clients to say, "Take me, I'm yours." The assumption being that most women aren't prepared to be physically aggressive. I'm not so sure.)

Men may not be racked with the same contrary pressures to attract and repel, but both sexes suffer when attraction is based only on certain characteristics and not on the whole person. One of my patients, married two years, recently said in despair, "How could I have fallen in love with that man?" Falling in love is an act of imaginative creation; the beloved is a forgery you need.

Testing for Receptivity

Getting to know somebody is exciting. The unknown opens the door to all kinds of possibilities. But as obviously important as it is to know the other person, it's equally important to let him or her know you. A strong relationship is formed when two people open themselves honestly, get to know and be known. If they don't, the result is a brittle, fragile thing. Too bad we don't choose a mate with as much care as we pick out a new car.

Courtship is an exciting game, but in the excitement it's easy to mistake the object of the game. Although young men may want "to score," at stake is more than sexual conquest and surrender. A woman may want "a relationship," but if she gets one based on her doing all the accommodating, she loses in the long run.

It's not just trying to "win" that beguiles players into revealing less than their true selves, it's trying to avoid hurt. By now it should be clear that there can be no intimacy without some personal disclosure, and there can be no personal disclosure without some misunderstanding and hurt. The secret of successful relationships is not avoiding hurt, but exposing ourselves to it judiciously. Shame occurs when we open ourselves and run right into rejection. The solution is not to avoid openness, but to open ourselves and become vulnerable gradually, testing for receptivity, expecting and learning to withstand some pain.

Ideally, intimacy evolves, gradually, out of reciprocal interest and shared trust. This mutuality forms an emotional bond, across which two people in love share themselves: reveal their own and appreciate the partner's real self. More often what we try to do is get the other person to like us—dress up, be agreeable, hold our feelings back. As a result, we don't fall in love with the whole and genuine person; we fall in love with what we see. For the self-respecting and secure this poses little problem—what you see is what you get. Not so with those who are afraid to be openly themselves. The folly of pretense was lampooned charmingly in Blake Edwards's film *Victor, Victoria* in which Julie Andrews practiced double duplicity, playing a woman who posed as a male transvestite. Our own duplicity is less deliberate and less complicated, but the results are also less amusing.

After a suitable amount (or an unsuitable amount) of shifting and testing to see if the other appreciates us, we relax into closeness. Two selves dissolve into a couple—two couples, really, "His" and "Hers." Some people in love are philanthropists: They want to give. Others are capitalists: They want to own. These differing impulses come close enough to fitting together to draw the lovers toward each other.

Closeness

In receiving adult love, we are made to feel worthy of being the primary object of the most intense devotion. (Our parents loved us, but they exchanged intimacies in a secret language and sent us to bed or hired baby-sitters so they could be alone together.) This intimate connection brings out the twin desires for merger and self-expression. Self-expression means exposure, and exposure has consequences. Once we expose our backstage self and unguarded sexuality to our partners, our silent plea is: "Please love me"; while in the back of our mind lurks the trembling dread: "Now he [or she] is going to despise me."

Remember the first time? Both partners are nude, exposed in a situation they want and fear, with few guidelines. Of course, it's easy! The lovers' minds brim with happy thoughts: *Will he turn me on? Will I turn him on? Will he please me? Will I please him? Will I be able to get and keep an erection? Is my penis big enough? Will I come too quickly?*

When we are joyfully accepted as a body by the partner, self-consciousness vanishes. Accepted and confirmed by being wanted, we cease to worry and begin to enjoy each other.

It's not surprising that profound emotions are awakened and expressed in sex. The trust involved in showing our pleasures, the vulnerability in letting another give us these and guide them—this does not come lightly. Nor are the emotions of passion always tender and loving. When the strongest and most primitive emotions are expressed, and accepted, passion becomes fiercer and less controlled. The depth of relaxation afterward is a measure of the fullness of the experience, and a victory over shame and guilt.

Tension

Perhaps it's been a while since the first time. (Perhaps it's been a while since the last time.) The progress of love is not smooth or steady, because it depends not on what a couple does but on what two separate people do. You can love someone who doesn't love you, or you can love someone who loves you but doesn't respond sexually on the same schedule. (In sex, like comedy, timing is everything.)

One reason we get too little out of love is that we want too much. When we look for perfect love, we're looking for someone who will allow us to express ourselves completely, without attack or rejection. We want a love that reflects our complete selves, and gives us complete validation. But no human being can sustain this burden. Other people have wills and counterwills of their own. In a thousand ways they can hurt us. That's why some people (married and single) never love. It's too dangerous.

Among the remedies for romantic passion, few are as effective as marriage. We enter marriage in order to get the security we need, in order to get relief from our anxieties, our aloneness, and self-doubt; but marriage also binds us to another person, who turns out to have a lot of cockeyed ideas. No wonder there's tension.

Tension in relationships comes from anxiety and interpersonal conflict, each fueling the other. Tension can be resolved in one of three ways: working it out, triangulation, or distancing. These responses are not, of course, mutually exclusive, but most people automatically lean toward one of them. (You and I prefer to work things out, at least we would if our partners were more reasonable.)

Working things out means moving toward, not against, your partner. The difference is between talking about your feelings and making requests versus criticizing and blaming. What counts is a nonjudgmental attitude of openness, rather than following a particular formula. However, let me give you some examples of what works and what doesn't.

"There's no reason for . . ." doesn't work. "Why?" (when it's an honest question) does. "You never . . ." doesn't work. "Would you please . . . ?" does. "You just lie there like a stone" doesn't work. Making the other person wrong never works. *The most* effective move you can make to ease tension is to invite your partner to tell you what's bothering him or her. Doing so introduces the goodwill that makes mutual understanding possible.

As we saw in the previous chapter, tension in a relationship often propels the partners to move toward a third party. It begins when one of the partners is upset or lonely and, instead of talking about it, turns to someone else. Friends are naturally sympathetic and don't always realize that listening to complaints about someone else may be a way of enabling a friend to complain about problems instead of solving them. What causes the most resentment are questions about the primacy of attachment: Who comes first? The person on the outside may be jealous and resentful, and inclined to criticize: "How come the kids always come first?" "You tell your friends more than you tell me." Remember two things. First, the need for selfobjects is lifelong. Don't criticize, consider: Could you do more to meet the need for understanding? Second, distances between three points of a triangle are interconnected. Don't criticize; move toward your mate *or* move toward the other corner of the triangle. Spending more time with the kids yourself frees your partner to be more available to you. Taking an interest in his or her interests also brings you together.

Distancers automatically move away from tension, but even people who aren't distancers get tired of having their feelings hurt, become resentful, bitter, and start to withdraw. To reduce your own distance, move toward your partner and talk about your feelings. To reduce your partner's distance, remember the First Law of Entomology: You catch more flies with honey.

REJECTION, WITHDRAWAL, AND ALIENATION

When we're single, rejection stings and can lead to withdrawal and alienation from the lover. When we are committed to staying in a relationship, rejection can lead to psychological withdrawal—alienation not only from the other but also from the self, in the form of disowning rejected qualities of the self, especially sexual desire.

As everyone knows, an affair or a marriage can leave bruises all over the psyche. Unless we appreciate the *reciprocity* of relationships, the mutual and unintentional giving and getting of bruises, we're likely to blame our partners for conflicts and tensions that are hard to avoid. Blame rubs salt in the wounds; understanding helps heal them.

Trust makes betrayal possible; the deeper and more intimate the trust, the deeper and more wounding the betrayal. That's why infidelity hurts so much, and it's why we're so vulnerable to shame from our intimate partners. The most radical shame is to offer oneself and be rejected as unlovable.

Moviegoers who saw *Fatal Attraction* responded to the unfaithful husband (Michael Douglas), identifying with his guilt and the horror of his lover's revenge. But why was the retaliation of Glenn Close's character so extreme? It would be easy to dismiss her as a lunatic, but that doesn't explain anything (it never does). What made her mad—a woman scorned—was the shame of rejection.

The fate of our relationships is very much a function of what we bring to them. Secure self-respect enables us to trust, to be open, to withstand inevitable hurts—the price we pay for being close. Insecurity and shame make us guarded and reactive. Not only do we have to deal with our own histories, but with our partner's as well. A woman may, for example, have to pay the price for rejection inflicted long ago on her man. He's jealous and demands to know where she was and who she was with. Or perhaps he reacts like a wounded child to the slightest criticism. If his jealousy and oversensitivity feel like an attack, she may be tempted to counterattack. But remember, symmetrical retaliation only escalates conflict.

Keep in mind that rage nearly always signals narcissistic injury. The reaction may seem disproportionately strong, but it *is* proportionate to the unconscious significance of the stimulus. You can guess that I recommend a complementary response: Make your partner feel understood, and he or she will be more willing to understand you later. And I can guess that there are times when this feels unfair ("How come *I* always have to be the one to be understanding?") and times when, right or wrong, you just can't take it. Perhaps more important than how you respond at any particular moment to a spouse's jealousy or prickly sensitivity is how you deal with the underlying insecurity.

As you'll recall, the roots of insecurity are not in active rejection or abuse, but in the failure to receive mirroring and reassurance. An elemental sense of being a neglected self precedes the adult experience of particular instances of rejection or neglect. For this reason, much of what happens to us as adults reminds us of those early feelings. We are attuned to repetitions of old hurts.

Knowing the problem points toward the solution. No, you are not responsible for your partner's insecurity, and no, you can't cure it; but you can reduce it. Demonstrate your appreciation for your mate's positive qualities, and demonstrate your acceptance of his or her inner experience by allowing him or her the right to complain.

The more secure we are the less likely we are to lash out at our partners when they show their upset. Try to avoid getting caught up in a reactive position; try to see past your partner's anger to the hurt beneath. If neither partner can break the cycle of misunderstanding, the relationship can break up.

Total rejection triggers total rage. In his heartbreaking ode to undying love, *Love in the Time of Cholera,* Gabriel Garcia Marquez described the reaction of a lover scorned. Rejected by the beautiful Fermina Daza, Florentino Asiza tries to distract himself, but jealousy, lying in ambush, takes possession of his soul.

He prayed to God that the lightning of divine justice would strike Fermina Daza as she was about to give her vow of love and obedience to a man who wanted her for his wife only as a social adornment. . . .

At times his solace was the certainty that during the feverish nights of her honeymoon, Fermina Daza would suffer one moment, one at least but one in any event, when the phantom of the sweetheart she had scorned, humiliated, and insulted would appear in her thoughts, and all her happiness would be destroyed.[3]

The person who cuts off the relationship cuts into the self of the one still coupled. The pain is excruciating, but it's clean and can heal. Less dramatic, but in some ways more hurtful, are the little arrows to the heart of everyday rejection and rebuff. These injuries kill trust, if not the relationship, and lead one or both partners to pull back out of range.

Each of us is torn between tremendous longing for love and tremendous fear of the merger love requires. If you look closely at the cycles of closeness and distance in a relationship, you'll see how shame pushes lovers apart. Frequent, yet always unexpected, humiliation from our partners cuts so deep because it comes from in so close. And yet, in the depth of our longing, we expose ourselves time and again. Yearning for acceptance draws us back to our partners; rejection drives us away.

Imagine a man making love to his wife. Suddenly he realizes that she's been turned off for quite some time. She's looking away, just hoping he'll finish. He's in the throes of passion and she's looking disgusted, impatient to have it over. Imagine his shame. Imagine how a woman feels when in the heat of an argument her husband throws up to her all those vulnerable admissions she's made to him. Imagine her shame. Imagine a self flayed regularly like this, and you can understand why so many people give up trying to restore their relationships in favor of protecting themselves.

Mutual withdrawal, frozen in place by compensating connections (her career, his hobbies; his career, her children), becomes the chronic condition of many marriages. More and more left unspoken; less and less lovemaking, until intimacy is lost and it's hard to remember what ever made them fall in love in the first place.

It's the otherness of lovers that make them so attractive, almost as though Nature's design to mix genes drives us toward mates who will fill out our missing spaces. Opposites attract, but they're hard to live with. When things are good, partners accommodate to each other's differences. When things aren't so good, they polarize each other.

THE NAGGING WIFE AND WITHDRAWING HUSBAND

I met Claire when she consulted me feeling "burned out, tired, and depressed." I met another side of Claire when, at my urging, she brought her husband to our sessions. The first Claire was sad. The second Claire was angry.

If opposites attract, it was no surprise that Claire and Arthur had been attracted to each other. She was expressive, open, and affectionate; he was steady, calm, and serious. When it came to conflict, her specialty was angry criticism, his was wounded silence. Worse, they found themselves married to someone who breaks the rules: She screams at him. He walks out on her. And, as so often happens, their differences polarized each other. The more angry and vocal she got, the more angry and withdrawn he became.

Arthur: "She's a shrew! Everything is my fault. She screams at me and says the most exaggerated things—I'm a heartless bastard, I never do anything—I'm sick of taking all the blame."

Nichols: "She's a shrew? How did you train her to be like that?"

Arthur: "It's not my fault. She's always been like that."

Nichols: "No, it's impossible, You're telling me a one-person story; in a marriage everything is a two-person story."

What did he do that infuriated her? He punished her with stone-faced silence. And how did she teach him it wasn't safe to say what he feels? Such questions suggest shifting blame, and couples often feel them that way, but my purpose was shifting focus from a linear view to a circular one. The point

*wasn't who started what, but what were they doing—each of
them—to contribute to the behavior they hated.*

Arthur picked Claire with all the intelligence his eyes could
muster. Just looking at her gave him that breathlessly anxious,
knocked-off-your-feet feeling—the fall of falling in love. His
imagination filled in the rest. She liked what she saw in him,
too. With the eyes of her heart, Claire saw in Arthur much that
was missing in her life: calmness, seriousness of purpose, and
above all self-sufficiency.

On their honeymoon, Claire discovered that Arthur was a
great lover—of reassurance. Ardent but inexperienced, he was
always in a great hurry. Afterward he wanted to know if she'd
had an orgasm. She never did. She was too anxious and too
annoyed to let go. At first it felt good to inspire so much fren-
zied passion, but it wasn't long before Claire got turned off.
Sometimes she said yes when she felt maybe, and sometimes
she said no. Claire's no's hit Arthur hard.

She started avoiding him, making excuses. When he asked
what was wrong, she told him. "I don't feel like you're making
love to me, just using me to get what you want." Arthur
couldn't hear what she was trying to tell him; he just felt humiliated. She wanted tenderness, affection, patience; she
wanted to know he cared. But instead of moving toward her,
he moved away: I'll never go near her again.

In matters of the heart, most of us are recidivists. Arthur
would stay away until he was overcome with desire. Then he
came at her with all the tenderness of a randy goat. Not wanting to be punished by another week of hurt silence, Claire
gave in. And responded with as much enthusiasm as anyone
who says yes and means no.

Things got bad and things got worse. Neither love nor longing was gone, but their marriage devolved into an unpleasant
routine of self-pity and recrimination. Once they'd talked for
hours. Now they drifted past each other without touching,
sealed inside their own private preoccupations. He thought a

*lot about his work and how unfair Claire was. She thought a
lot about her work and how unfair Arthur was.*

*Until Claire became aware that feeling hurt and showing
anger only drove Arthur away, she would continue to do so.
Until Arthur realized that he alternated between avoiding
Claire and then defending himself, rather than ever complaining himself or actually listening to her complaints, he would
continue to do so.*

*I confronted them with what they were doing, and they lis-
tened. Things got better. But sex continued to be a problem.
The sad thing was, shame kept them from talking about it.
Most of the action in the bedroom took place in their minds.*

*Claire wished he would just hold her. She could come over
to him, but he'd misinterpret the gesture and be all over her.
So she did nothing. Arthur would lie there in the dark looking
at Claire with mute urgency, longing to touch her, to arouse
her ardor, and perhaps have it returned. He imagined sliding
his hand over her breast—and her pulling away in disgust. It
killed him to lie in bed and have the cure for what ailed him
within reach:* Why couldn't she cooperate?

*I was rough on him. "So when she rebuffs you, you get hurt
and stay away until you can't stand it any longer. Then it all
starts again. You two have this down pat. I have no doubt you
can keep it up."*

*Arthur: "So what can I do about feeling hurt when she re-
jects me?"*

Nichols: "Not a damn thing."

Arthur: "You mean there's nothing I can do?"

*Nichols: "I didn't say that. I said there's nothing you can do
about your feelings."*

Arthur: "Well, what should *I do?"*

Nichols: "I don't know. Ask Claire."

*Opening up the subject of sex was a first step. My contribu-
tion was confronting both of them with what they were doing
to perpetuate a problem. After that, they talked about their
feelings, which removed quite a bit of bitterness, and then they*

talked about what they wanted from each other. Things got
better—not great, but better—and it made a big difference.

It's easy to think of the disengaged husband as not involved.
Actually, he's very much involved, brooding over his private
thoughts, nursing his wounds. Hurt and anger kept Arthur away
from Claire until sexual frustration drove him back. Arthur's defense against the shameful feeling of rejection was withdrawal;
Claire's was attack. And these complementary defenses polarized
them in a mutually frustrating arrangement.

Blind to the self-perpetuating patterns they're caught up in,
many married people become obsessed with bitterness and blame,
voiced or unvoiced. Each one feels hurt, let down, deserted,
abandoned—and is tortured by the knowledge that the other one
could be, if only he or she would be, a perfectly satisfactory person. Instead of a refuge from humiliation, the relationship becomes a source of it.

The self-perpetuating pattern I just referred to is a cycle of
distance, loneliness and longing, then closeness, which produces
conflict and leads to rejection and shame and more distance. If you
think about your own relationship, it's not very hard to figure out
what your partner does that feels like rejection and makes you
bitter—not very hard and not very useful. If, instead, you consider
how you seek closeness and why that might not suit your partner,
you could try something different. For example, the man who tries
to talk to his wife when he comes home from work but usually gets
ignored could figure out when she might be more receptive to
talking. The woman whose husband never seems to want to do
anything with her might consider joining him at something he
likes. Thus, for example, instead of asking him to go to the movies
with her and the kids, she might ask him to pick out something for
the two of them to do together next weekend.

Before I offer more concrete suggestions, I want to drive home
the point of this section: The key to getting unstuck in relationships is to shift your perspective and see that the two of you are
caught up in a destructive cycle *that both of you perpetuate.* One
pursues and the other distances. More pursuit propels more dis-

tance, and more distance propels more pursuit. Eventually, shame makes the pursuer cut off, "Who needs it?" Then the distancer feels, "Well, I tried," and gives up. Insecurity and shame drive the cycle toward bitterness—and the anesthesia of despair. You know what your partner does that makes you unhappy. What you have to become aware of is what you do that pushes him or her to behave that way, and how you react that somehow keeps it going. *That,* you can change.

When things go bad in a relationship, we have a choice between protection of a depressed and vulnerable self or restoration of the relationship. There are times when we hurt too much and there is no choice. And there are times when we hurt and there is a choice.

INTIMACY, LOST AND FOUND

Relationships can be restored, however impaired they may be. But let me be honest, it isn't easy. Tunnel vision and our own emotions hold us back. Most of us are already doing the best we can. We may be frustrated and disappointed, but we keep trying, accepting what we must and doing what we can. Unfortunately, most of our efforts are simply more of the same. More of the same strategies that carry us so far and no farther. And perhaps the greatest stumbling block of all in relationships: Most of us can't stop wishing our partners were different, alternately trying to change them and feeling bitter that they remain who they are.

Revitalizing intimate relationships is possible if you understand three concepts: *reciprocity, blurred boundaries,* and *anxiety.* By now you understand something about how shame holds you back from trying new things and how couples polarize each other. Efforts to renew intimacy in relationships must take both things into account.

Reciprocity

The governing principle of relationships is reciprocity. This doesn't mean exchanging favors or operating according to the

Fairness Doctrine. It simply means that in a relationship one person's behavior is functionally related to the other's.

As long as we remain trapped in the illusion of unilateral influence, it's hard to get past thinking how unfair others are and wishing they would change. Once you realize that two people's behavior in a relationship is reciprocal—linked in an ongoing circular pattern—you can stop worrying about what's fair and who started what, and start figuring out what to do to change the pattern. The alternative—thinking only about what's missing ("We don't have sex much anymore") or the annoying things your partner does ("He's so unaffectionate")—leaves you in a position of wanting to change something without realizing what you are doing to keep it going.

Here's a simple example. Suppose a woman is angry at her husband because he never gets around to doing the chores he agrees to do. She's tried everything, from asking to nagging, still, she ends up having to do everything herself. It's not fair and she's bitter. She might be able to change this pattern by looking at her part, which comes before and after the "He never . . ." (Having to scheme to get him to do his share is not fair but may work.) First, get a clear agreement. Husbands often grunt a perfunctory "sure" to household requests, as much to end the conversation as because they actually intend to do what's asked: "Honey, the faucet in the kitchen is leaking, do you think you can fix it or should we call a plumber?" "When do you think you can have it done by?"

And after? Unfortunately, most husbands don't feel the consequences of unfinished household chores, and most wives end up taking care of what the husbands don't. If the only shower in the house was broken and nobody fixed it, he'd get it taken care of. But regardless of who says what, most husbands know that if they don't get around to fixing a faucet or cooking supper, their wives will. Persist. If you're going to give up overfunctioning, you have to wait long enough for your partner to feel the consequences of not living up to his agreements. He may not change until it becomes clear that if he doesn't do his share it won't get done. Try a little "strategic helplessness." It's harder to argue with "I can't" than "I won't."

Housework—isn't that a mundane subject for a chapter on love and sex? Yes, and the longer we fail to meet our partner's mundane expectations the less we'll have to worry about love and sex because there won't be any.

Blurred Boundaries

Mending relationships takes *individuation* and *empathy*. Individuation means relating to each other as separate selves. Self-respect generates individuation: Belief in yourself makes it easier to stand up for yourself. And efforts to individuate generate self-respect: Standing up for yourself makes it easier to respect yourself. In an intimate relationship, self-respect translates into claiming your rights and not being defensive.

To say that each of us is a separate person, a person of worth and with rights, seems obvious and simple. Unfortunately, we tend to lose sight of this when we're caught up in the emotions of intimacy. We need to clarify in our minds what our legitimate wants and needs are. Until we are clear about what we think and feel, we cannot differentiate between what we and what our partners expect us to think and feel and want.

When we experience ourselves as a subject-of-needs, we may think of others as objects for the satisfaction of needs. This doesn't mean we're tempted to use and abuse them, only that our need makes us long for unqualified love. It's this longing that creates unrealistic expectations and leads to bitterness in the face of frustration. Mature love carries the burden of accepting and bearing bonds with a unique and independent human being, someone we do not control and from whom we are quite different.

In frustrating relationships, we tend to dwell on the awful, unfair things the other person does, alternately enduring and protesting. One thing we rarely stop to ask is "Why?" It doesn't take much to ask "Why must she always . . . ?" or "Why doesn't he ever . . . ?" Turning these rhetorical questions into real questions that are worth answering takes empathy.

Empathy creates deeper leverage for change than reciprocity. Reciprocity enables you to analyze behavior: how yours evokes and maintains your partner's. Changing your behavior interrupts the cycle. Empathy, understanding the inner experience of another, gives you the power to unfreeze conflict by getting beneath your partner's behavior, some of which may be defensive, to a more genuine level of feeling.

Couples rarely speak in the language of feeling and need. Instead of saying, "I feel . . ." or "I want . . . ," it's likely to be, "You always . . ." or "You never . . ." Criticism and demands polarize couples into mutual antagonism. I've already suggested that you should figure out what you feel and want, and say so. Empathy enables you to make this translation for your partner. Instead of being put off or bewildered by his or her annoying moods, you can figure out what's behind them. Ask yourself: "Why does he [or she] need to behave this way at this moment?" Because he's mean, selfish, and pigheaded? Come on. Put yourself in the other person's shoes. What would make *you* act that way? (If you come up with "nothing," try again.) Here's an example from a couple I'm treating.

Graham is a Methodist minister beloved by his parishioners, who consider him a dedicated, selfless, truly caring person. His wife, Sheila, admires him and the work he does, but wishes he had more time for her and the children. He usually comes home late for supper and then goes out again for Bible study classes and counseling sessions and committee meetings. The couple spend less and less time together, and both of them are feeling worn-out and unappreciated. So much to do and so little time. Yes, but perhaps more to the point, so little understanding.

Like many dedicated professionals, Graham works hard— he's a workaholic—but part of what keeps him going is the elixir of appreciation. His reward for making so many hospital calls is hearing "how wonderful he is" and how the sick person "couldn't have made it without him." He uses time he might otherwise spend with his children to work extra hard on his sermons, but the beaming faces and warm greetings ("Oh,

*what a wonderful sermon; it was just what I needed to hear")
keep him at it. What wife can compete with the narcissistic rewards available to the "selflessly" dedicated professional man?*

*And Sheila, what about her? She works just as hard as Gra-
ham, doing the endless things a wife and mother must do. No
matter how many times he's been late, when suppertime
comes she's hungry for a little adult conversation. By the time
he finally gets home, she's hurt and angry. She doesn't say
much about it, but then she doesn't say much about anything
else either. Graham is worn out and wants peace and quiet.
So there they sit at the dinner table, five feet away and miles
apart.*

*It isn't too hard to figure out how Graham and Sheila could
show a little empathy for each other. They both need the same
thing: appreciation and attention. Even as simple a thing as
asking, "What did you do today?," and then listening attentively for a few minutes would make a big difference. (If your
partner complains about work, just listen sympathetically,*
don't offer unsolicited advice.)

No, it isn't hard to figure out how Graham and Sheila could show
a little empathy for each other, but what about you?

Empathy takes just a little more than sympathy. It takes figuring
out what the other person is feeling. Here are a couple of clues.
The three most powerful individual issues in human relationships
are: wishing for pleasure; getting angry when frustrated; and longing for appreciation. These motives are constant, but most of us
lead with our defenses. The person who shows anger probably
feels neglected and hurt; the person who acts hurt is probably
frustrated and angry. Rage protects the self but precludes comforting. Likewise, the hurt withdrawal of a depleted self is protective but may obscure the need for responsiveness.

When you extend your understanding to your partner, remember, the person who's hurt and angry is swollen with bitterness.
The first sensitive probe may air out some of the acrimony, before
the person softens. When you say, "You feel bad, don't you?" don't
expect the first response to be, "Yes, aren't you kind for noticing."

Overreactions are understandable if you ask yourself what would explain them, or to whom and under what circumstances might such a reaction make sense? The woman who was humiliated unpredictably by her father will naturally be highly reactive to criticism. The man who feels devastated by any rejection may have been punished as a boy with profound and prolonged rejection. It's not just us our partners react to; we abrade each other's insides because they were rubbed raw long ago.

Over the years, an accumulation of hurts, large and small, wounds us and makes us sensitive. We overreact because we're primed for a possible repeat of a humiliating attack on the self. Shame makes us anxious.

Shame and Anxiety

When anxiety seeps into the sexual act, it can spread and rot out the whole erotic relationship. Once a lover becomes apprehensive about the usual poking and panting, thereafter when the other makes a bid for sex it will arouse anxiety instead of ardor. In a similar fashion, anxiety also becomes attached to intimate conversation. It takes a little longer for this to happen, because most people have a greater backlog of experience with anxiety-free conversation than with anxiety-free sex, but the process is the same.

Anxiety becomes attached to—infects is more like it—actions and settings. First consider getting together in a relatively anxiety-free setting. For example, the safest place for most couples to have a relaxed and friendly conversation is in a comparatively conflict-free setting, like a restaurant. And if your erotic relationship is in bad shape, it may be a good idea to begin by showing gentle affection in places other than the bedroom, places where a kiss or a hug doesn't automatically imply the next step.

Now, action. There are gradations of intimacy, from the least to the most intense, and anxiety only comes in at a certain level. Even the most conflicted couples can talk about superficial subjects, and if sex is a major problem, holding hands or hugging may not be. The best way to resolve anxiety is to think of graded levels of intimacy, and then proceed to *just before* the first level of anxiety. First talk, then touch.

Make two lists, one a hierarchy from the least to the most intimate subjects of conversation, the other a hierarchy from the least to the most physical intimacy. The first list might go something like this:

1. Chat about the weather
2. Conversing about a third person
3. Impersonal talk about yourselves—for example, what you did today
4. Personal talk about yourselves—for example, hopes and plans for the future
5. Light problems about the relationship
6. Heavy problems about the relationship

The second list might go like this:

1. Sitting in the same room together
2. Sitting or walking next to each other
3. Holding hands
4. Hugging
5. Kissing
6. Hugging in bed
7. Caressing each other, without touching breasts or genitals
8. Caressing breasts and genitals
9. Masturbating your partner with your hand
10. Coitus
11. Genital kissing

Obviously, these lists are meant only as examples; they may not fit your feelings. Work out your own lists. Use some imagination. Don't settle for a short list of "what we usually do." Make it longer and more interesting.

Then get busy. Move down the list until you or your partner become anxious. It's best to stop just short of this point, but if you can't, just back up a little; if shame and anxiety make you back off, remember for the next time. Practicing safe intimacy will gradually melt anxiety, and you can gradually become more intimate—*gradually!*

One of the problems that complicates this approach is that married partners *know* each other. She knows that if they do Number 5, that means wham, a quick jump to Number 10. He knows that going for a walk with her means having to endure complaints about the relationship. There's no easy way around this problem, except to go slow and do what you can to wear away the assumption that doing Number 2 automatically leads to Number 5. (One reason teenage sex was so thrilling was that we could neck and pet with full passion, without having to worry about what comes next—as long as we knew we weren't going to go all the way.)

Note that although these activities can lead to a progression from less to more intimacy, thinking of them merely as stepping-stones robs them of pleasure and you of happiness. Happiness is feeling complete: You have something you want and no other want comes crowding in.

Focus on the present. We each have our own ways to impair our ability to focus on immediate sensory experience. Some of us are too preoccupied with other things—or with what comes next—to let go and give in to the moment. Others are too easily distracted. If your thoughts drift off, drift back; if your focus is broken, refocus.

As long as you avoid crossing the double line into anxiety, you can focus on your feelings—talking and touching. Satisfying sex requires coordination and cooperation. Are you ashamed to say what you like and don't like? Ashamed to make time for yourselves? Ashamed to talk about the anger that makes you not in the mood? Try to overcome your own shame enough to say what you need to say, and try to overcome impatience and anger enough to hear your partner out. Think about the qualities that make a sexual experience satisfying for you. Is it the setting? What you did before and afterward? Make sure you can arrange the setting so that it's conducive.

Reducing anxiety frees up the capacity for sexual pleasure; full engagement realizes that pleasure. The fullest enjoyment comes with the fullest involvement. There is a flow to any activity you enter into fully. This flow is a merging of action and awareness. There's no duality; you're aware of your actions but not of the awareness itself. You can cultivate this flow by immersing yourself in what you're doing; avoid giving in to negative and self-doubting thoughts. This self-forgetfulness becomes easier as one gains more self-respect: You don't have to hold back and worry if you know you're basically okay. But regardless of how much self-respect you have, you can enhance pleasure by focusing your awareness on what you're doing, not on yourself.

Sex, like play, is most fun when we're concentrating on what we're doing instead of worrying about the self doing it. In the normal waking state, our minds are full of worry. Deep-flow activities, like play and sex, are, or can be, a wonderful escape and release. Give up worry and control by letting go. Go with the flow.

And remember that sex means touching, being affectionate, and being close, as well as "doing it." When it comes to touching, experiment attentively. Take your time. Notice what gives pleasure and linger there. Let your partner know what you like. Focus on the feelings.

Falling in love is easy; staying in love is hard. Recall that shame guards the boundary around the private self, and you'll immediately understand how the intimate other we allow inside our boundaries has the capacity to heal shame or inflict more. We hurt each other when we lead with our defenses. One of the secrets to a successful relationship is learning to rise above hurt, vulnerability, and rejection long enough to reach out with understanding. When we see our partners' defensiveness as cruel and mean, we're tempted to attack or retreat. Try to remember what it feels like to be hurt and ashamed. Our partners aren't mean; they're only lonely.

Self-respect enables us to live more honestly and fully. We don't need to apologize for ourselves or put on an act. We can be who we are. Breaking through insecurity to get to self-respect means discovering our authenticity and then expressing it. Self-discovery takes understanding. Self-expression takes action. Both take courage.

Insecurity fuels, and is fueled by, anxious self-centeredness. Confidence helps us focus outward, and focusing outward helps us build confidence. But self-respect is more than confidence. It also means having ideals, ideals that take us beyond the sphere of the self.

EPILOGUE

■■■■■■■

Value and Meaning

Thus far I haven't said much about the relation of value and meaning to self-respect. After all, I'm a psychologist, not a philosopher. Now, however, I feel I must touch on this subject briefly because self-respect cannot be understood from an entirely egoistic perspective—namely one that says our actions, including relationships with other people, are important only as they benefit or enhance the self.

Self-respect demands that our lives have value and meaning. Meaning involves making a contribution that goes beyond the limits of the self. But what is that meaning and where do we find it?

Generations of philosophers (and college sophomores) have asked, "What is the meaning of life?" Religious belief supplies the answer to some people, while others look for answers in pure reason or science. When it comes to this all-important question, psychology has no answers, only conjecture. My own hunch is that there isn't one. Meaning isn't given or found, it is constructed.

Our values and ideals are a unique expression of the self. That's why living up to them gives us a feeling of satisfaction. But the good life takes us beyond the self. The antidote to morbid inwardness is engagement in the world—doing things and being with people, instead of worrying about why we can't. The good life also includes commitment to an ideal, a motivating principle beyond simple wishes and desires. An ideal is an image of something higher, transcending the self, and pursuing our ideals lifts us higher, too.

Living up to our ideals takes us beyond the self, but it is important to realize that *having* ideals is an essential part of what it means to be a self with respect. The source of self-worth is acceptance, but self-respect also includes visions of goodness that shape our lives. These visions stabilize and inspire us, giving us an inner sense of continuity and worth.

The movement and direction of our lives can be charted by the satisfaction of our desires in work, personal relations, and leisure. But self-respect is a deeper measure of satisfaction, which cannot be achieved without a personal commitment to values and ideals that extend beyond and outlast the self. Goals and ideals are not noble products of piety—like the charity of the rich—they are essential to our identity, and our self-respect.

Among our goals and ideals we must choose a contribution that outlasts the self—leaving children behind, or advancing a cause, such as civil rights, or creating a lasting work—or confront when we're old the bitter shame of having lived a life without meaning.

Cynics (and second-semester sophomores) question that sense of meaning by reflecting that nothing really has any lasting significance, since a hundred years from now no one will care whether we lived or not, and a million years from now this earth will likely cease to exist. Maybe. But maybe each of us can find meaning in our own ways. Mine is to try to make things a little better for other people. Most of my days are spent taking care of my obligations and looking after myself. The time I spend counseling people, supervising students, and listening to my children is part of my job as a psychologist and a father. I may be helpful, but I don't think of it that way. I'm performing functions that go with roles I've chosen to express and fulfill myself. It's when I extend myself beyond this, doing a little extra, showing someone a small kindness, that I feel a sense of adding something to the larger community of persons. Could *that* be the meaning of life, adding a little kindness to the world? I don't know. I only know it gives me a sense of purpose.

*   *   *

Greater respect for ourselves and others brings new freedom and responsibility. On the one hand, freedom to be ourselves and allow others to do the same; on the other, recognition of our connection to and responsibility for what goes on in the world around us. This recognition brings with it a greater willingness to provide for the care and welfare of others. Not because we're noble, but because self-respect demands it.

The same solipsistic view of the self that isolates some of us from family and friends can also isolate us from our communities. Many of us relate to perceived needs of the community as just another set of external expectations and obligations. Either we dutifully comply or we rebel. Often missing is a sense that we are all linked together.

Most of the time we're too busy looking after ourselves to accept a broader responsibility as human beings. The history of our nation parallels our personal development. Old-style rugged individualists of the American frontier used a racist form of social Darwinism to justify their political irresponsibility. Implied in the slogan "manifest destiny" was the idea that America's native inhabitants deserved to lose their land because they were ignorant savages. We did this when our nation was young and weak. In young adulthood many of us are similarly selfish, too busy trying to get ahead to care about the plight of anyone outside our immediate orbit. Now we can. By asking, "What can I do to make things a little better?" we may discover a fulfilling sense of purpose. But it is not selfless. Caring about other people is the fullest expression of a rich and complete self.

When we ignore our responsibility, we ignore our nature. All living things are an interdependent web. The average American's involvement with crime illustrates the point.

Most of us hate and fear crime. Though we aren't sure what to do about it, we believe that it is not a problem of our making. The problem is the criminals'—or society's. It is the responsibility of police, politicians, and the courts. We despise and sympathize with the underclass that menaces us on the street. We depend on and mistrust the police. The tension we feel between our fear of government and our fear of crime helps us avoid accepting personal responsibility. Those liberals among us who blame crime on poverty and discrimination are not really assuming responsibility any more than those conservatives who would like to unleash the police from civil-rights restraints —"Execute the drug lords."

Most of us grew up in relative safety, feeling entitled to it. We ignore breaches of the law when we consider them trivial—subway turnstile jumpers or rural vandals—or when we profit—someone gives us some computer software or shows us how to "cut corners" on our taxes—or when we're afraid to intervene—when we witness a drug sale or purse snatching. Our passive participation in these crimes illustrates, in a narrow way, how we allow crime to flourish and, in a broader sense, how we divorce ourselves from our communities: "It's not *my* problem." "What can *I* do?" My point is not to offer suggestions for solving the proliferation of crime—I wish I had some—but to remind the reader that there's no way not to be involved. Either we're involved in an active effort to make our world a better place, or we're involved in passive acquiescence to selfishness and greed.

It's all too easy to extol and trivialize community commitment as an idealistic but impractical expression of doing good. To mistake concern for social justice and the relief of suffering with selflessness. It isn't. Contributing to the collective good is part of the fulfillment of the self.

It isn't a meaner and more selfish outlook that makes us hostile to the aspirations of those less fortunate. It is a shameful sense of powerlessness, and a false and self-defeating notion of self-interest. Cynical self-absorption grows on us gradually, from our idealistic years in school to a life progressively swallowed by immediate career and family concerns. If, in turning inward, we become inured to other people's suffering and overwhelmed by our burdens and sense of powerlessness, our self-respect is under-mined by the very efforts we make to bolster it.

We've come to understand the global ecology that means the smokestacks of Detroit and Chicago are poisoning lakes and killing fish in Quebec and New Hampshire. In the political realm, we've seen how a cartel of Arab oil states can conspire to fix prices resulting in hour-long lines at American gas stations. These devel-opments make us angry, but they seem to be the product of large forces well beyond our control. This thinking allows us to forget our moral responsibility to those with fewer advantages, and ob-scures the larger truth of the interdependence of all humanity. And so we now have hundreds of thousands of our own citizens lying around the streets of American cities, sleeping in doorways and occasionally reaching out to us, begging with Styrofoam cups. Many of us are tempted to turn away. The homeless are a source of collective shame.

Solutions to the problems of poverty and hunger and drug ad-diction will come when we rediscover the disadvantaged, not as alien "others" or even as objects of sympathy but as part of our communities and potential allies in a struggle to curb the inordi-nate and growing power of the corporate elite. I'm not talking about a revival of conscience but a realization that a respect for ourselves means a universal respect for human dignity.

I've emphasized our connection to community and the sense of purpose that comes from extending kindness to others, because this gives me a sense of meaning. Whether you find it in religion or in your parents' teaching or in your own heart, finding and serving an ideal is part of what it means to have self-respect.

In the ordinary way we make sense of our lives, there is a ten-sion between the claims of individual self-expression and the claims of universal benevolence and justice. One of the great par-adoxes of human nature is that we are propelled by two powerful motives that seem to point in opposite directions. On the one hand, we have a compelling desire to identify with larger human wholes—friends, lovers, families, clans, communities; to join ourselves with others. On the other hand, we want to be unique. Special.

The second motive—to develop a powerful and unique self, to stand out and be admired—is really a partial motive, representing one way to fulfill the desire to be loved and to belong.

One of the ways we strive to overcome shame—our sense of unworthiness—is by idealizing the self, aiming to become heroic, truly extraordinary. The natural urge to individuate is realized when we discover our unique talents and then express them. It is a matter of completion and fulfillment—self-satisfaction, not self-inflation.

Individuation carried to its logical extreme creates precisely the isolation that we cannot stand. But a more complete self-understanding includes an appreciation of our collective nature. And this is where belonging and making a contribution come together in the fullest expression of self-respect.

Discovering our human interdependence gives us a sense of self-expansion and a feeling of transcendent value. The power of self-transcendence is joy and love. When the question of who we are and how we should live alerts us to our interconnectedness, we may discover that collective respect liberates us from collective shame.

NOTES

. . . .

1. The Search for Self-respect

1. Jean-Paul Sartre, *Being and Nothingness* (New York: The Citadel Press, 1964), p. 235.
2. Ibid., p. 236.

2. Shame: The Alienating Emotion

1. Hunter Thompson, *Generation of Swine: Tales of Shame and Degradation in the 80's* (New York: Summit Books, 1988).
2. Tennessee Williams, *Memoirs* (New York: Doubleday, 1976), p. 12.
3. Leon Wurmser, *The Mask of Shame* (Baltimore: Johns Hopkins University Press, 1981).
4. Franz Kafka, *The Diaries of Franz Kafka* (New York: Schocken Books, 1965).
5. S. J. Perelman, "In Pixie Land I'll Take My Stand," in *The Rising Gorge* (New York: Penguin Books, 1987), pp. 242–243.
6. Nathaniel Hawthorne, *The Scarlet Letter* (New York: Perennial Library, 1967), p. 49.

3. The Adaptive Function of Shame

1. Carl Schneider, *Shame, Exposure, and Privacy* (Boston: Beacon Press, 1977), p. 37.
2. Ruth Benedict, *The Chrysanthemum and the Sword* (Boston: Houghton Mifflin, 1946).

3. R. D. Laing, "Mystification, Confusion and Conflict." In *Intensive Family Therapy,* eds., Ivan Boszormenyi-Nagy and James Framo (New York: Harper & Row, 1965).

4. Gershen Kaufman and Lev Raphael, "Shame as Taboo in American Culture," *Forbidden Fruits: Taboos and Tabooism in Culture,* ed., R. Browne (Bowling Green, Ohio: Popular Press, 1984), pp. 57–66.

5. Gershen Kaufman, *Shame: The Power of Caring* (Cambridge, Mass.: Schenkman Books, 1980), p. 29.

6. Ernest Becker, *The Denial of Death* (New York: The Free Press, 1973), pp. 30–31.

7. Plato, *Apology & Crito of Plato* (Lawrence, Kans.: Coronado Press, 1980).

8. Ibid.

4. The Mechanisms of Defense

1. W. J. Weatherby, *James Baldwin: Artist on Fire* (New York: Donald I. Fine, 1989).

2. Fyodor Dostoyevski, *The Brothers Karamazov* (New York: Penguin, 1958), p. 46.

5. Living in the Shadow of Insecurity

1. Anita Brookner, *Hotel du Lac* (New York: Dutton, 1986), p. 133.

2. Erving Goffman, *The Presentation of Self in Everyday Life* (Garden City, N.Y.: Anchor Books, 1959), p. 75.

3. Wurmser, *The Mask of Shame.*

6. You Can Run But You Can't Hide: Distracting Ourselves from Insecurity

1. Philip Zimbardo, *Shyness: What It Is, What to Do About It* (Reading, Mass.: Addison-Wesley, 1977).

2. Anthony Storr, *Solitude: A Return to the Self* (New York: The Free Press, 1988).

3. Robert Bramson, *Coping with Difficult People* (Garden City, N.Y.: Anchor Press, 1981).

4. Susan Cheever, *Home Before Dark: A Biographical Memoir of John Cheever by His Daughter* (New York: Pocket Books, 1985), p. 165.

5. Margaret Mead, "Sex and Censorship in Contemporary Society," in *New World Writing* (New York: The New American Library of World Literature, Third Mentor Selection, 1953), p. 18.

6. Harold Nawy, "In the Pursuit of Happiness: Consumers of Erotica in

San Francisco," *Journal of Social Issues* 29 (1973): 147–161. The quote is from Philip Zimbardo's summary of the results, *Shyness,* p. 101.

7. Keith McWalter, "Couch Dancing," in "About Men," *New York Times Magazine,* December 6, 1987.

7. The Anatomy of Shame

1. Sigmund Freud, "The Interpretation of Dreams," Chapt. 7 (1900), *Standard Edition,* vols. 4 & 5 (London: Hogarth Press, 1953), pp. 1–626.

2. Sigmund Freud, "The Ego and the Id" (1923), *Standard Edition,* vol. 19 (London: Hogarth Press, 1955), pp. 1–60.

3. Sigmund Freud, "Three Essays on the Theory of Sexuality" (1905), *Standard Edition,* vol. 7 (London: Hogarth Press, 1953), pp. 135–243.

4. Sigmund Freud, "Civilization and Its Discontents" (1930), *Standard Edition,* vol. 21 (London: Hogarth Press, 1961), pp. 64–145.

5. Alfred Adler, *The Science of Living* (New York: Greenberg, 1929), and *Understanding Human Nature* (New York: Fawcett, 1981).

6. Daniel Stern, *The Interpersonal World of the Infant* (New York: Basic Books, 1985).

7. Helen Block Lewis, *Shame and Guilt in Neurosis* (New York: International University Press, 1971), p. 30.

8. Ibid., p. 86.

9. Erik Erikson, *Childhood and Society* (New York: Norton, 1950).

10. Michael Nichols, *Turning Forty in the Eighties* (New York: Fireside/ Simon and Schuster, 1987), pp. 148–149.

8. Love and Worth: The Foundations of Self-respect

1. Carl Rogers, *Client-Centered Therapy* (Boston: Houghton Mifflin, 1951).

2. Donald Winnicott, *The Maturational Process and the Facilitating Environment* (New York: International Universities Press, 1965).

3. Margaret Mahler, Fred Pine, and Anni Bergman, *The Psychological Birth of the Human Infant* (New York: Basic Books, 1975); Donald Winnicott, *Collected Papers* (New York: Basic Books, 1958); Harry Guntrip, *Psychoanalytic Theory, Therapy, and the Self* (New York: Basic Books, 1971).

4. Stern, *Interpersonal World of the Infant.*

5. Jerome Kagan, *The Nature of the Child* (New York: Basic Books, 1984); T. Berry Brazelton, "Joint Regulation of Neonate-Parent Behavior," in *Social Interchange in Infancy,* ed., E. Tronick (Baltimore, Md.: University Park Press, 1982).

6. Stern, *Interpersonal World of the Infant.*

7. Kagan, *Nature of the Child,* p. 51.

8. Winnicott, *Maturational Process and the Facilitating Environment.*

9. John Bowlby, *Attachment and Loss, Vol. II, Separation: Anxiety and Anger* (New York: Basic Books, 1973), p. 203.

9. Why We're Insecure: The Introduction of Shame

1. Harry Stack Sullivan, *The Interpersonal Theory of Psychiatry* (New York: W. W. Norton, 1953).

2. Stern, *Interpersonal World of the Infant,* p. 222.

3. Heinz Kohut, *The Restoration of the Self* (New York: International Universities Press, 1977), pp. 55, 56.

4. Shere Hite, *Women in Love* (New York: Knopf, 1987).

10. The Humiliations of Childhood: School, Church, and Play

1. Dietrich Bonhoeffer, *Ethics* (New York: Macmillan, 1955), pp. 18, 19.

2. Friedrich Nietzsche, *Thus Spake Zarathustra* (New York: Penguin, 1978), Part 4, p. 378.

3. Charles Darwin, *Expression of the Emotions in Man & Animals* (Chicago: University of Chicago Press, 1965), p. 332.

11. Adolescence: That Awful, Awkward Age

1. Simone de Beauvoir, *Second Sex* (New York: Knopf, 1953), pp. 287–288.

2. William Schonfeld, "Primary and Secondary Sexual Characteristics: Study of Their Development in Males from Birth Through Maturity, with Biometric Study of Penis and Testes," *American Journal of Diseases of Children* 65 (1943): 535–539.

3. Alfred Kinsey, William Pomeroy, and Charles Martin, *Sexual Behavior in the Human Male* (Philadelphia: W. B. Saunders, 1948).

4. Erikson, *Childhood and Society.*

12. Positive Parenting

1. Harold Brodkey, "A Story in an Almost Classical Mode," in *Stories in an Almost Classical Mode* (New York: Vintage, 1989), pp. 258–259.

2. Erikson, *Childhood and Society.*

14. Making Friends with Yourself

1. Morton Lieberman, Irvin Yalom, and Matthew Miles, *Encounter Groups: First Facts* (New York: Basic Books, 1973).

2. Harriet Markus, "Self-Schemata and Processing Information About the Self," *Journal of Personality and Social Psychology* 35 (1977): 63–78; Daryl Bem and Andrea Allen, "On Predicting Some of the People Some of the Time: The Search for Cross-Situational Characteristics in Behavior," *Psychological Review* 81 (1974): 506–520; Jean Piaget, *The Child's Conception of the World* (Paterson, N.J.: Littlefield, Adams, 1960).

15. Kinship and Friendship

1. Michael Nichols, *The Power of the Family* (New York: Fireside/Simon and Schuster, 1988), pp. 136–137.

16. Overcoming Shame in Love and Sex

1. For a philosophical discussion of interpersonal boundaries see Robert Nozick, *The Examined Life* (New York: Simon and Schuster, 1989); for a more pragmatic discussion of boundaries in family life see Nichols, *The Power of the Family*.

2. Heinz Kohut, *The Analysis of the Self* (New York: International Universities Press, 1971).

3. Gabriel Garcia Marquez, *Love in the Time of Cholera* (New York: Knopf, 1988), pp. 145–146.

INDEX

■■■■■■■

ABOUT THE AUTHOR

■ ■ ■ ■ ■ ■ ■

Michael P. Nichols is Professor of Psychiatry at Albany Medical College, where he practices and teaches family therapy and psychoanalytic therapy. He is the author of *The Power of the Family, Turning Forty in the Eighties,* and other books. He lives outside of Albany, New York, with his wife and two children.